# THE GERMAN
# ARMY LEAGUE

# THE GERMAN ARMY LEAGUE

## Popular Nationalism in Wilhelmine Germany

MARILYN SHEVIN COETZEE

New York   Oxford
OXFORD UNIVERSITY PRESS
1990

Oxford University Press

Oxford   New York   Toronto
Delhi   Bombay   Calcutta   Madras   Karachi
Petaling Jaya   Singapore   Hong Kong   Tokyo
Nairobi   Dar es Salaam   Cape Town
Melbourne   Auckland

and associated companies in
Berlin   Ibadan

Copyright © 1990 by Oxford University Press, Inc.

Published by Oxford University Press, Inc.,
200 Madison Avenue, New York, New York 10016

Oxford is a registered trademark of Oxford University Press

Library of Congress Cataloging-in-Publication Data
Coetzee, Marilyn Shevin, 1955–
The German Army League: popular nationalism in Wilhelmine Germany
Marilyn Shevin Coetzee.
p.   cm.
Includes bibliographical references.
ISBN 0–19-506109-8
1. Deutscher Wehrverein.   2. Germany—Politics and
government—20th century.   3. Nationalism—Germany—History—
20th century.   I. Title.
DD228.5.C63   1990
943.08′4—dc20            89-37128   CIP

Photographs courtesy of the Hoover Institution

2 4 6 8 9 7 5 3 1

Printed in the United States of America
on acid-free paper

For my parents

# Acknowledgments

The history of the Army League might have remained untold had it not been for the generous financial and moral support of many institutions, friends, and colleagues. I am especially grateful to the Alexander von Humboldt Foundation of Bonn, West Germany, and, in particular, to its Klaus Epstein Memorial Fund, which enabled me to undertake the research for this book in Germany during 1980–81. I should also like to thank the staffs of all the archives I visited in the Federal Republic for their assistance and for their permission to quote from materials in their custody. The Hoover Institution and its Western Collection's curator, Agnes Peterson, deserve recognition for the kind assistance they provided me in the form of a travel grant as well as for their permission to reproduce the photographs contained in this book. Martin Blinkhorn, the editor of *European History Quarterly,* was kind enough to permit me to draw upon material originally published in that journal.

Special thanks also go to Gerd Keim, the grandson of the Army League's founder, August Keim, for allowing me access to his grandfather's small collection and for sharing with me more personal recollections of his family. I cannot overlook the hospitality of Margaret and Kurt Wolf of Bielefeld, and Lutz and Pamela Haber, currently of Bath, who made my stays in Germany and England extremely pleasurable.

Margaret Lavinia Anderson, David Blackbourn, Roger Chickering, Richard Evans, James Sheehan, and Hans-Ulrich Wehler read the manuscript, and I profited from all their suggestions. In no way, of course, should they be held accountable for the views expressed in this book. I am indebted to William Becker of George Washington University, not only for the grant he secured for me from the university to cover the expenses of typing the manuscript, but also for his friendship and assistance in ways only he knows. Thanks go as well to Jean Moser for her diligence in typing the manuscript. I also owe a special debt to Paul Kennedy of Yale University who offered his support in a variety of ways. My mentor and friend James Sheehan of Stanford University has served as a model of inspiration since my undergraduate days at Northwestern University. I hope this first book meets his standards.

It has been a pleasure to work with the members of Oxford University Press—

Marion Osmun, David Roll, and Rosalie West—who treated my manuscript in a professional and efficient manner. Above all, Nancy Lane has been a model editor who deserves the highest praise.

I offer this book to my parents with gratitude for all their time and effort in supporting my development as a historian. Without their constant financial and moral backing and the intense love of learning that they instilled in me, this book could not have been written. I hope they realize how much I appreciate everything they have done. Last, but certainly not least, my husband and fellow historian, Frans, read and breathed every word and version of the Army League from its inception until its appearance as this book, and offered encouragement and love. For the years he was forced to share the stage with those confounded popular nationalists, I apologize, and hope that future books will be less demanding.

*New Haven, Conn.*                                                    M.S.C.
*September 1989*

# Contents

# THE GERMAN
# ARMY LEAGUE

# Introduction

This book is a study of image and reality, a reassessment of the role of one of Wilhelmine Germany's most prominent popular nationalist associations, the *Deutscher Wehrverein* or German Army League. While this study of the Army League explores the rising tide of German militarism before the First World War, it also confronts the equally significant issue of popular political mobilization in the Wilhelmine age. As an extraparliamentary pressure group designed to strengthen the German army and along with it the patriotic fabric of the nation, the Army League competed with the spectrum of preexisting political parties, in particular the National Liberals, for the affection and support of the German public in safeguarding the state from internal subversion (by Socialists, pacifists, and Left Liberals), in sharpening its citizens' political and national consciousness, and in expanding the nation's ability to compete with and eventually surpass its European rivals in the realm of foreign politics. The Army League was the last of the patriotic societies to emerge after the mid-1880s and develop a highly confrontational critique of Wilhelmine governmental policies on issues of both domestic and foreign significance.[1] We can only begin to appreciate its contribution, though, by first sketching, however briefly, the basic contours of Germany's prior associational development.

Associations, of course, were by no means solely a late nineteenth-century phenomenon. In the late eighteenth century, literary and social clubs provided models for the gymnastic, choral, and cultural societies that emerged during the Restoration era in such rapid succession that one prominent historian has labeled the 1840s the "age of associations."[2] Even the contemporary Russian novelist Nikolai Gogol, in his novel *Dead Souls,* recognized Germans' affinity for associational life.[3] The expansion of associations in the early and mid-nineteenth century reflected the transition of German society from a corporate to a class structure. In a way, voluntary associations served as surrogates for the old guild system; they fostered a sense of community and catered to their members' needs in much the same fashion as had the guilds, but without the stigmas of exclusivity and resistance to change.[4]

The associational explosion of *Vormärz* also paralleled the rise of the liberal

3

movement. Prohibited by the state from establishing their own political network, liberals sought refuge in a spectrum of nonpolitical associations that functioned as "training schools" in which "the first generation of liberal leaders learned to think and act politically."[5] The philanthropic organizations and chambers of commerce of the 1840s, for example, owed their existence to the liberals. They were established not in opposition to the state and its policies, but in a "compensatory and complementary relation to it," for "only with the cooperation of the state was the dissolution of the old feudal bonds achieved. . . . The state was not the opponent but the inaugurator of bourgeois society; it was an agent of freedom."[6]

Political repression following 1848 only temporarily curtailed rather than extinguished the development of Germany's associations. After 1850 many urban areas witnessed a revitalization of their associational networks; in Munich alone the number of associations increased nearly twentyfold between 1850 and 1900, from some 150 to approximately 3,000.[7] Unlike their predecessors, which had been primarily local in orientation, the post-1850 associations branched out regionally, with credit, savings, insurance, and trade associations leading the way in this efflorescence.[8] Internal migration, economic diversification, and urbanization all stimulated associational growth. For example, *Knappenvereine* (miners' associations) and *Kolpings-Gesellenvereine* (journeymen's associations), which catered to workers seeking diversions from the tedium of industrial employment and the anonymity of urban life, specifically offered activities "designed to be carried out on Sundays and weekday evenings, the available free time of the urban laborer."[9] By 1870 it was estimated that every other German was a member of an association.[10] This momentum persisted after unification. Demographic growth ensured a continuing supply of potential members, while the extension of the railways, the postal service, and the popular press all facilitated the formation and maintenance of organizational contacts. Moreover, the gradual reduction of the average workweek and the corresponding increase in leisure time also contributed to the continuing vitality of associational life in Imperial Germany.

During the last two decades of the nineteenth century, a new genre of associations emerged, the patriotic societies or *Nationale Verbände*. Although shaped to some extent by the associational traditions of the past, they nonetheless represented a distinctive departure in German public life. In terms of their sheer size, national breadth and exposure, social heterogeneity, and predilection to criticize the state, the patriotic societies differed from their predecessors. These associations included the Colonial Society (1882; consolidated 1887), the Pan-German League (1891), the Society for the Eastern Marches (1894), the Navy League (1898), the Imperial League against Social Democracy (1904), and the Army League (1912).[11] By the eve of the First World War, the patriotic societies could muster impressive membership totals: the Colonial Society (42,000), the Pan-German League (18,000), the Imperial League against Social Democracy (221,000), the Navy League (331,000), and the Army League (90,000).[12] They appeared to be particularly successful in mobilizing members of the middle classes whose apparent mania for associational participation was evoked by Paul Wriede's caricature entitled "Vereinsmeier" (1908)[13]:

Am Montag sprach Herr Meier: "Du,
Mein Weib, ich muss jetzt fort,
Wir haben Vorstandssitzung heut',
Im "Halbmond" ist der Ort."

On Monday Herr Meier said: "See here,
My wife, I leave in haste,
We have an executive meeting t'day,
The Halfmoon is the place."

Am Dienstag sprach er: "Hör, mein Schatz,
's ist unbequem und schad',
Ich kann heut' nicht zu Hause sein,
Hab' Ausschusssitzung grad'."

On Tuesday he said: "I say, my dear,
It really is too bad.
An all-day meeting of the board
Will keep me from home, egad."

Und Mittwoch sprach er wiederum:
"Es tut mir furchtbar leid,
Die Hauptversammlung lässt mir heut'
Kein halbes Stündchen Zeit."

And Wednesday he said anew:
"It certainly is a crime.
The general meeting leaves me t'day
But half an hour's time."

Am Donnerstag Herr Meier rief:
"Schnell meinen Rock, im Flug!
Ich bin ja Delegierter heut',
Um sieben geht mein Zug."

On Thursday Herr Meier cried,
"Quickly my coat, I'm late.
My train departs at seven sharp;
T'day I am a delegate."

Am Freitag flötet Meier süss:
"Heut' ist Kommers bei Witt,
Adieu, klein Frau, nu wein' man nich',
Ich bring' Dir auch was mit."

On Friday Meier cooed lovingly:
"Tis alumni night chez Witt;
Adieu, sweet wife, now don't you fret,
I'll bring you some little bit."

Sonnabend Katerschoppen war,
Sein Fehlen würd 'genier'n,
Und Sonntag für 'ne Herrentour
Müsst er 'rekognoszier'n.

Saturday's drink to clear the head,
Too awkward just to flout it.
As to Sunday, for the men's field day,
He's obliged to see about it.

Und wo es irgend angebracht,
D'rauf konnt man sicher bau'n,
Da sprach er einen Damentoast:
"Ein dreifach Hoch den Frau'n!"

And anytime it seemed apropos,
It was as sure as Hades
That he'd propose a gallant toast:
"Hip hip hurray for the ladies!"

Late for a meeting and in great haste, Wriede's bourgeois, Herr Meier, scurried from the dinner table, groped for his coat and hat, and bid his dutiful wife farewell as he dashed out the door. Days of the week took on meaning for Herr Meier when he could relate them to his associational activities. Only during the fleeting moments snatched between his numerous commitments did he stop to recall his domestic responsibilities. Evidently, attendance at a meeting had become for the average bourgeois as common an after-dinner ritual as drinking a stein of hearty lager and smoking a pungent cigar.

Channeling this associational mania of the Bismarckian and Wilhelmine eras into concrete political achievement was the aim of the patriotic societies. These societies were apprehensive concerning Germany's ability to acquire and maintain the respect, colonial empire, battlefleet, and superior army consonant with the status of a great world power, and they feared the implications of an organized socialist movement, especially after the anti-Socialist legislation was rescinded in 1890. Of course, these suspicions reinforced one another and drew upon a host of other contributing factors, but they all pointed toward the potential, indeed the necessity, of rallying the nationalistic groups in society to preserve Germany's military power and social order. Coming as it did at the end of this developing series of patriotic societies, the Army League affords an admirable opportunity to assess the wider dimensions of the now extensive historiography regarding the role of the patriotic societies in reshaping the Right in Wilhelmine Germany and thereby recasting the political system as a whole.

## I

During the past fifteen years the historiography of the Wilhelmine era has undergone as rapid and tumultuous a transformation as some historians have attributed to the Wilhelmine economy itself. In the vanguard of this historiographical reorientation is Geoff Eley, who, since the mid-1970s, has engaged in a running critique of prominent historians such as Fritz Fischer, Hans Rosenberg, and Hans-Ulrich Wehler. Eley believes that these historians have viewed the Wilhelmine era from a teleological perspective, as but one link in a chain in the perplexing "problem of continuity of German policy from the First World War to the Second."[14] For Fischer, Rosenberg, and Wehler, Wilhelmine Germany—with its "entrenched authoritarian feudal elites," debilitated liberal movement, and a public easily aroused by patriotic symbols—offered evidence of a peculiarly distinctive German path, or *Sonderweg,* whose ultimate resolution was the Nazi episode.[15] Those entrenched elites were not irrelevant vestiges of feudalism but retained their political, social, and economic base through policies designed to protect German agriculture and contain the expansion of socialism. By erecting tariffs, constructing a battlefleet, and acquiring colonies—all aspects of social imperialism—these elites manipulated the malleable masses, diverted internal tensions outward, and stifled the emergence of political consciousness from below. As a consequence, German liberalism was severely handicapped and proved unable to resist the kinds of ultranationalist appeals that culminated in the rise of German fascism. Thus the patriotic societies both exemplified the fateful susceptibility of the German public to nationalist agitation, and the ability of Germany's ruling elites to preserve their position by a second "revolution from above" against forces for progressive change.

This suggestion of continuity, of an unbroken path from Bismarck to Hitler, came under attack in the 1970s by a group of young German historians from England, including both David Blackbourn and Richard Evans as well as Eley himself. These "revisionists" challenged the approach of the so-called new orthodoxy school. They assailed its members for what they perceived to be their narrowly conceived theoretical basis, which overemphasized the dominance of Prussian Junker elites and underestimated the extent of regional diversity and the contribution of the other federal states to the character of German development.[16] Eley initially put the older school's conclusions to the litmus test in his doctoral study of the German Navy League (founded 1898), one of the many patriotic societies that emerged in the tense atmosphere prior to the First World War.[17] Rather than confirming contentions about the role of associations like the Navy League in serving to perpetuate the domination of Prussian elites over the German public by appealing to their nationalistic sentiments, Eley instead offered evidence of a self-mobilized, popular nationalist association which was not only critical of governmental naval policy but which also, he suggested, illustrated the participation of newly emergent social groups that challenged the elitist hegemony.

In line with these assertions, Eley dismissed the idea of *Sammlungspolitik* as a successful policy pursued by Wilhelmine elites to keep the masses in check.[18] This policy of "gathering together," described by historian Eckart Kehr as Minister Miquel's attempt to gloss over the considerable differences that separated the interests of agrarians and industrialists by using the navy as a rallying point, seemed to Eley "to impute too much unity and coherence to the empire's 'ruling elites' and too much manipulative farsightedness to politicians like Bernhard v. Bülow and Alfred v. Tirpitz."[19] Eley argued that *Sammlungspolitik* was indeed a failure because not even the issue of the navy (let alone the broader issue of nationalism) could in 1897–98 negate the economic as well as political differences that divided the bourgeois Right.[20]

Eley used his empirical research on the Navy League to lay the basis for a broader study that would engage the historical profession in what he considered to be a more significant issue—the reshaping of the Wilhelmine Right. In his book entitled *Reshaping the German Right,* Eley argued that the Navy League was not an aberrant or isolated example of the limits of "elitist manipulation"; quite to the contrary, it represented part of a wider, independently mobilized populist movement of which the other patriotic societies, the Pan-German League and the Army League, in particular, were manifestations.[21] According to Eley, the populist impulse found in the patriotic societies emerged around 1890 when Germans were affected by a variety of far-reaching technological and educational advances that would have bearing on their political mentality. These patriotic societies thus offered proof that Wilhelmine society was far removed from the stagnant and depressing portrait painted by members of the "new orthodoxy" school and well beyond the grasp of the presumed iron rule of the "old order."[22] The Wilhelmine era was much more fluid and complex than previously assumed. As Eley contended:

> Somewhat against the grain of much Wilhelmine historiography I have conceived the post-Bismarckian period—inaugurated by processes of accelerated capitalist development, the end of the depression and the passage to imperialism—as one of far-reaching political change, in which the entire structure of the public domain was re-ordered. The particular history of the nationalist pressure groups only makes sense in the context of change: namely the decomposition of one structure of politics, and its gradual, uneven replacement by another.[23]

The structural base of German agrarian elites was gradually eroded by the advent of a new group of political activists who stemmed primarily from the middle classes but whose political locus was not the party system but rather the patriotic societies. These associational enthusiasts, Eley pointed out, represented a counter-political culture, termed "radical nationalism," which emerged to challenge the parliamentary system during the 1890s amidst growing political and economic expectations among Germany's population. Radical nationalism "entailed a populist commitment—a systematic appeal to the people, not just as a formality of public agitation, but as a constructive ideological assault on the old order, its parliamentary practices and forms of legitimacy."[24] It signaled, according to Eley, the demise of traditional *Honoratiorenpolitik* (the politics of notables) as practiced by the political parties since the mid-nineteenth century.[25] *Honoratioren* were "amateurs, who could afford to hold political office without financial reward . . . notables, whose social status was not defined by their political role" and who lived "for politics," not "off politics."[26] Unlike the *Honoratioren* of the parties, the new breed of associational activists that Eley describes did not remain indifferent toward their constituents but rather became vigorous and vociferous populist agitators who sought to involve the public in important national issues from which it had been excluded in the course of party debate. Eley concludes that the radical nationalists used the hypnotic appeal of nationalism as a stimulus for raising the political consciousness of the German middle classes and as a political battering ram with which to bring down the system of *Honoratiorenpolitik*.

Eley's corrective of previous historiographical accounts of the Wilhelmine period rests upon two specific components—the demise of *Honoratiorenpolitik* and the failure of *Sammlungspolitik*. For Eley the patriotic societies are a symptom of the political, social, and economic transformation in the two or three decades prior to World War I. They "registered a profound seismic shift at the base of German society, which sent heavy tremors of social aspiration upwards to the political surface of the new German nation-state."[27] Moreover, these populist associations prompted the parties of the Right to transform their unresponsive platforms, a process that occurred, according to Eley, in several stages.[28] After 1879 the failure of the established parties of the Right (the Conservatives, Free Conservatives, and National Liberals) to incorporate the interests of "new popular forces for recognition—the petty bourgeoisie in town and country, the peasantry, the professional and administrative strata" led to the formation of extraparliamentary societies, the patriotic associations as well as a host of economic interest groups, which stood "in opposition to the established conservative parties as 'parties of order.' "[29] Eley insists that the years between 1879 and 1908–9 witnessed the "rise of the petty bourgeoisie, which laid down its own organizations and forged its own distinctive ideologies, whose common characteristic was a militant populist nationalism, and whose point of negative departure was the political exclusiveness of the established party-political oligarchies."[30] Thus this populist impulse from the middle classes was clear proof that the Wilhelmine system was not held captive by feudal elites and that, therefore, it would be erroneous to imply that the "relationship of the so-called 'traditional élites' to the peasantry and petty-bourgeoisie was unproblematic."[31]

## II

Although Eley is by no means the most concise of historians, this brief outline summarizes what I believe to be the thrust of his powerful analysis. The breadth and scope of his argument are impressive; the contribution to the profession undeniable. Indeed he has broadened our perspective about the Wilhelmine epoch and has demonstrated that every historical age must be allowed to yield its own particular story rather than to be confined as a mere appendage to a specific historical event, in this case Nazism. Thus what I find most compelling about Eley's thesis is the role he assigns to the patriotic societies as mobilizers of a new kind of patriotic and political movement, independent of government control. Clearly, the aggressive policies on military and colonial issues (and on socialism as well) that were pursued by the patriotic societies to the consternation of the government point to a certain degree of popular extraparliamentary political mobilization and repudiate the notion that Wilhelmine society could offer no resistance to the firmly established control of feudal aristocrats. Beyond this, however, Eley's account of the reasons for this populist upsurge and the social origins of its leaders is not entirely convincing.

Both issues are in fact interrelated. By examining the origins of this populist movement through a "top down" approach, Eley attempts to confront the question of why the middle classes suddenly felt the urge to break ranks with the government's nationalist policies in the 1890s. Although emphasizing that "attention is rarely devoted to the internal relations between leaders and led, Berlin and the branches, the centre and the periphery," he unfortunately ignores his own advice, falling somewhat short of the localized study required to flesh out these themes.[32] Instead he draws his observations from the experiences of the leaders of the associations, in part because of the lack of readily available information about the social background of the rank and file membership. Yet even from the material at hand, Eley's assertions are at best contradictory. First, he differentiates between what he calls "old" and "new" populist agitators. The old or "moderate nationalists were invariably established at a pinnacle of achievement and social prestige (normally inherited), while their opponents [the "new"] were invariably outsiders with a reputation and political career still to make."[33] In fact, as I suggest in a later chapter, many of what he terms "new" or "radical" nationalist—individuals I would define as those for whom the patriotic societies had a raison d'être beyond the formalities of associational structure—did indeed stem from well-established middle-class (and even upper-middle-class) families with traditions of service, learning, and prestige.[34] They were not, as his book initially implies, drawn exclusively from the petty bourgeoisie. Yet Eley then contradicts himself by conceding that "the radical nationalists were composed not of the casualties of Germany's over-rapid but distorted modernization, but precisely those who by family, education and general cultural background were most comfortably integrated into Wilhelmine society."[35]

If, as I argue in this book, a considerable portion of what Eley calls radical nationalists came from upstanding households, then what were their reasons for dispensing with tradition and establishing their own independent course? Eley's thesis is that "radical nationalists were a group of people for whom conventional orientations towards the parties or older corporate institutions like the Army or civil service mattered relatively little."[36] While he provides examples of individuals who rebuked partisan politics and severed their ties with the parties of the Right with which they had formerly been associated, he also admits that the patriotic societies frequently attracted members of the National Liberal and conservative parties.[37] In fact, those nationalists who considered partisan politics to be paramount to "cattle trading" coexisted, if on a rather tenuous basis, with others who were ardent supporters of the parliamentary system, as the cases of both the Navy and Army leagues suggest. Moreover, contrary to his belief that radical nationalists disdained the twin pillars of the Prussian state, the army and bureaucracy, and publicly assailed their shortcomings, they nevertheless were the very same individuals who flaunted their military or bureaucratic status. Whether retired from or remaining on active military duty, army officials who were members of the patriotic societies took great pride in their service, and their stinging criticisms of the army (or navy) can be seen as a way in which to elicit reform. Given the curious lack of coordination between various departments within the military and bureaucracy, it is perhaps less surprising that these men were forced to make public their criticisms through the medium of the patriotic societies. Thus, the patriotic societies incorporated various segments of the middle strata (and occasionally of the nobility) whose notions concerning partisan politics were as diverse as their agenda for nationalist consensus. In this sense, then, nationalism was less a unifying factor than a divisive one.[38]

This disunity ultimately resulted in a split in the Navy League's ranks in 1907–8, as dissident radical nationalists seceded and searched for other avenues. The thrust of Eley's arguments regarding the aim of the patriotic societies revolves around events leading up to the Navy League crisis. Quite understandably, he chose to appropriate the contemporary phrase *National-radikaler Oppositionsorganization* to describe the process of nationalist fermentation occurring within the association and to apply it likewise to the other patriotic societies.[39] Radical nationalism suggests extremism—a kind of uncontrollable patriotic virus that ravaged the body politic, a radical departure from the basic patriotic loyalties individuals had displayed toward their country. Radical nationalism, however, is an appropriate term only when used to describe the motives of a minority, those associational activists who tended the machinery of the patriotic societies, who disseminated their propaganda, who carefully crafted their image, and who sought to ensure that all Germans embraced the need for national rejuvenation. Radical nationalists, therefore, believed that their job was never done; even when their association's particular tangible goals were met—perhaps the passage of naval or army bills—they nonetheless continued to support that association in the belief that there was a larger commitment required, less tangible, perhaps, but no less critical. Without this attention to a radicalized patriotism, the patriotic societies would probably not have appeared to hold their innovatory significance.

The term "popular nationalism," I would argue, has a broader application. While it incorporates the motives and actions of radical nationalists, it also implies a more sensitive appreciation of the role of the individuals who joined these associations. The popular nationalist label could apply to those who pledged themselves to one or more of the patriotic societies, who supported their tangible aims but who rarely participated once those aims were accomplished or sufficient progress toward them was perceived. In short, their ideological commitment to a broader reconstruction of nationalist politics in Imperial Germany was minimal, and their radicalism in this context, therefore, similarly limited. Patriotic societies offered to these people a way to make their voices heard on these issues, but beyond that failed to provide an alternative for the parliamentary system. As Eley correctly argues, popular nationalism was not primarily fervor orchestrated by the German government to rally the public around its domestic and foreign policies; Germans were not, to use the prevalent phrase, "mobilized from above" by government officials in the sense that they were manipulated like marionettes on a string and forced to perform perfunctory rituals of support (such as voting or membership). But, on the other hand, it was not merely a movement—as Eley portrays it—whose sole significance was the attempted demolition of traditional patterns of political behavior in which the mobilization of support for very specific issues (such as military expansion) figured almost as an accidental byproduct incidental to the larger goals in mind.

In testing the strength of the popular nationalist movement, its ability or inability to reconstruct the German Right and to impose a more responsive and populist platform upon the traditional parties, one must examine the last distinct phase in the evolution of the Imperial German Right, the years between 1909 and 1918. Theoretically, popular nationalist ideas should have been most attractive during these years, given the intense military and economic rivalry between Germany, Britain, and France.[40] Yet five years transpired between the unceremonious departure of the Navy League radicals and the emergence of the German Army League in January 1912. These were the years, according to Eley, "in which the right engineered a further feat of self-orientation no less far-reaching than the earlier one of 1878–79. It was characterized by a further ideological compromise, this time with the freshly mobilized petty bourgeoisie, and by the decisive acquisition of a genuine popular base. . . . The nationalist panacea supplied the ideological fixative which aided the integration of previously discordant forces."[41] The development of the Army League during this period, though, discounts this notion of the complete reconstitution of the German Right, suggesting instead the continued fragmentation of the "old" and the "new" Right.

### III

While the Navy League has attracted a good deal of attention, the Army League has escaped critical assessment. Over the years historians, regardless of their historiographical bent, generally have accepted precisely the image the Army League sought to project—of a nationalistic, highly influential association that had access to the highest corridors of power and tapped a deep reservoir of popular support. A few scholars have gone so far as to suggest that the league's political influence even exceeded that of its vaunted sister association, the Navy League.[42] The passage of successive military bills in 1912 and 1913, the presence of prominent notables on the league's national and regional executive committees, and a formidable membership of hundreds of thousands of German citizens certainly helped to create this aura of power. But these impressions are based primarily upon a narrow range of evidence derived largely from the league's highly visible national army campaign, and thus are misleading. A complete and accurate assessment of the league must consider other equally important but less visible aspects—its propaganda and the extent of its appeal and, correspondingly, the experience of associational life for the rank and file membership. Impressive membership figures and prominent names alone cannot do justice to the complexities and richness of local patterns of sociability. To accept the Army League's image at face value might be likened to diagnosing a patient without the proper instruments. Much escapes detection, for the naked eye and gentle touch of probing fingers are no substitute for the thorough examination.

Perhaps it would be more fruitful at this juncture to discuss what the Army

League actually was, rather than what it appeared to be. Founded in January 1912 and dissolved in 1935, the Army League represented the last link in a long chain of Wilhelmine patriotic societies dedicated to the revitalization of the German patriotic and militaristic spirit. With an immediate goal of securing German military preparedness through the quantitative expansion as well as the qualitative improvement of the army (i.e., the passage of the 1912 and 1913 army bills), the Army League's long-term aim was substantially broader and as such more revealing: the inculcation of the German populace with the spirit of nationalism and "proper" German morals, and the "neutralization" of any opponents of this schema. Two obvious targets of the league's campaign were the socialist and pacifist movements, which actively and vociferously condemned the growing militarization of German society as a vice, whereas the Army League hailed it as a virtue. As a separate subculture, the socialist movement resembled a nasty wound that resisted healing; it was a constant reminder of the persistence of class divisions within Wilhelmine society and of the clear limitations of the use of nationalism as a unifying element. Whereas another patriotic society, the Imperial League against Social Democracy, overtly sought to eradicate the socialist menace, the Army League shrouded its antisocialist vendetta in its militaristic rhetoric.

The establishment of the Army League in January 1912 was an event wholly independent of government involvement. As the league's founder and president, retired General August Keim, was eager to point out, the Army League was the creation of a group of concerned, independently minded, and nonpartisan citizens critical of governmental military policy. The government, in fact, saw no need for the Army League's existence, maintaining that the government alone had the army's best interest at heart, and it initially entertained the hope that the league would fail. Army League strategists placed moderate government officials who opposed their methods of regenerating the army and rejuvenating German society in the same category as the political left, as traitors to the national cause. The government's middle-of-the-road approach to the nation's military deficiencies and domestic problems, the league's leaders asserted, was simply incompatible with the dictates of foreign policy. What was required, they insisted, was swift, decisive, and radical action to avert an impending foreign and domestic crisis.

Creating the impression that government army policies were inept and insufficient while the league's were the most feasible for averting military disaster was the job of its propaganda machine. Once the presses were set into motion in January 1912, they spewed forth tens of thousands of copies of the league's monthly journal, *Die Wehr,* as well as pamphlets, circulars, commemorative medallions, stamps, and postcards, all generated for consumption by the masses. Three-quarters of the league's annual budget was expended on propaganda, prompting General Keim to declare that the Army League was not a *"Sparverein"*—a savings institution—and that its purpose was not to turn a profit. Propaganda was the sine qua non of the Army League's existence; it acted as a lifeline between the national association and local affiliates and between potential members and diehard supporters.

While taking into account the dimensions of foreign and military affairs, this book will be much less concerned in the strictest sense with military history, with analyzing the minutiae of the league's arguments on issues such as troop maneuvers or military technology, than it will be with assessing the league's wider impact on the political mobilization of the masses and hence its role as a popular nationalist association. Whereas previous accounts of the Army League have been concerned with its role in national affairs and the conduct of its leadership, this study seeks to transcend the narrow confines of nationalist politics by also examining the local and regional dimensions of popular nationalism. The massive propaganda blitz that the Army League launched in 1912 reached a point of diminishing returns by the end of 1913, corresponding to a stagnation in the league's membership. Why the Army League's seemingly invincible propaganda machine began to sputter, why Germans suddenly appeared less enthusiastic about the league in general after 1913, what it meant to be a member of the Army League, what level of commitment membership demanded, and how the views of the league's leaders corresponded with those of the rank and file are all issues that will be addressed, and their resolution will help clarify some of the misconceptions about the league and about the nature and appeal of popular nationalism.

# CHAPTER 1

# The Founding of the Army League

Wilhelmine Germans, one might argue, took their army for granted. To some extent, this was to be expected given the army's historic role as the nation's first and only line of defense. Periodic setbacks aside, the army somehow always managed to assume its responsibility to the nation and secure the necessary funding to maintain itself. Germans were accustomed to periodic increases in indirect taxes to provide for their army's upkeep. In 1898, however, the army found its unique position threatened by the building of a German battlefleet. Under the vigilant guidance of Admiral Alfred v. Tirpitz, the navy emerged as a rival to the army. Not only did the navy challenge the army for the public's affection, but it also competed for limited resources. Winning the public's hearts was one thing, tapping their pocketbooks another. The Reich's precarious financial state intensified this rivalry. While Germany's appetite for achieving the status of a world power (*Weltmacht*) grew, the resources available to finance its foreign ventures did not keep pace. Nearly 90 percent of the Reich's budget was expended on both branches of the military, and between 1896 and 1908 total armaments expenditures nearly doubled.[1] The largest portion of these expenditures, though, went toward underwriting Tirpitz's five naval bills, which received Reichstag approval between 1898 and 1912.

The two decades prior to the First World War witnessed a "complete militarization" of Imperial finances without concomitant fiscal reform.[2] In 1909, Secretary of the State of the Treasury, Adolf Wermuth, warned of the dire consequences likely to result from continued unrestricted military spending: "the internal structure of the Reich, its defense capabilities and its external prestige demand not merely a standstill, but an energetic reduction of [our] expenditure . . . [otherwise] the development will end inescapably in the complete collapse of our finances and all national activities stemming from them."[3] In the past, the government generally had resorted to higher indirect taxes to finance the military; but the strain that these taxes placed, in particular upon the workingman's budget, and the furor that they provoked among the Social Democratic Party (SPD), made government officials increasingly reluctant to impose any further such tax increases. The government did give serious consideration to the idea of direct taxation in the form of death or property taxes. It encountered stiff opposition, however, from the federal states, which sought to preserve their constitutional right to levy direct taxes, and from agrarian interests, which feared that augmenting the powers of the Reichstag in any way would both erode their critical base of authority in the local assemblies and increase their share of the nation's financial burden.[4] As a result, the government found itself wedged between irreconcilable forces. If the government raised indirect taxes, it would offend the average consumer and possibly provoke internal dissension; if it levied direct taxes, it threatened to unleash a furor among defenders of state's rights and the conservative agrarians. In 1906, however, the Reichstag was able to pass a law, with the support of the Catholic Center Party, which imposed a death duty on distant relatives. Nevertheless, this tax alone was insufficient to produce the necessary funding for such enormous military expenditures.[5]

The matter of Reich financial reform reached a climax in 1909 when Chancellor v. Bülow was forced to devise a fresh approach in order to fund Tirpitz's spiraling naval demands.[6] Bülow was intent on raising 80 percent of the necessary revenue from new indirect taxes and 20 percent from a death duty on inherited property.[7] On this occasion, the Conservatives mustered the support of the Catholic Center to stymie Bülow's efforts. They rejected the National Liberals' demand for the introduction of a direct tax and an increase in indirect taxes on liquor. With the defeat of these measures in July 1909, the Bülow bloc collapsed and Bülow himself resigned as chancellor. His successor, Theobald v. Bethmann Hollweg, would not find it any easier to reverse or even stem the increases in Germany's budget deficit.

Bethmann's concern for the state of the Reich's finances (and domestic tranquility) can be seen in his skepticism of Tirpitz's "luxury fleet." The Chancellor remained unconvinced that the Admiral's 2 : 3 ratio (for every three capital ships the British constructed, the Germans would build two) could be attained. The British stubbornly refused to relinquish naval mastery to the upstart Germans by maintaining their own "two power standard," i.e., building two additional ships for every one produced by Germany. Tirpitz, he suspected, was engaged in a futile exercise that would not only further escalate tensions between the two nations and possibly lead to war, but would also leave Germany's foremost line of defense, the army, denuded. Tirpitz's fleet was diverting critical funds that might have strengthened the army and thus was threatening to undermine the nation's position on the Continent. "Germany can conduct a strong policy in the sense of *Weltpolitik* only if she maintains her power on the Continent," Bethmann told the Reichstag, and the Chancellor was not alone in his thinking.[8] Officials in the German General Staff, in particular Erich Ludendorff, viewed Germany primarily as a Continental power whose geographic location in the heart of Europe, surrounded on all sides by enemies, dictated a strong, well-equipped army. In a series of articles published in *Militärwochenblatt,* Ludendorff argued that Germans were mistaken to presume that their fleet could ensure national security. It was the army, he stressed, that demanded immediate attention and not the navy. As another observer aptly put it, "battleships can't climb hills."[9]

The second Moroccan Crisis of July 1911 brought home this point. The German navy simply was not ready to fight the British, who threatened to intervene on

France's behalf (according to Lloyd George's Mansion House Speech of 21 July 1911) following Germany's abortive play for French Morocco. Spending more money on the navy and risking war with Britain was, for Bethmann, unthinkable. By the end of November moves were already underway within the government to secure a new army bill. In a memorandum of 29 November 1911, Major General Wandel, the director of the German War Department of the Prussian Ministry of War, surveyed Germany's position in light of Morocco.[10] He concluded that Britain would likely intervene in support of France and Russia should Germany go to war and that therefore the German army should prepare as rapidly as possible for the eventuality of a two-front conflict. If Germany was to become a true world power, it would have to prove its superiority on the Continent first. The reorientation of German armaments policy was a welcome turn of events for the Chancellor, members of the General Staff, and the leaders of the nascent Army League. For General August Keim, the Army League's founder and president, it was an opportunity to secure through the medium of an army league the nationalistic aims he had been advocating throughout his tenure in the Navy League and Pan-German League.

As the last of the patriotic societies, the Army League's relationship with its predecessors was significant. It would profit from their mistakes and capitalize upon their successes; it could expand the ranks of its own membership (and thus maximize its public visibility) by tapping the preexisting public sentiment toward popular nationalism; and in any event, it would operate within a milieu shaped, above all, by its two formidable mentors. It was the Pan-German League and Navy League that set the standards against which other patriotic associations were measured, and it was primarily their members who formed the ranks of the Army League.

Inaugurated in April 1891 as the General German League (*Allgemeiner Deutscher Verband*), the Pan-German League came to envision itself as "the purest embodiment of the nationalist cause, standing above the political parties and their conflict, the supreme coordinator of individual nationalist campaigns."[11] The league's exuberant confidence in its later years certainly belied the uncertainties that plagued its formative development. For two years (between 1891 and 1893) structural and tactical issues within the league tended to have a divisive rather than a unifying effect. Disputes over membership rights (i.e., whether Jews were eligible to join), financial woes produced by legal restrictions and excessively low dues (one mark minimum), and poor communication between the national organization and local branches all threatened the league's tripartite program of developing German national consciousness, defending the rights of ethnic Germans living abroad, and advocating an aggressive foreign policy.[12] In 1893 the league was forced to reorganize when members broke ranks over the issue of whether the association should evolve into a political party modeled after Bismarckian principles, as a "union of all patriots, not on the basis of a feckless program of mediation . . . but a firm and decisive intervention," or adopt a nonpolitical (*überparteilich*) stand.[13]

New leadership and a name change (to the Pan-German League) in 1894 enabled the league to embark on a fresh course. Two friends, Ernst Hasse and Adolf Lehr, cooperated to provide the association with firm and enthusiastic leadership. To restore lost confidence, the two men solicited substantial contributions from wealthier members to improve the league's finances and repaired the communication breakdown between the national association and local affiliates by establishing a weekly journal, the *Alldeutsche Blätter*.[14] Membership figures responded in a positive fashion to these measures, and old chapters were now revived as well as new ones founded. Still, the Pan-German League attracted only a limited following and in all the years of its existence never achieved the mass backing enjoyed by the Navy and Army leagues. At its height in 1901, Pan-German membership stood at an estimated twenty-two thousand, as opposed to the hundreds of thousands who flocked to the other two patriotic societies.[15]

What the Pan-German League lacked in popular appeal, however, it compensated for in the breadth of its platform. It was clearly a multidimensional league; by virtue of its broadly nationalistic platform the league was able to target as worthy of its attention any issue remotely related to German patriotism. In particular, the league focused upon two national issues, the Eastern Marches and the navy, although it was eventually forced to share the limelight for these concerns when organizations devoted specifically to these issues were founded, the Eastern Marches Society (*Deutscher Ostmarkenverein*, 1894) and the Navy League (1898). Nevertheless, the competition served to underscore the need for a concerted "national front" at whose forefront the Pan-Germans hoped to be. Pan-Germans thought of themselves as superpatriots and loyal monarchists whose duty it was to level harsh criticism of governmental policy when it fell short of the mark.[16] By proclaiming itself as the guardian of the "national interest," the Pan-German League felt obliged to pursue its goals, secure in the knowledge that German public opinion, that mighty weapon in the arsenal of the popular nationalist movement, was on its side.

By the mid-1890s popular enthusiasm for the naval issue provided the league with an opportunity to agitate for a massive program of naval construction and thereby strengthen its influence in national affairs. Divisions within the Navy Office over the lengths to which this naval expansion should proceed and the repercussions thereof served to underscore Pan-German assertions about the government's indecisiveness regarding national matters. The league responded by offering the Naval Office its services in orchestrating broader popular support for Germany's naval program. Charged in 1897 with the duty of bolstering Germany's fleet, Admiral Tirpitz turned down the league's offer of assistance, preferring instead to steer what he considered to be a smoother, more gradual course than the one the Pan-Germans demanded. What ensued in 1898 was a scramble by several pronavalist groups for validation to acquire the right to rally public opinion. One of the groups, which was supported by heavy industry and led by journalist Victor Schweinburg, perceived the navy not simply as a national issue but also as a possible financial bonanza. Although committed to naval expansion, the Schweinburg group retained complete confidence in the decisions of the Navy Office and refused criticism of its policies.[17] A second navalist group, which was led by the Berlin cod-liver-oil magnate, J. E. Stroschein, and included independent nationalist thinkers as well as some Pan-Germans, viewed the purpose of naval agitation in a completely different fashion. Its objective was to mobilize public support for a far-reaching and aggressive naval building program and to resort to open and active criticism of government naval policy. A third navalist group, the Pan-German League itself, "saw their own organization as a perfectly adequate base for future naval agitation" and viewed the Stroschein initiative with considerable apprehension.[18]

In April 1898, with the tacit support of Admiral Tirpitz, the Schweinburg circle stole the march by founding the Navy League.[19] Not to be upstaged, the Stroschein and Pan-German League factions put aside their differences to reconstruct the Navy League along more "populist" lines in order to "carry the naval idea to the people."[20] In 1899 Stroschein and Heinrich Rippler, a Pan-German and editor-in-chief of the nationalist *Tägliche Rundschau,* spearheaded a drive to divest the Navy League's executive ranks of "governmentalists" and replace them with "populists." Using the press as their forum for debate, the "populists" demanded that the Navy League desist from being "an 'agitation team' for heavy industry and government and become instead 'a free association of all nationally-minded German men friendly to the fleet, a *Volksverein.*' "[21] Their campaign succeeded in removing from the Navy League some of their more prominent opponents. In 1899 secretary Schweinburg departed and in 1901 both his successor, Carl Wilhelm Freiherr v. Beaulieu-Marconnay, and Navy League president Prince Wilhelm zu Wied resigned.[22]

As a result, the Navy League underwent a transitional period between 1901 and 1903. At first membership declined from over 238,000 in 1901 to slightly over 233,000 by 1903, but by 1904 it began to rebound, partly in response to the league's new constitution (1902), which provided a tighter organizational framework.[23] The year 1904 marked as well a turning point in the outlook of the Pan-German League and Navy League. Dismayed by stagnant membership and resentful of the Navy League's expanding membership, the Pan-German League assailed the German public for failing to recognize its importance as a warehouse for the export of nationalist ideology. The league claimed to devote itself to all worthy national causes—not one to the exclusion of the other—and as such believed it offered Germans a wider inventory of patriotic options from which to choose. In contrast, the Navy League and the Eastern Marches Society were, in the Pan-German League's estimation, one-dimensional organizations. The Pan-German League's leadership could not comprehend why the other two competing associations would appeal to a broader segment of Germany's populace when its association could not. Disillusioned by the Pan-German League's fall from national prominence, its president, Hasse, accused Germans of lacking political acumen (they were, according to him, "dull-witted" and "politically childlike") and added that they deserved the government they had.[24] Popular nationalists in the Navy League, on the other hand, offered a different assessment. A politically mature but underrepresented German public awaited its leader; popular nationalists and their medium, the Navy League, had arrived to provide Germans with a platform from which to express themselves politically. Making the political system more responsive to the desires and needs of the people by seeking to dismantle the remaining vestiges of *Honoratiorenpolitik* was the approach that the popular nationalists of the Navy League pursued, while the Pan-German League relied on resolving issues of national importance through a socially more restricted base.

The critical contest for control of the Navy League's agitational direction occurred between 1904 and 1908 and involved a struggle between two internal factions, the moderates (governmentalists) and the radicals. The moderate wing, led by a Catholic nobleman from Bavaria, Freiherr v. Würtzburg, insisted that the Navy League restrict its activities to enlightening the public on naval matters rather than engaging the Naval Office in running battles over the size of the fleet.[25] Würtzburg welcomed the league's aim of constructing a broad alliance of Germans, with the exclusion of the SPD, but believed that if any national consensus was to be reached, it would have to include the Catholic Center Party. After all, the Center was the pivotal party in the Reichstag, holding one hundred or more seats in every election with one exception since 1890. Therefore, he believed, the league should accommodate it. General August Keim, a leader of the populist faction, took issue with these assumptions. First of all, Keim was irreconcilably opposed to any suggestion that he refrain from placing further demands on the government and Naval Office. Educating the public was not a passive task, according to Keim; rather it involved active political discourse directed, when necessary, against any party or governmental agency that refused to recognize the urgency of expanding the fleet. Second, Keim's attitude toward the Center differed markedly from Würtzburg's. The general bitterly resented the party's tactic of using "its parliamentary strength to deter the government from bringing in a vital measure for national defense," of placing confessional and political considerations over national ones.[26] Keim and his supporters regarded the Würtzburg group as "defenders of the existing social and political order," who upheld the *Honoratioren* system, opposed budgetary reform, and had "no desire to abandon agriculture by making Germany into a purely industrial state."[27] In more specific terms, the conflict within the Navy League revealed the rising tension between the defenders of the conservative agrarian order and status quo and their bourgeois, populist challengers.

Keim, who was at the center of the internal crisis, would found the Army League in 1912. A champion of the populist cause, General Keim was a fiercely independent, strong-willed, and hot-headed maverick (a "*Feuerkopf*") whose commitment to nationalism and whose experience in military affairs made him one of the most colorful figures of the popular nationalist movement.[28] Born into an old Hessian military family in 1845, Keim followed family tradition by becoming a career soldier. In 1862 he entered the army as a cadet in the same infantry regiment to which both his father and grandfather had belonged. He subsequently served in the Wars of Unification (Austro-Prussian and Franco-Prussian) and was wounded in the line of duty, an injury that would later cause him considerable discomfort and interfere with his associational duties. A fondness for history, particularly military history, led him at age thirty-three to interrupt his military career briefly to join the staff of the *Kölnische Zeitung* and *Hamburger Nachrichten* as a military correspondent. In 1881 he returned to serve on the German General Staff but retained his penchant for journalism by continuing to do freelance work. A newspaper article in which he criticized current government military policy as being deficient and unresponsive to the need for army expansion resulted in Keim's demotion to field officer in Alsace in 1889 and in Celle in 1891. The experience of being dressed down by his military superiors left Keim with a bitter taste toward authority.

The incident, rather than ending Keim's military career, actually provided him with a new avenue to pursue his military crusade. Keim's deep concern for the condition of the German army captured the interest of Chancellor Leo v. Caprivi, who engaged Keim as primary spokesman for the 1893 Army Bill.[29] It was Keim's responsibility to administer the publicity campaign for the bill, for which he put his journalistic talents and persuasive abilities to work, publishing a series of pamphlets on the urgent need for army reform and lobbying Reichstag delegates on the bill's merits. Impressed by the general's tireless and successful efforts to nurse the bill's passage through the recalcitrant Reichstag, Chancellor Caprivi awarded him the Order of the Crown, Third Class, in July 1893. Keim, reluctant to abandon the limelight, returned to penning articles for prestigious military journals, including v. Loebell's *Jahresberichten über die Veränderungen und Fortschritte im Militär-wesen,* and the *Militärwochenblatt,* always seeking to fine-tune his criticism of army policy and find a suitable outlet for his cause. In all of his articles one finds the recurrent theme of the need for the army to undergo routine and periodic vigorous "check-ups" to prevent it from falling behind its Continental counterparts. In 1899, at the age of fifty-four, Keim retired from the army with the rank of major-general. Why Keim took an early retirement is not at all clear, although the likelihood of further promotion appeared remote, given the general's penchant for criticizing military policy. If Keim indeed stepped aside for this reason, then this could explain at least in part his antipathy toward the practice of *Honoratiorenpolitik.* For it was he, who by dint of his opinions and bourgeois roots, was being excluded from the decision-making process by the patrician military elite.

At age fifty-four, however, Keim was hardly ready to retire to quieter pastures. The patriotic societies offered him a ready-made forum in which he could pursue his nationalistic goals. In 1900, at the invitation of league president Prince Wilhelm zu Wied, the general joined the Navy League and immediately sought to entrench himself in its leading circles. Within months of joining, he succeeded in getting himself elected to the Presidium, and in 1902 he took charge of the league's propaganda. As a result, Keim was able to expand his political network to include other popular nationalists who in time would form the core of the Army League.[30] By 1904 Keim was directing the Navy League's ambitious naval expansion campaign and was eager to resolve the dispute within the association between "governmentalists" and "populists." For the general, there was only one logical choice—a populist program that would enable him and other sympathizers to continue to assault the government with their demands for a more substantial naval program. Keim's insistence on molding the Navy League into an aggressively independent association and his intolerant and obtrusive personality set him on a head-on collision course with the governmentalist faction. To Würtzburg's followers, Keim was an agent provocateur who attempted to use "the movement for political ends, to make it serviceable to certain political interests at the pleasure of individual leaders."[31] In 1907 the dispute finally exploded when it was revealed that Keim, at the behest of Chancellor Bülow, had engaged in secret electioneering against the Catholic Center Party in the 1907 Hottentot elections and had used Navy League funds in the process.[32] By involving the Navy League in political affairs and by undermining the Center's parliamentary position, Keim clearly had made a mockery of the league's nonpartisan vow.

Letters purloined from Keim's office provided damaging evidence of the covert affair and were published in February 1907 in a number of newspapers with close ties to the Center Party. Not only did the letters demonstrate Keim's antipathy toward the Center, but they also smacked of religious bigotry, earning him the title of "Furor Protestanticus."[33] The major embarrassment that the entire affair's revelation undoubtedly caused Keim only served to reinforce his determination to regain the upper hand. One of his first steps was to mend fences with the Catholic community, starting with Cardinal Fischer, an eminent figure in the Church: "That during the elections I should have said or written anything which would be taken as showing animosity towards the Catholic Church or my Catholic compatriots is not at all true!" he lied to the Cardinal. "I am especially outraged by the defamatory remarks because I am the son of a Catholic mother and my sisters are also Catholics and married Catholic husbands. One sister . . . died in a convent. As a young officer I used to visit at the home of Bishop Köttler [sic? Ketteler]. For all these reasons, it is incomprehensible for an upstanding man like myself to have fostered such ill-will towards my fellow Catholic citizens."[34]

This confession of innocence fell on deaf ears. Calls by Catholic Navy League members for his removal from the Presidium were accompanied by a chorus of vociferous condemnations of his clandestine activities by Center Party and Socialist delegates in the Reichstag. Yet it was not simply the Bavarian Catholic faction that felt besieged and betrayed by Keim and his followers. There was considerable dissent, too, among other high-ranking league officials who accused the general of seeking to negate all of the Navy League's accomplishments. For example, Prince Karl v. Urach, president of the league's Württemberg Federation and a respected public figure, charged the Keim faction with political "terrorism" in trying to strangle its opposition.[35] In a poignant letter to *Geheimer Kommerzienrat* Alexander v. Pflaum, honorary president of the Württemberg Federation, Urach warned of the severe repercussions should Keim be allowed to pursue his "political course" and asked his colleague despairingly why the general was so determined to make "our poor association" a political one. The entire crisis, the prince concluded, had been cleverly orchestrated at the highest levels and reflected the selfish wishes of a minority, not the approval of the majority. He pronounced Keim to be a purely "party man and a born politician."[36]

Because Keim believed that the interests of the nation took precedence over the interests of the few, he forced the final showdown between the opposing factions within the Navy League. His election as Navy League executive chairman in December 1907 triggered the penultimate series of events leading to the split in the league's ranks. In January 1908 the Catholic (Bavarian and governmentalist) delegation withdrew from the emergency Congress held in Cassel, taking with them more than eighteen thousand members.[37] From 1908 onwards the Navy League had a new president, Admiral Hans v. Koester, and toed an independent line, irrespective of government policy.

With the Navy League crisis now resolved, Keim moved on to what he hoped would be more fertile pastures. By mid-February 1908 he had found a new outlet for his popular nationalist impulses—the Pan-German League. The general's membership in the Pan-German League, however, did not appear to have been necessarily an expression of ideological sympathy with the association's platform. Although he supposedly confessed to its leader, Heinrich Class, that he "now knew where he belonged" and that he wanted to spend the rest of his life in the league's service, it is indeed questionable how sincere Keim's profession of faith really was.[38] It was natural for Keim to have gravitated toward the Pan-German League upon leaving the Navy League, given that the Pan-German League supported the same kinds of nationalistic endeavor as did Keim and was a kind of think tank for popular nationalists. But for Keim, the Pan-German League would serve only as a temporary holding tank whereby the general could launch a series of patriotic societies based upon his populist visions. The Pan-German League's social basis was simply too restrictive and its membership too limited for the aims that Keim sought to achieve. The general's alliance with the league, therefore, was a marriage of convenience.

Keim was certainly not a passive bystander; he belonged to the world of movers and shakers. He was a demagogue—a skilled orator and manipulator who learned how to push all the right buttons, as he had demonstrated in his rapid rise to the top of the Navy League.[39] In the Pan-German League he followed the same pattern, getting acquainted or becoming reacquainted with leading Pan-Germans in order to facilitate his election or appointment to the league's powerful ruling bodies and to convince them of the efficacy of his nationalist plans. In the first year of his association with the league (1908), the general campaigned for the idea of a *Nationaler Bund,* a kind of umbrella organization for the patriotic societies that was to be funded by the Pan-German League. Class and other league officials rejected Keim's idea, but the general refused to allow this temporary inconvenience to derail his project.

Keim's true intentions were not lost on some Pan-Germans. Alfred Geiser, league secretary, commented on the general's activities to president Class: "I don't know whether Freiherr v. Stössel has already informed you about Keim's intentions concerning the *Nationaler Bund.* . . . Keim has obviously resolved not to leave center stage [*nicht von der Bühne abzutreten*]."[40] The league wanted to avoid at all cost Keim's bid to steal its spotlight and to cast it squarely upon himself. It feared that Keim's renewed visibility, coupled with the founding of a successful new organization, could leave the Pan-German League high and dry (as had nearly happened with the establishment of the Navy and Eastern Marches leagues).[41] On the other hand, should Keim's new organization fail, it would reflect poorly on the Pan-German League, not simply on Keim himself. This, too, would deal a potentially devastating blow to its image and reputation. Class, therefore, implored fellow Pan-German Ernst Graf zu Reventlow to convince Keim to abandon his plan: "In your discussion with Keim I request that you make him aware of the dangers to his political reputation which would result from another associational failure. On the contrary, he can make himself quite useful here in the Pan-German League where he can find his desired independence."[42] The absence of funding rather than the fear of failure forced Keim to abandon his plans temporarily in 1908.

Some Pan-Germans thought the only way to prevent Keim from founding a separate organization was to elect him to the *Vorstand,* thereby forcing him to be responsible to the organization as a whole. Yet even his election to this powerful board in 1909 did not satiate his voracious appetite, as Heinrich Pohl, Pan-German journalist, explained to Class in April 1909: "I know very well that at present he is still not Pan-German through and through and that he is neither a leading spirit nor a dispassionate politician."[43] How to harness the general to the Pan-German cause and simultaneously satisfy his excessive ego was the challenge that Class faced. *Rechtsanwalt* Putz, a loyal Pan-German and former Navy League activist, understood Keim's character but was far from sympathetic to what he considered the general's selfish intentions. "I am very critical of Keim and am totally convinced . . . that he only can, and desires to be, more useful where he can experience the adulation he desires," Putz revealed to Class. "He first revealed his Pan-German heart only after he was excluded from the Navy League."[44] The "Old Man's [*der Alte*]" writings, according to Putz, also demonstrated his "boundless vanity and self-centeredness."[45] Once again, in February 1910, the idea was discussed whether to place Keim on the *Geschäftsführender Ausschuss* (executive committee) as a reward for serving the league rather than his own individual interests. This time the suggestion of promotion met with considerable resistance, as reflected in one member's warning to Class against pursuing such a measure:

> I want to dissuade you strongly from electing General Keim to the *Ausschuss*. Apart from the fact that he is a hothead who enjoys banging his head against the wall, I observed at the previous *Ausschuss* meeting that although he is an experienced soldier, he lacks all understanding for discipline and parliamentary procedures. I believe that we have better candidates . . . for this position. It should lie in your best interest not to have Keim in the *Ausschuss*.[46]

Although Keim clearly had many enemies, he nonetheless managed to get himself elected to the *Ausschuss* in 1910, and one year later was installed in the league's highest governing body, the *Hauptleitung* (presidium).[47] For Keim to have overcome the opposition, he must have enjoyed the support of president Class. Even though Keim and Class did not necessarily agree on the means by which their nationalistic goals could be realized, they nevertheless had respect for each other's opinions, from which a friendship developed.[48]

Not that friendship or receipt of a high-ranking position in the association would dissuade Keim from pursuing his quest of establishing new patriotic societies. Between 1908 and 1910 he launched the Patriotic Book League (*Vaterländische Schriftenverband*), the General German Writing Association (*Allgemeiner Deutscher Schriftenverein*), and the German Youth League (*Deutscher Jugendverband*).[49] The first two served primarily as clearing houses for the public distribution of pamphlets and books deemed by Keim to be of patriotic significance.[50] Unlike the others, however, the Youth League had the potential of becoming a mass association. Its intention was to instruct the nation's youth in the virtues of patriotism by combining physical exercise, which would build muscle and promote discipline, with intellectual development through the study of patriotic books (to be provided, of course, by Keim's own Patriotic Book League and General German Writing Association).[51] Dues for the Youth League were set at a minimum of four marks for individuals and ten marks for corporate associates. The founding of *Jungdeutschlandbund* (Young Germany) by General Colmar von der Goltz in 1911 and the establishment of its dues at a one mark minimum soon overshadowed Keim's Youth League and eventually forced him to cooperate with von der Goltz's league.[52] Recalling some of the earlier predictions by Pan-Germans about the general's associational activities, it would appear in retrospect that Keim's ventures fell wide of the mark and did little to enhance his own personal stature or the reputation of the Pan-German League itself.

Although the three associations failed to attract a wider audience, they nevertheless provided the general with a ready-made forum with which to test his ideas on another nationally related interest—the military and spiritual preparedness of the nation. Having begun his career as a spokesman on army affairs, he now returned to resume his crusade for army expansion within the Pan-German League. In 1910 he proclaimed himself the league's expert on army affairs and sought to convince fellow Pan-Germans of the expeditiousness with which the army's deficiencies must be redressed. Since Pan-German sympathies lay with the navy, Keim was forced to wage an uphill struggle. Earlier efforts by Pan-Germans such as Graf zu Reventlow (an ardent naval enthusiast) were unsuccessful in persuading their colleagues of the importance of balancing the needs of both the army and navy so that neither would suffer at the other's expense. In 1906 and again in 1908 Reventlow called upon fellow Pan-Germans to augment Germany's naval program with army expansion and the fulfillment of universal military service.[53] His warnings against the myopia of according the navy financial primacy remained unheeded until Keim took up the army's cause in 1910. Throughout that year and into 1911 Keim reiterated his message that the German army could no longer rest upon its laurels and would have to struggle to catch up with its Continental rivals. Keim argued that Germany would have to possess a strong, formidable army whose quality would have to be maintained regardless of financial considerations.[54] In 1910 the foundations for the Army League were being laid, but it took the Second Moroccan Crisis of 1911 to secure them.

The failure of Germany to secure territory in Morocco at France's expense in July 1911 brought the nation to the brink of war and provoked further criticism of the government from popular nationalist circles.[55] The lead article in the *Alldeutsche Blätter* announced: "We can now see clearly that we cannot rely on our government to advance the Fatherland's world prestige."[56] Through indecision and incompetence, the government, the Pan-German League insisted, had failed to prevent Germany's nightmare from becoming a reality: the nation stood alone in the heart of Europe with enemies poised on all sides and fielded an army that was insufficiently prepared. Something had to be done to prevent the nation from becoming further entangled in the web spun by its foes; since the government had demonstrated itself incapable of handling both foreign and domestic affairs, the time had come for Pan-Germans to assume these responsibilities. "Ministers come and go but the *Volk* remains. And it is this *Volk,* amidst all the hopes of the second half of the year, which must be wiling to be led forward. . . . It [the *Volk*] is the pioneer of our great future."[57] The government's mishandling of the Moroccan Crisis provided the Pan-Germans with additional ammunition for rallying patriotic Germans around the league and breathed new life into dormant chapters.[58] It also provided Keim with the opportunity to launch his new patriotic association, which he christened the *Deutscher Wehrverein* (German Army League).

Preparations for the Army League were underway sometime during July or August 1911.[59] As a high-ranking official in the Pan-German League, Keim now had access to men who shared his national vision and who would fill the ranks of his new organization. Not all of the Army League's officials and ardent supporters, however, boasted membership in the Pan-German League; many who joined initially were old friends of Keim from his Navy League days or acquaintances he had made through his journalistic ventures. Although the Army League attracted many Pan-Germans and was founded while Keim was active in the Pan-German League, it was not, as some historians have argued, a Pan-German enterprise. The Army League was Keim's, not Class's, brainchild and its platform was undeniably Keimian, despite aspects of Pan-German ideology. Keim had nurtured and created the idea of an army league, most likely even before his association with the Pan-German League. In many ways, it was a natural culmination of Keim's concerns. Class was simply its godfather; he supported the Army League's efforts but played only a minor role in its development.[60]

Keim used the auspices of the Pan-German League but jealously guarded his precise plans for the Army League from other members, Class included. Sometime during the spring/summer of 1911 Keim offered the position of business manager (*Geschäftsführer*) to Theodore Bassler, editor of the *Alldeutsche Blätter* from October 1910 through May 1911.[61] Bassler accepted the post without Keim's having consulted the editor's former boss, Class. Upon learning of Keim's arrangement with Bassler, Class expressed his displeasure with the general's clandestine offer, writing: "I am glad that your relationship with Bassler is satisfactory. I did not expect it to have been any other way but I am only puzzled as to why you engaged him without consulting me beforehand."[62] Unfortunately, neither Keim's nor Class's correspondence reveals the reason behind Keim's maneuverings or choice of Bassler as business manager. It would appear, however, that Bassler's brief stint as editor of *Alldeutsche Blätter* may have been an indication that Class was dissatisfied with his employee's performance. As one Pan-German suggested in a letter to Class: "Keim is very demanding, and it is doubtful whether Bassler will suffice for him in the long run."[63] Indeed, Bassler served Keim for only one year.

The case of Bassler was not the only indication that Keim was determined to maintain complete control of the Army League. Certainly the general realized that he required the financial help of the Pan-German League to see the new league to fruition; thus, he could not afford to alienate its leaders to the point that they would refuse him initial aid. After all, as an officer of the Pan-German League, Keim was most likely aware that plentiful funds were available for such purposes and was eager to ensure that some of the surplus found its way into the Army League.[64] Honing his skills as a successful fundraiser (demonstrated during the 1893 Army Bill campaign), he obtained from the Pan-German treasury an unspecified amount designated to offset the basic costs associated with the organization's founding. When, however, these initial funds were exhausted, Keim requested but was denied access to an additional 7,000 to 8,000 marks. Writing apologetically to his friend,

Class explained: "Whether I will be able to aid you in your financial woes appears doubtful, although I will certainly try my best. Because of the statutory provisions I am unable to give you money from the *Wehrschatz*. Nevertheless, I will attempt to contact certain individuals who, although not Pan-German Leaguers, may be interested [in funding the Army League]."[65] The *Wehrschatz,* to which Class referred, was a fund established in 1903 to which wealthier Pan-Germans contributed voluntarily and whose resources were used in the aid of "German national endeavors" but not toward defraying the cost of running the Pan-German League.[66] Theoretically, then, the Army League should have been eligible for *Wehrschatz* funds. Certainly the Army League's goals fell squarely within the category of "national endeavors." If the Pan-German League was behind the association's founding and was using Keim as a front man, the additional funding that Keim sought would have contributed to the image the Pan-German League relished, that of an umbrella association coordinating and administering national causes. It seems out of character for the Army League to have been denied its share of the financial resources.

To lessen the sting of refusal, Class fulfilled his promise to Keim to recruit potential contributors. Among them were two Pan-German industrialists, Emil Ludwig Possehl, a wealthy iron magnate with extensive holding companies in Russia and Norway, Senator, and an original member of the Pan-German League; and Johann Neumann, a senator from Lübeck, one-time Mayor of that city, close friend of Class, and Pan-German League executive member.[67] Convinced that he had sold Senator Possehl on the Army League, Class reported optimistically to Keim that Possehl was "so enthralled that he most certainly and immediately will make a large donation."[68] In contrast to Possehl's apparent enthusiasm, Senator Neumann appeared less taken with Keim's association and chose to donate 80,000 marks to another national cause.[69] Enraged by Neumann's and other unnamed individuals' refusal to aid his league, Keim accused industrialists of flaunting their patriotism and of failing to follow through with their nationalist commitment in financial terms. In less elegant terminology, Keim demanded that the industrialists "put up or shut up." Individuals of this kind were, in the general's words, "stupid" (*"Die Leute sind eben alle wie vor den Kopf geschlagen"*).[70] Feeling betrayed and fearful of failure, Keim made one last plea to Class, requesting his aid in obtaining an interest-free loan (*"zinseloses Darlehen"*) from the Pan-German League, which the general promised would be repaid as soon as the Army League was on firm footing.[71] In Keim's inability to secure Pan-German funds gratis is yet another indication of the tenuous relationship between the new league and Class's association.

Equally significant is the length to which the Army League went to avoid giving the public the impression that it was a Pan-German satellite. In certain circles, the Pan-German label suggested a kind of nationalism practiced by an elite minority with a limited understanding of Germany's domestic and foreign affairs. The future of Germany's military (and hence the future of the German nation), Keim reckoned, depended upon the support of all nationally minded Germans, and he believed the government was more likely to ignore the demands of a small group of superpatriots than it was to overlook the wishes of an entire nation. Thus, in order to create the optimum conditions for the success of his league's goals, Keim necessarily denied any ties with the Pan-German League. Local Army League branches, in fact, practiced a process of subtle disassociation. In Hamburg, for example, the local secretary/treasurer, Dr. Warner Poelchau, director of the Hamburg branch of the Deutsche Bank, took special pains to reassure potential members and apprehensive government officials that the association did not adhere to "Pan-German ideology [*alldeutsche Ideen*]"[72] One member of the Bremen branch, C. Adolph Jacobi, confided to a colleague that he had joined the Army League under the assumption that it was in no way associated with Pan-German ideals: "Upon the persuasion of an acquaintance, historian and *Geheimrat* Dr. Dietrich Schäfer, I pledged my interest in its goals but with some reservation because, as you know, I have always avoided anything which even remotely appeared to be chauvinistic or Pan-German in character."[73] By asserting the Army League's independence from Pan-German tentacles, Keim sought to resume the position he had relinquished following the Navy League Crisis—as the fulcrum of a distinctive popular nationalist movement.

Initial preparations for the Army League now squared away, Keim at age sixty-six took his army campaign to the public through the medium of the press in November 1911. The campaign was strategically timed to harness the pent-up resentment that followed the failure in Morocco and to coincide with the initial preparations accompanying the upcoming Reichstag elections of January 1912. The Moroccan Crisis had proved that the German navy alone was incapable of defending Germany's interests abroad and at home; only a revitalized army in conjunction with a strong German fleet could protect the nation from its surrounding enemies. This was the message that resounded in Keim's articles and speeches throughout the end of 1911 and beginning of 1912, and it was one that Keim expected the nation's voters to implement at the polls.[74]

Independent newspapers like *Der Tag* provided a forum for the Army League, as did those with ties to the Pan-German League, such as the *Tägliche Rundschau, Die Post,* and the *Rheinisch Westfälische Zeitung.* In fact, the first announcement of the Army League's founding appeared in the *Tägliche Rundschau* in the form of an open letter.[75] Not until two weeks after this announcement did the *Alldeutsche Blätter* mention the new league's existence.[76] In each of the articles Keim reiterated his demand for an end to the government's practice of *Vogel-Strauss Politik* (literally, "ostrich politics"), of burying its head in the sand at a time when Germany required strong leadership. According to the retired general, now was the time for the government to redress the army's weaknesses by providing it with the substantial funding and technological improvements required of a top-flight fighting force. Using the French army as a comparison, Keim argued that the German army at present was inferior on several counts.[77] First, he maintained that the French peacetime army was larger than that of the German: he calculated that the French force stood at 1.4 percent of the French population, whereas the German army's strength was only 0.94 percent of Germany's nearly 65 million inhabitants.

The general's calculations, however, were based on erroneous figures. In 1910 France's population stood at 39 million, not the 25 million figure Keim had used. Of course, the smaller population figure served Keim's (and the Army League's) purpose since it created precisely the image that its founder sought to create—that of France as military aggressor, ready at a moment's notice to do battle with a militarily inferior and unprepared Germany. His figures, too, pointed up the fact that Germany had strayed from the stipulations of Bismarck's famous "One Percent Law," which stated that a minimum of 1 percent of Germany's actual population must serve in the army.[78] Second, he insisted that French soldiers received better and more efficient training for combat than did their German counterparts. And as a result of more extensive and intensive training sessions, French recruits were, on the whole, healthier as well. On both counts the German army paled in comparison.

Few German newspaper readers could fail to understand the general's seemingly simple and supposedly accurate calculations denoting Germany's unenviable position as a second-class military nation. Germany had wandered from the path that its greatest military monarch, Frederick the Great, had paved. Restoring the German army's health would require grave sacrifice on the part of the nation. Aside from throwing their complete support behind the new army bill of 1912, Germans, Keim argued, might have to consent to paying additional taxes or even a special military tax (*Wehrsteuer*) so that the German sword would be "as razor sharp in peacetime as it is during war."[79] "We have the people and the money. We are lacking only in the determination to place both at the service of the Fatherland," the Army League founder complained.[80] The army belonged to the nation, and for this reason, the league's membership was open to any patriotic German who was willing to sacrifice for the "good of the nation."

On Sunday, 28 January 1912, the anniversary of the capitulation of Paris (Franco-Prussian War), a crowd of nearly a thousand, by league accounts, gathered in Berlin to mark the official founding of the Army League.[81] Socialists reacted to this occasion by assailing the league as a militaristic monster. The *Leipziger Volks-zeitung* proclaimed that "aside from professional warmongers and a few ultra patriots there was no one to speak of [in attendance]. A handful of National Liberals, Herr Paasche and Herr vom Rath, naturally could not pass up the opportunity of demonstrating their deeply rooted fixation with the military."[82] Nor did the fledgling association strike a responsive chord within the nationalist camp. In particular, supporters of the fleet worried that the Army League would take the wind out of the Navy League's sails and jeopardize the navy's portion of the forthcoming military budget. Keim's league threatened to compete with its sister association for the affection of the German populace, and naval enthusiasts feared that the nation's love affair with the navy would disappear as rapidly as it had begun.

Throughout January 1912 the issue of the validity of Keim's new league was debated in the nonpartisan newspaper, *Der Tag*. Rear Admiral Schlieper, representing the navalists' viewpoint, argued that it was a superfluous association; its founding would impair the Navy League's efforts at securing vital funds for Tirpitz's fleet and thus severely hinder Germany's ability to defend itself in the upcoming war.[83] Schlieper recognized that an uncompromising insistence upon the navy's unchallenged right to primacy in military funding would only strengthen the case of those agitators who argued that for years the army had been unfairly reduced to second-class status. In an effort to appear more conciliatory, Schlieper conceded that "neither should the army be placed in an inferior position," yet he remained determined to ensure that new allocations to the army would not entail corresponding reductions in the funds granted to the fleet.[84] He was especially apprehensive about the appearance of the volatile Keim as president of the Army League, for he was all too familiar with the general's idiosyncratic, yet persuasive, agitational techniques.

Eight days following the publication of the Admiral's editorial, Major General v. Gersdorff, an Army League spokesman, countered Schlieper's criticism. Rather than accusing the Admiral of myopia, Gersdorff adopted a more conciliatory tone. He stressed the Army League's role as a necessary counterweight to the Navy League rather than as its rival.[85] Citing the lessons of history, Gersdorff emphasized that Germany's success or failure as a Continental power depended upon the quality of its army. Here he echoed the view of Lord Roberts, president of the British National Service League (roughly the English counterpart of the Army League) and a highly respected retired general, that "the fruits of Trafalgar were not reaped until Waterloo."[86] The Major General appealed for cooperation from the navalists with the Army League's campaign to bring Germany's other line of defense—the army—up to par with its navy and in so doing provide the coherent deterrent that the nation so urgently required. Interservice rivalry, he warned, would only prove counterproductive and would foster the impression that Germany lacked unity and resolve. Gersdorff was also quick to remind Schlieper that at no time had the army ever challenged the navy's image as the "darling [*Schosskind*]" of the German nation.[87] Even Keim was to emphasize the complementary rather than the antagonistic nature of the two associations, announcing that the Army and Navy leagues should "march together as good comrades."[88]

The debate reflected two overriding concerns in 1912: first, whether Germany could continue to fund both services accordingly, given the deteriorating state of the Reich's finances; and second, whether the army, rather than the navy, should now be accorded precedence in budgetary considerations in view of the shift away from colonial interests and the return to Continental politics. The Army League's founding thus came at a critical juncture in the nation's military strategy. It was Keim's intention, therefore, to orchestrate the new demands for the army's revitalization through the medium of his new league and thereby return himself to the center stage of popular nationalist politics.

# CHAPTER 2

# The Politics of Military Despair

Si vis pacem, para bellum
ARMY LEAGUE MOTTO

"The German army . . . appears to . . . be living on a glorious past and to be unequal to the repute to which it is commonly held."[1] Such was the pronouncement of the respected military correspondent of *The Times,* Charles à Court Repington, in October 1911. In the journalist's remark was a sense of déja vu, for it had been the very same newspaper that only a half-century earlier had contended that despite its reputation and size, the Prussian army was in no condition for fighting. In 1911 *The Times*'s assertion struck the same responsive chord as it had in 1860. Repington's stinging critique, coming as it did on the heels of Morocco, lent credence to the Army League's call for expansion and provided Bethmann with greater maneuverability in trying to limit Tirpitz's grandiose naval plans. What neither Bethmann nor his conservative supporters expected, however, was the length to which the Army League's leaders were willing to go to place the German army in a position of superiority over its European rivals.

In November 1911 the General Staff proposed that a new army bill should redress both the qualitative and quantitative deficiencies of the army. Not only did it urge the creation of additional army corps on both the western and eastern fronts so as to facilitate mobilization, but it also demanded that the army's peacetime strength be augmented by approximately 24,000 men, 5,200 noncommissioned officers, and 1,500 officers.[2] The proposed 1912 army bill would be the largest since 1893. Securing funding for this expansion would require raiding the naval budget, a move that Admiral Tirpitz vigorously opposed. In an attempt to protect his precious navy from plunder, Tirpitz first sought to convince War Minister Josias v. Heeringen of the futility of increasing tension between the two military services by sacrificing one budget for the other. When that failed, Tirpitz sought the ear of the Kaiser himself.

The Chancellor decided that the announcement of the impending military bills be postponed until after the January 1912 elections to avoid controversy over the taxes for the new bill. Sensing the likelihood of increased taxation, Conservatives advocated financial restraint in the upcoming military budget. While the Conservatives intended to forestall new taxes that might be levied against them, the Chancellor in the meantime aimed at reducing the number of capital ships in the upcoming naval bill and convincing the Kaiser that the army must now take precedence over the navy.[3] He succeeded on both counts. Bethmann related to his War Minister that in his meeting with Wilhelm, the Kaiser was emphatic that "when it came to the necessary strengthening of the army and the navy, the army must absolutely have priority."[4]

In persuading the Kaiser of the priority of army reform, the Chancellor was hopeful that he had improved the chances of a rapprochement between Germany and Britain. "If we did not now construct any additional dreadnoughts," Bethmann reportedly exclaimed, "we would be in a position to create a great colonial empire . . . [and] drive a wedge between the Triple Entente."[5] His optimism, however, was based on the mistaken assumption that in return for containing German naval construction, the British not only would remain neutral in a war that involved either France or Russia but also would acknowledge Germany's right to colonial acquisitions in Africa. These hopes were dashed with the failure of the Haldane Mission in early 1912 and with subsequent diplomatic efforts between Germany and Britain.[6] In early February 1912 the naval bill was published, and one month later the Chancellor presented both military bills to the Reichstag.

In the early months of 1912, with parliamentary discussion of the army bill imminent, the Army League set about trying to assure the bill's ultimate passage. Intent on establishing its credibility before the public on military matters, the league published a series of pamphlets that drew (or claimed to draw) upon the professional expertise of a number of its own members (usually retired army officers) as well as sympathetic individuals within the military. Its first publication, entitled "Why must Germany strengthen its army? [*Warum muss Deutschland sein Heer verstärken?*]," was designed to educate Germans about the army's deficiencies, as the Army League interpreted them. The pamphlet—some thirty-five thousand of which were circulated—argued that most Germans overlooked the dangers inherent in a potent Triple Entente, a badly understaffed and sorely inefficient army, and the country's disadvantageous geographic location. The Army League estimated that in both peacetime and war the combined strength of the Russian and French armies outnumbered that of the German and Austrian forces by a margin of nearly two to one.[7] As for Germany's position in the heart of Europe, surrounded by enemies— this problem could not be resolved without the creation of a larger army to prevent Germany from becoming another stomping ground of Europe as it had been in the seventeenth century.

France served both as a model to be copied and a foe to be detested. The league alerted the German public to France's intention to seek revenge for its defeat in 1870 and for Germany's annexation of Alsace-Lorraine. Not only was France reorganizing its own army in preparation for the inevitable war with the Fatherland, but it also intended to lure able-bodied young Germans into the French Foreign Legion so as to sap Germany of its military potential. "Why must Germany strengthen its Army?" called attention to France's intensive training programs for both officers and enlisted men and its determination to supply its officer corps with younger, better qualified candidates who could achieve promotion more rapidly than their German counterparts. The issue of reinvigorating the officer corps with fresh blood, especially from the middle classes, was one that the Army League also believed must be addressed. There was no place for elitism within the officer corps given the seriousness of the threat to the nation's existence. "Prussia's catastrophe of 1806 was to a large part the fault of aging [*Ueberaltung*] of the officer corps," the pamphlet concluded. "France's army was defeated in 1870/71 because of a breakdown . . . of its officer corps, and Russia's defeat in 1904 can be explained in part by the aging of its officer corps."[8]

In attempting to drive its point home, the league distorted the French case. Of course, it was to the league's advantage to make the German army appear inferior. There is evidence to suggest that the French officer corps, for example, was in no better shape than its German counterpart, a fact that the Army League could have noted had it perused contemporary French newspapers or military journals. In his analysis of the French army, historian Douglas Porch has stressed that France's officer corps was a debilitated gerontocracy. As of 1 November 1910, 30 generals, 25 lieutenant colonels, 80 majors, and 100 captains were physically incapable of campaigning, while "one of two generals chosen to lead a maneuver army each year between 1909 and 1914 had reached the retirement age."[9] Not only were some French officers ready for the geriatric ward, but they also lacked the skill to compensate for their greying beards and shaky limbs. Contemporary French newspapers testified to this problem as well. "When you compare the generals of fifteen or twenty years ago to those today, you are struck by the inferiority of the latter" the Conservative organ *Porte-Voix* lamented in 1912. "Line officers are frequently amazed by the feebleness of their appointed leaders. Ill at ease in the field they were utterly incompetent."[10] Nor was the opportunity for promotion as available as the Army League professed. The French army, like the German, faced a shortage of noncommissioned officers (NCOs) because officer pay and reenlistment bonuses were poor. As a result, training of enlisted men was often left to an inexperienced minority. One high-ranking French general admitted that "the quality of our professional NCOs has dropped in the last few years. Today the cadres are stuffed with too many NCOs who are old, tired, who have lost their enthusiasm but do not want to retire and so stop promotion."[11]

A more recent study of the French army by Gerd Krumeich confirms Porch's assertions. Krumeich, in fact, argues that the Moroccan Crisis functioned as a catalyst for French military expansion because it demonstrated that the "French army was not really prepared for action."[12] Indeed, throughout the 1890s and into the first decade of the twentieth century, the fallout from the Dreyfus affair, which intensified the basic distrust between the army and civilian authorities and damaged the army's image, helped to perpetuate shortcomings within the French army. It took the combination of the "nationalist revival" in France with provocative plans for German military expansion to reinvigorate the French army. Nevertheless, the Army League viewed with grudging admiration but suspicion its counterpart's reorganization program after 1911, especially the improvements in its infantry (the 1912 infantry cadres law), artillery (the famous 75-mm gun), the training of its reservists, and the extension of its railway network.[13]

To bring home to the German public the potential danger and deviousness of French intentions, the Army League fastened upon the French Foreign Legion. The Army League was not the first to call attention to the Legion's alleged temptation and mistreatment of young German recruits. Already in 1908 an Anti-Legion league was founded by a former Legion officer and born-again German patriot, Fritz Ohle, who sought to alert inexperienced German youth to the dangers of joining the Foreign Legion.[14] Every German who entered the French Foreign Legion was a double loss to the German army, Ohle argued, because each recruit added to the strength of the enemy and by his absence deprived the German army of another soldier. Ohle's crusade, however, made little impact at the time; the Lord Mayor of Crefeld, for example, maintained that Ohle's charges were exaggerated and offered as proof the fact that his city, despite its proximity to the border, had lost only a mere handful of recruits to the Legion.[15] In February 1911 interest in the activities of the Legion was rekindled by Center Party Reichstag representative Matthias Erzberger's blistering condemnation of the Legion's promotion of "white slavery," its inhumane and immoral treatment of recruits, and its illegal recruitment of German citizens. Erzberger urged War Minister Heeringen to take swift and direct action to halt the Legion's practices, and his remarks struck a sympathetic chord with the German press.[16] French public opinion suspected the direction the agitation would take, for as the German ambassador to that country, Wilhelm Freiherr v. Schoen, explained to Bethmann, many Frenchmen displayed a "nervous uneasiness [*nervöse Unbehagen*]" and "even in the most placid and level-headed circles a feeling of fear was widespread that the Imperial Government, in light of the 'difficulties' surrounding the upcoming parliamentary elections, might use [the issue of the Legion] to arouse the patriotic sentiment of the German nation."[17]

Keim especially welcomed the assault on the Foreign Legion since in the Pan-German League he had railed against it. He charged that half of the Foreign Legion consisted of young German recruits, of whom nearly half again (45 percent) were from Alsace-Lorraine, a fact that he claimed attested to France's desire to retake the *Reichsland.* To prevent the Legion from pursuing a policy of subversion in the *Reichsland* and wooing young, impressionable Germans seeking adventure, the Army League advocated the passage of legislation that would prohibit Germans from joining the Legion and wearing Legion uniforms and dissolve all existing Legion veterans' leagues. It also proposed to strip all returning German Legionnaires of their citizenship.[18] One of the Army League's most vociferous spokesmen against the Legion was Dr. Ferdinand v. Papen, who toured league branches on a regular basis to popularize the league's anti-Legion stand.[19] A resourceful fact collector, v. Papen supplied the Army League and his audiences with an impressive array of statistics. For example, he insisted that the Legion recruited between 2,000 and 3,000 Germans yearly, and that nearly 90 percent of the Legion was composed of Germans (including Swiss and Austrians).[20]

His figures, however, were far from accurate. According to a government memorandum of April 1912, the Foreign Legion consisted of roughly two infantry regiments of approximately 10,000 to 12,000 soldiers and officers.[21] Its officers were primarily French, although some were German (mostly from Alsace-Lorraine), Swiss, Danish, and Swedish, while NCOs were by and large German. A report of October 1913 offered more specific details. The Legion's first regiment with 5,390 men was composed of 47.8 percent Frenchmen, 6.5 percent Alsatians, 15.7 percent Germans, and 30 percent others.[22] Thus, at most 22.2 percent of the Legion consisted of German recruits, not nearly 90 percent as the Army League proclaimed.

While statistics were employed to substantiate the Army League's case against the French Legion, vivid descriptions of Legion life were coaxed from former German recruits to illustrate its indictment. The League chose the starkest revelations for its billboard posters, which adorned railway stations and factory walls in the Rhineland. One particularly descriptive poster affixed to a wall in the Gutehoffnungshütte in Oberhausen read:

> For a wretched four pfennig a day you do intolerable tasks and menial slave work. After endless maneuvers in the scorching heat of the African desert, you are left to languish, if you have not already succumbed to merciless enemies or predatory animals. . . . Punishments . . . are beyond belief. One is sentenced to years for what normally would carry [a maximum] penalty of several days. . . . If by chance you have survived five years in the Foreign Legion, your health would be permanently ruined. Once released [from duty] and shoved over the French border, you will be received by your fellow Germans as a cripple and beggar. . . . Therefore, German compatriots, do not heed the enticements of unscrupulous recruiters, do not sign up at recruitment offices. Do not be misled by promises of a high bounty for enlisting and carefree days to follow: they are but lies and deceit.[23]

The none-too-subtle implication here was that German workers in this case should not seek greener pastures elsewhere, and certainly not through enlistment in the Legion, whose allure was merely a mirage. Rather they should rejoice in their own German citizenship and recognize the benefits they received from the existing socioeconomic system.[24] By publicizing the dangers that faced the Reich along its western frontier, the Army League hoped that the government could be persuaded to implement the necessary remedial legislation in the form of a major and far-reaching army bill.

In April 1912 the government revealed its three primary objectives with regard to army reform. They included an expansion of the total number of enlisted men and officers available for military duty, improvements in the army's mobility and firepower, and an increase in the salaries of enlisted men. The Chancellor defended the bill's provisions, stressing, "We need to arm ourselves sufficiently not only to safeguard against a possible invasion but also to maintain the peace to ensure our future welfare."[25] In Bethmann's estimation, any military reform should be moderate in nature and predicated upon fiscal responsibility. More extreme measures, as proposed by exponents of a "misplaced patriotism [*missverstandener Patriotismus*]," would aggravate rather than solve the problem.[26] Disappointed by the bill's moderate objectives, the Army League vowed to press for the inclusion of additional reforms, among them the implementation of actual universal military service (the Army League insisted that the so-called One percent Law be fulfilled), the training of additional reservists, the more extensive and intensive training of reserve officers, and the immediate formation of cavalry divisions.[27]

By the time the bill went before the Reichstag for approval in the spring of 1912, the lines of debate were already clearly drawn, with Socialists decrying the ever-rising tide of militarism and the Army League that fostered it, and National Liberals and Free Conservatives praising army expansion and the league's diligence in bringing this critical issue to public attention. Socialist representatives accused the government of supporting the aims of the Army League and warned that further unnecessary military increases would disable Germany's economy and result in war. "I can only hope that the Army Administration will choose not to acquiesce in the Army League's program," Socialist Daniel Stücklein proclaimed to the Reichstag. "The Army League, a creation of General Keim, is an *Agitationsverein* in every sense of the word. It is most regrettable that a number of such organizations exist in Germany—some demand more ships, others clamor for more soldiers. If only other organizations could be founded whose goals would be to create the money necessary for these demands."[28] National Liberals Ernst Bassermann and Hermann Paasche countered that France, not the Army League, was the aggressive party and that the league was simply doing its patriotic duty in demanding significant army reform. Paasche felt compelled to justify his support for the Army League and his participation in it, stressing that "moderates" like himself could advocate the league's cause: "At the request of others . . . and because [I am] a moderate politician who could perhaps exercise a moderating influence on political firebrands [i.e., Keim], I joined the Army League. I truly believe the Army League is headed in the right direction . . . when it seeks to make the *Volk* aware of the dangers which threaten it, [and] of the armaments build-up of foreign nations."[29]

The equally loquacious Eduard v. Liebert, Free Conservative, an Army League member and president of the Imperial League against Social Democracy, provoked a round of hisses from the Socialist deputies with his assertion that the army was the nation's first line of defense (against domestic enemies as well) and thus it had to be fortified regardless of the cost. Despite the Left's protest, the army bill received overwhelming approval on 21 May. Although it augmented the army's peacetime strength by 29,000 men and increased the number of infantry and field artillery units, the bill failed to provide for the implementation of universal military service, the expanded use of the automobile and airplane, and the expansion of the engineer and supply units as the Army League had insisted. For Keim, the reform was too little, too late, and was further proof of the present government's inability to come to grips with military realities. With his goals unfulfilled, the general intensified his campaign, seeking yet another army bill that would address the needs of the nation.

The outbreak of the Balkans War in October 1912 brought a renewed sense of urgency regarding the preparedness of the German army. As Austria-Hungary's alliance partner, Germany was theoretically bound to aid its ally should Austria-Hungary enter the conflict on the pretext of protecting its own interests in southeastern Europe. With the Balkan League's quick victory over Turkish troops and the balance of power in the region destroyed, the Empire's intervention became increasingly likely. Austro-Hungarian officials realized that the Balkan League's victory would serve to strengthen the Slavic nationalist movements within the Empire and could lead to further internal unrest. Austria-Hungary, therefore, saw restoring the balance of power in southeastern Europe as essential to preventing the dissolution of its own Empire.

For Germany the situation was not as straightforward. Of course, strategically it could not afford to lose a reliable and sympathetic partner by refusing to commit its own troops to its Austrian allies. On the other hand, Germany's unequivocal support for Austria-Hungary in the Balkans would undoubtedly widen the conflict to include Russia and perhaps England as well. Since Bethmann had been unsuccessful in securing British neutrality, the likelihood of a war between Germany and England seemed greater. But was Germany willing to risk an all-out war over the Balkans? There was another aspect to be considered here. Certain government officials and leaders of the patriotic societies contemplated the creation of a *Mitteleuropa*, a German customs union which would stretch from Central Europe to Baghdad and which would afford Germany a more competitive edge against its British and American rivals.[30] But regardless of whether German officials preferred to concentrate on propping up the Austrians or on expanding to the east, or even if they preferred to remain aloof but exercise authority and influence, they could do so only to the degree that the German army was capable of achieving military victory.

To underscore the seriousness of the situation and the pressing need for a larger army bill for 1913, the Army League dispatched General Litzmann to the Balkans in October 1912 to observe the war and to compile data on Russian troop strength.[31] While on assignment Litzmann met with King Carol I of Romania, a Germanophile and great admirer of the general's writings, to exchange views on the crisis.[32] Litzmann's activities were closely monitored by the German Foreign Office, since his visit did not receive official governmental sanction. The results of Litzmann's mission, subsequently published in *Die Wehr,* purported to demonstrate Russian military superiority. The Army League drew parallels with earlier officers whose advocacy of military reform went unheeded, resulting in Prussia's humiliating defeat at the hands of Napoleon. In 1913 Germany could not afford to repeat that mistake.

A reassessment of German military power was simultaneously underway within governmental circles. The Kaiser expressed his fear that in light of the Balkans crisis, the "military balance of power was shifting rapidly to the detriment of the Triple Alliance" and that, therefore, a new army bill must be prepared.[33] In October the War Minister disagreed with his superior's assessment and insisted that Germany's military situation had in fact not deteriorated. One month later, however, Heeringen reversed himself and conceded that a new army bill was necessary. Nevertheless, he entertained serious reservations about the government's ability to finance the increases. The War Minister's perception of the financial and social obstacles to expansion carried little weight with most members of the General Staff, especially with Helmut Moltke and Erich Ludendorff, who discounted such objections as subsidiary to the necessity of increasing the army (even if this meant "diluting" the officer corps with bourgeois entrants). On 2 December Heeringen warned Bethmann that the new army bill would cost between 200 and 300 million marks and expressed his apprehension as to "how it could be reconciled with the present principles of our financial policy."[34] On 4 and 5 December both the Chancellor and War Minister met independently with the Kaiser to discuss the army bill.

Three days later, on 8 December, Wilhelm summoned his Chief of the General Staff, Moltke; the Secretary of the State for the Navy, Tirpitz; the Chief of the Admiralty Staff, August v. Heeringen; and the Chief of the Naval Cabinet, Georg v. Müller, to discuss the military situation in light of Britain's recent "change of heart" toward Germany.[35] Only days earlier British officials had notified Germany that if Austria-Hungary invaded Serbia, the British would not stand by idly, for under no circumstances would they permit themselves to be "confronted by a united continental group under the leadership of a single power."[36] The German meeting of 8 December in response—the so-called War Council—essentially accepted the inevitability of a future (and probably imminent) war and underscored the need for Germany promptly to fortify its army in preparation for that conflict. The discussion, therefore, strengthened the position of the General Staff and weakened the ability of Heeringen to resist their demands for immediate and substantial military expansion.

The debate over the army bill intensified throughout the winter and into the spring of 1913. Moltke's memorandum of 21 December to Bethmann reiterated his belief that war was inevitable and stressed that in any conflict between the Triple Alliance and the Triple Entente, the former would have the greatest disadvantage because the Alliance was a purely "defensive union."[37] Germany, he went on to point out, could not count on complete support from Austrian troops, since a considerable portion were stationed in the Balkans (in Serbia), nor could it expect the aid of its other partner, Italy. Thorough and rapid army expansion was, therefore, essential to the nation's survival, and the Chief of the General Staff suggested an additional 150,000 recruits per annum, thereby raising the army's peacetime strength from 620,000 to 920,000 men. In addition, he demanded the creation of three new army corps and the expansion of the cavalry, field artillery, communications (and telegraph) troops, and the nascent air force.

Another point of contention concerned the expansion of the officer corps. Moltke and Ludendorff argued that the German army's success depended not only on its technological superiority but also upon the quality of its officers.[38] Since the army had experienced a decline in the numbers of NCOs and officers, both men conceded the need to recruit new candidates from among the middle classes. General Keim concurred with this suggestion and called upon the government to ensure better pay and promotion opportunities for NCOs (thereby making the position more attractive to middle-class candidates).[39] Heeringen rejected their proposals, offering instead a substantially smaller increase in troop strength (35,000–40,000) and stressing that the recruitment of large numbers of new officers was undesirable because it would undermine "the political reliability of the army and the homogeneity of the officer corps."[40]

The fate of the army bill was held hostage by two seemingly irreconcilable forces. At the one extreme were men like Ludendorff and Keim, who were unwilling to compromise the nation's security (and their own principles) to social or financial considerations. They were "the embodiment of a new kind of officer, who viewed the interest of the military as an end in itself above the interest of the state."[41] At the other extreme were the Conservatives, who opposed either expanding the army or altering its composition, both of which they feared would jeopardize their traditional base of authority. This polarity has been described as the "dual militarism [*der doppelte Militarismus*]."[42] A vigorous "bourgeois" militarism, espoused by the leaders of the Army League, regarded no obstacle as too great to be overcome with regard to the nation's defense, in sharp contrast to the more traditional militarism of German Conservatives whose commitment to army reform was guided ultimately by their appreciation of the likely implications for their own domestic position. In their view, the new "bourgeois" militarism was embodied in the Army League's unbridled nationalism, its clamor for more troops, its raucous insistence on the infusion of the officer corps with middle-class candidates, and its intemperate criticism of government military policy, all of which combined to subvert the monarch's unique constitutional authority in military matters.

Arguing along these lines, a Conservative Reichstag deputy, A. v. Graefe, condemned the Army League's propaganda, alleging that it fomented unrest among the troops (by challenging the basis of military discipline) and raised illusory hopes of national reconciliation (by promising the eventual mitigation of domestic class conflict).[43] General Keim, never one to sit silently in the face of criticism, responded two days later. In a sharply worded letter to a National Liberal party official, he characterized v. Graefe's charges as a "carefully conceived device of the Conservative agrarians" intended to disrupt relations between the National Liberals and the Army League.[44] Keim also proposed that the official broach to his party's leader, Bassermann, the possibility of a press campaign directed against the Conservatives.

Keim recognized, however, that Conservative opposition was especially troublesome in that it was likely to influence the government's response. Indeed, shortly before v. Graefe's criticism, the Army League's Kurd v. Strantz already had been "explicitly summoned" to the Chancellory to clarify the league's position. The interview was necessary, v. Strantz explained, "because apparently the Chancellor believed that we were undermining the confidence in the army."[45] His vigorous assurances to the contrary were intended to pacify the Chancellor, yet they were also intended for the consumption of v. Strantz's childhood friend, Gottlieb v. Jagow, the current Secretary of the Foreign Office.

The War Minister's and the Conservatives' intransigence toward the league's extensive program of army reform continued to pose a major obstacle. This, however, did not dissuade the league and its supporters (Moltke and Ludendorff) from persisting in their campaign. In a memorandum dated 22 January, the two men implored Heeringen to reconsider their demands, upon whose implementation depended "Germany's victory in the next war."[46] Nettled by his colleagues' barbs, Heeringen retaliated by taking his case directly to the Kaiser, whom he persuaded in favor of a more limited increase. Ludendorff was reassigned to a regimental command in Düsseldorf on 27 January, his demotion a signal to those who persisted in their criticism.[47] Moltke's resolve, however, was not so easily shaken, and three days after his colleague's transfer he wrote to Bethmann urging that the army bill at minimum provide for the sizeable troop increase that he had originally suggested. On 28 February Bethmann approved a version of the new army bill that increased the army's peacetime strength (by 117,000 men, 15,000 NCOs, and 5,000 officers) but nevertheless fell short of the 300,000 man increase recommended by the General Staff.

With the bill scheduled for parliamentary discussion in April and May, the Army League extended its own public campaign, despite the setback its more radical proposals had just received. The "government's proposals" were now defined as "the very least we can accept."[48] No further qualitative or quantitative compromises were to be permitted, "in view of the ongoing armaments buildup of our neighbors."[49] In effect, this meant that financial considerations were no longer legitimate; any reservations on that score would have to be subordinated to the absolute necessity of ensuring the nation's military preparedness against its steadily arming opponents. Such an uncompromising attitude, however, was bound to bring the Army League into conflict with the intentions of the Lex Bassermann-Erzberger. This amendment, which had been ratified along with the previous army bill, stipulated that by 30 April 1913 the Reichstag must institute a general tax on various forms of private property.[50] Another confrontation with the Conservatives over the issue of direct taxation, therefore, seemed inevitable.

On 11 March the Bundesrat approved Bethmann's appropriation for funding the proposed army bill. A one-time military contribution (*Wehrbeitrag*) would cover the expenses of the bill's nonrecurring military costs, while a subsidiary income tax (on increases in wealth) would be levied to pay for the annual expenses or to provide a reserve in case the matricular contributions of the individual states proved insufficient.[51] The nonrecurring contribution had an element of patriotic sacrifice about it and meshed neatly with the patriotic fervor rekindled by the centennial celebrations of Prussia's victory over France in the Battle of Leipzig in October 1813. The Army League applauded this idea and appealed to the patriotic consciousness and civic responsibility of all Germans. "Let 1913 be a year of sacrifice," it urged, "as today the times are no less treacherous than they were one hundred years ago."[52]

The idea of a one-time military contribution was by no means novel. It had been discussed three years earlier by popular nationalists, including Keim, Litzmann, v. Liebert, and even Paasche, as the least controversial and most lucrative financial avenue for raising revenue for the military. In April 1910 the Reichstag dismissed the suggestion, leading Keim to charge that it was pathetic for a nation to spend 3 million marks on alcohol but remain unwilling to pay for the maintenance of its own national defense. He blamed the Reichstag's opposition on "bureaucratic intransigence" ("*bürokratische Unzulänglichkeit*").[53] In 1913 the Army League renewed its call for the introduction of the *Wehrbeitrag*, emphasizing that the tax was the only "comprehensive levy which would bring in millions," and which could equalize the burden of the military:[54] "One must be willing to [accept] all that is virtuous—love for the Fatherland, honor for the nation, and willingness to sacrifice [for the good of] the community. In times of peace the army is the educational institution for the youth. Those who pay the *Wehrsteuer* contribute to a kind of school charge which benefits the entire civilization. Everyone gives willingly what he can: either sons or money."[55] Any German who opposed the army bill and its accompanying financial provisions, the Army League warned, would be "committing a crime against the German people."[56]

On 7 April Bethmann introduced the army bill as a "defensive and peaceful" measure aimed at redressing Germany's military imbalance with its neighbors and not at provoking a military confrontation.[57] It was essential, therefore, that the Reichstag approve the bill without dilution or substantial amendment, and that it make adequate financial provision for the bill's implementation. Bethmann surmised that while a majority in the Reichstag accepted the necessity of another military bill, their reservations about the financial implications might cripple it. Nevertheless, the Chancellor was hopeful that his proposal of a nonrecurring tax might elicit the support of the Conservatives, who might warm to a broadly based tax and hesitate to further alienate themselves from the government's position.[58] Yet the Conservatives refused to compromise, fearing repercussions from below. Despite their opposition, on 30 June 1913 the bill and its concomitant tax provisions were approved by the Reichstag (with even the Socialists voting in favor). The bill's passage was greeted with jubilation by the nationalist press, which lauded the Army League for its vigilant and vigorous advocacy of army reform. An aura of self-congratulation, though, could not conceal the widening fissures between conservative and bourgeois militarists.

The Army League celebrated the unceremonious departure in July of Heeringen, whom it had castigated as an exemplar of the ossified Conservative thinking that inhibited the expansion and modernization of the German military. The league's press chief, Hermann Müller-Brandenburg, recalled that "the army would have been much better off if v. Heeringen had never set foot in the War Ministry," and that it remained beyond his "comprehension how a man who in December 1912 continued to fight tooth and nail against the plans for a larger army bill could introduce the legislation before the Reichstag."[59] The unfortunate fact was "that v. Heeringen in his colorless room on the Leipzigerstrasse made the Army League a necessity."[60]

Mistakenly, the league assumed that Heeringen's replacement, Erich v. Falkenhayn, would prove more receptive to its viewpoint. But the league had no intention of renouncing its commitment to further quantitative and qualitative military reform. It pointed to the passage by France in August 1913 of a Three-Year Law and an increase in the number of Russian fortifications as proof that the German army must be prepared to fight at a moment's notice.[61] In September 1913 the Army League requested and received a secret meeting between its twenty-seven-year-old press chief, Müller-Brandenburg, and the War Ministry's press agent, Major Deutelmoser. The league hoped to ascertain the Ministry's current views on actual universal military service, French and Russian army expansion, and the military training of Germany's youth. On 25 September Müller-Brandenburg met with Deutelmoser for an hour, posing specific prepared questions, and on the twenty-sixth Deutelmoser provided the Army League official with replies from the Ministry.

During the course of the first meeting Müller-Brandenburg solicited the War Ministry's position on the reduction of the length of service for enlisted men to one year, the extension of reservist training from five to six months, the creation of new cavalry divisions, the addition of support trains, and the aging of the officer corps. While Deutelmoser promised the War Ministry's cooperation, he reminded Müller-Brandenburg that the "War Ministry has no intention whatsoever of influencing the Army League." Nevertheless, he expressed the War Ministry's hope that the Army League "would focus its attention in the near future on those issues which the War Ministry believed were necessary and attainable."[62] He cautioned the league about demanding too much of the Reich's limited financial resources since "such a move could turn the nation against the army, . . . [and] in times as serious as these, it is difficult to know when one will be forced to draw the sword."[63]

On the following day Deutelmoser presented the War Ministry's official response, the contents of which, he warned, were to be held in the strictest of confidence. Not even the league's executive council members were to be privy to these discussions. Once again Deutelmoser urged fiscal restraint. No new units could be considered before 1915 since "the financial burdens at present [were] too enormous for the economy to bear and any agitation in this direction would add grist to the mills of the Social Democrats, Left Liberals, [and] a large portion of the Center."[64] In any case, Germany did not expect a war with France until 1916, by which time it would be ready to do battle. On the other hand, the War Ministry agreed with the Army League about the importance of achieving complete universal military service and supported the infusion of younger blood in the army. The Army League could do the War Ministry and the nation great service, Deutelmoser suggested, by stepping up "its publicity demanding the training of youth for military and patriotic services."[65] While there was no direct reference to the possibility of diluting the "purity" of the officer corps through universal service, it was clear that the Ministry regarded the league's youth training program (like the army itself) as a means by which the lower classes could be inculcated with patriotic fervor and purged of any revolutionary inclinations.

It would be a mistake, however, to view these free exchanges on the state of the army as a sign of significant reconciliation between the Army League and the War Ministry. Keim's claim that under Falkenhayn the War Ministry was more receptive to the league's demands is by itself insufficient proof.[66] Nor is it likely that the War Minister alone determined the direction of military policy; if Falkenhayn, unlike his predecessor, found the league's suggestions more appealing, he still was skeptical of the impact of extensive reform on the Reich's precarious finances. Although the War Ministry seemed to moderate its opposition to the infusion of new blood into the officer corps, it nevertheless continued to resist other league demands for quantitative measures. (Qualitative increases of the kind that involved the actual training of soldiers and reservists the War Ministry could and did consent to, since these were manageable without raising the specter of new taxes.[67])

To observers not privy to the confidential discussions and memoranda between the government and the Army League, further evidence of reconciliation seemed to be forthcoming in the so-called Zabern Affair, which was sparked on 28 October 1913 when a derogatory comment made by a German Lieutenant Reuter to an Alsatian citizen infuriated the local Alsatian population. The affair illustrated the insularity of the German army and the haughty superiority with which it so often regarded civilian authorities[68] and it caused dissension within German military, administrative, and political circles. General Berthold v. Deimling, commander of the Alsatian corps, condoned the heavy-handed actions his troops had taken in the wake of the incident to restore order. Yet Count Karl v. Wedel, the German civilian administrator, denounced the army's unnecessary use of force against the native population and its contemptuous dismissal of the administration's legal authority. The Kaiser and the Chancellor found themselves on opposite sides of the issue; the Kaiser upheld the army's position, while Bethmann was inclined toward Wedel's assessment. So as not to impugn the reputation and authority of either the army or the Kaiser, however, Bethmann conceded and defended the military before a hostile Reichstag. The affair demonstrated the continued tension over civil-military relations in German society.

From December 1913 through the spring of 1914 Bethmann's efforts to protect the army's flank provoked renewed assertions by the Socialists and Left Liberals that the government and the army were conspiring to militarize German society. Heinrich Schulz (SPD) accused the government of succumbing to the Army League's militaristic propaganda and being manipulated by that association like a wooden marionette: "General Keim, who is known affectionately by his friends as the father of the previous army bill, gives the command . . . 'Eyes open, Herr Chancellor! Ears attentive, Herr War Minister!' Herr General Keim makes demands and that is very important! "[69] "The military administration . . . has not yet had the courage to combat openly [the league's] agitation," echoed Progressive deputy Ernst Müller-Meiningen. "It often appears nowadays that the retired generals—not the people, prince, or diplomats—are the greatest enemies of world peace."[70] As in the case of Zabern, the question of who was formulating German policy—the government or the army—required an answer. Bethmann's sudden advocacy of the army's position in Alsace made it appear to the political opposition that the army, not the Chancellor, exercised the initiative and that the Army League and General Keim were partly responsible for this shift in policy.

A powerful indictment of the Army League's role in this process of militarization was undertaken by Matthias Erzberger of the Center Party.[71] He added his voice to the chorus of criticism of the Army League's malign influence in the highest governmental circles. Erzberger found particularly distasteful the Army League's corrosive impact on the army's commitment to the idea of nonpartisanship. The participation of officers and enlisted men in league activities, especially in Alsace-Lorraine, implied that they subscribed to the league's warmongering and that they sought to disseminate such beliefs among the civilian population. General Deimling's active participation in the league's Alsatian association, he contended, was an example of how the Army League undermined the local German administration's efforts to maintain good relations with the Alsatians. Charging that the Army League was by no means the nonpolitical association it claimed to be, Erzberger urged the Chancellor to restrict the league's political activities and prohibit the membership of military men. The Centrist deputy concluded that Keim's association did not merit the praise it had received from the nationalist press regarding its role in improving the army's condition; on the contrary, the league had done a great disservice to Germany by always ascribing "superior qualities to the army of our potential opponent and publicly reveal[ing] deficiencies in our army organization."[72]

Falkenhayn responded to these charges of collusion by reemphasizing that "the administration maintains no relationship with the Army League and emphatically denies being responsible for it in any way or exerting influence over it."[73] Of course, he continued, both parties shared the same concerns about the army's ability to defend Germany's Continental interests, but that was where the relationship ended. "The fellows of the Army League are extraordinarily proud of their independence,"[74] Falkenhayn added, and so long as the league's goal, "the improvement of the Empire's army, coincides with that of the administration," the league could persist in its agitation.[75] For critics to demand that the administration take an "antagonistic attitude instead of a neutral one" toward the league and "disassociate itself from every retired officer" would be inappropriate.[76]

Falkenhayn's protestations of innocence failed to convince his opponents that the league and the government were not one and the same warmonger. A middle-of-the-road stance that neither condoned nor condemned the association remained the path of least resistance. To side with the Army League would further hinder the efforts of Germany's diplomats to secure British neutrality in the event of war; to denounce the association would further strain an already tenuous relationship between moderate Conservatives and popular nationalists. But if the government found itself constrained, so too did the Army League. With the passage of two consecutive army bills, further calls for reform resembled the effect of the little boy who continually cried wolf. To European observers, though, Germany appeared as the wolf itself preparing to prey upon its weaker neighbors. After all, the Army League made no secret of its intent to go beyond the mere redress of the nation's military deficiencies to lay the foundation of a physically and spiritually rejuvenated patriotic social order. To achieve these broader sociocultural aims, however, the Army League would have to identify the wider benefits of martial virtues and intensify the techniques for their dissemination.

# CHAPTER 3

# Creating an Image

In late nineteenth-century Germany the techniques of propaganda were being revolutionized by a constellation of political and social changes, especially the emergence of the literate and mass electorate.[1] Campaign literature and memorabilia were produced far more effectively and effortlessly than before. The patriotic societies, in particular, took advantage of these improvements by churning out millions of patriotic pamphlets for mass consumption. The Imperial League against Social Democracy, to take but one example, published nearly 50 million copies of 170 antisocialist pamphlets, or roughly one pamphlet for each German citizen.[2] An upsurge in newspaper circulation combined with an extended news coverage of politics offered both patriotic societies and the political parties a ready-made forum from which to dispense propaganda. Newspaper coverage of local, regional, and national elections of the 1870s and 1880s was relatively sparse in contrast to the 1890s, when it was substantially more extensive as evidenced by the greater length and frequency of articles.[3] As the parties began to devote more time to preliminary campaigning, the press responded in kind by devoting more space to them. Kaiser Wilhelm II was especially sensitive to the way the press portrayed his actions and described the attitudes of others toward his efforts.[4]

In the mid-1890s a new kind of propaganda emerged with the invention of the cinema, whose ability to reach a geographically wider and more heterogeneous audience was potentially greater than even the newspaper. Many Germans found viewing moving pictures or slides far more entertaining, informative, and inexpensive than reading tedious columns of densely packed newsprint. The cinema, as Gary Stark put it, "was . . . an undemanding, totally passive medium, one that barely required concentration, much less sophisticated interpretation."[5] Slide shows proved to be immensely popular, as was suggested by the frequency with which slide collections were rented for use at local organizational functions. The Navy League, for example, recorded that the number of slide rentals doubled between 1910 and 1912, from 631 to 1,216.[6]

Armed with these new techniques, the Army League hoped to create the public image or images it wanted to project and simultaneously spread the ideology of popular nationalism. Because the Army League's survival depended to a large extent upon the amount of public support it received, the league created its own propaganda network financed primarily by membership dues. Its propaganda machine produced an impressive array of patriotic literature, including reproductions of keynote lectures, historical speeches, military anecdotes, nationalistic poems and songs, colorful buttons and medallions, and, of course, its monthly journal *Die Wehr*, an annual *Wehrkalender*, and the *Nachrichten des Wehrvereins*, a weekly newsletter. That the league was "not a savings association [*wir sind kein Sparverein*]" was indisputable, judging from the depth and quantity of the material produced on a regular basis.[7] Yet, by being forced to rely so heavily on one resource—the consistent payment of dues—to maintain its propaganda machine, the Army League was ultimately unable to continue to project the image it had struggled so hard to build—that of an invincible association beholden to no one but itself and capable of providing leadership for a nation deprived of forceful leaders and national unity.

## The Issue of Nonpartisanship

*Überparteilichkeit* (nonpartisanship), one of the most frequently uttered catch phrases in the popular nationalist vocabulary, symbolized the ideal of national unity, of a Germany solidified by selfless sacrifice to the Fatherland and one embraced by all Germans regardless of age, class, or political or religious outlook.[8] The adoption of nonpartisanship as the Army League's motto was in part a reaction by the patriotic societies to what they viewed as a stagnant political system unable and unwilling to respond to the needs of its electorate and bogged down by selfish, petty interests. Political parties' determination to continue to appeal to the interests of specific segments of Germany's populace precluded, the patriotic societies maintained, the formation of a broadly nationalistic platform that could benefit the nation as a whole. Inter- and intraparty bickering and the practice of *Honoratiorenpolitik* by the parties helped foster the impression that Germany was incapable of handling its affairs, an image that might belie the nation's apparently whole-hearted support for *Weltpolitik*. When discussing the significance attached to this nonpartisan label, historians generally suggest that the slogan was used to demonstrate the patriotic societies' antiparliamentary proclivity. But might not these associations, the Army League included, have been trying to prod the parties into revitalizing their efforts in line with the example already before them, namely the patriotic societies' demonstrated ability to tap new issues and new members? Throughout the 1890s the Protestant parties of the middle and the right found themselves competing for a limited pool of voters from the middle classes. Rather than cooperating, the bourgeois parties moved further apart, thus undermining the potential for any middle-class consensus. It seems possible that National Liberals and Conservatives who joined the Army League did not necessarily regard their participation as a rejection of the parliamentary system but rather as a means by which to prod their parties into a broader social and ideological resonance. Prominent in the Army League were National Liberal Reichstag deputies Hermann Paasche and Karl Heckmann, Conservative Reichstag representative Karl Franz v. Böhlendorff-Kölpin, and Free Conservative and member of the Prussian House, Otto v. Dewitz.[9] Politicians were equally visible in league branches. In Hamburg, for example, among them were Syndikus Dr. Diestel, Dr. v. Melle, v. Berenberg-Gossler, J. F. C. Refardt, Dr. Sthamer, Dr. Westphal, Rudolf Mönckeberg, Alexander Schön, Adolf Stürken, and Rudolf Sieverts.[10] A similar observation could be made about England, where parliamentary government was firmly rooted.[11] As president Keim asserted: "In the Army League there are no Liberals and no Conservatives and no parties whatsoever. There are only 'good Germans.' "[12] The league's objective was simply to convince Germans and their parties that military matters belonged to nationalist politics and thus had to remain beyond the realm of partisan politics. "Military issues," Keim explained, "have absolutely nothing to do with party politics."[13]

By placing the nation's interests "above politics," the Army League hoped to use patriotism as a common denominator to attract members and subsequently to increase its visibility in and bargaining power with the government. The league sought to make it abundantly clear that its keynote was independence. As a nonpartisan association, its first responsibility was to the wishes of the people, and it claimed the right (as had some in the Navy League) to criticize government military policy and the opinions of so-called military experts who formulated it when military matters were found wanting. By impugning the government's attitude toward national defense, the Army League made the government appear incompetent before its citizens and the world community and sought to lend the distinct impression that it, not the government, exercised an informed influence on military affairs.

Having been burned before by Keim's pyrotechnics, the government was quick to repudiate the league's claim to have a better grasp of the nation's security requirements. "[The Army League] goes against the grain of Prussian sensibility," the *Kreuzzeitung* warned. "We cannot submit to organized agitation which seeks to interfere with the army administration fulfilling its most important and sacred duty."[14] Rear Admiral Schlieper echoed this sentiment precisely when he wrote, "If the Army League [intends] to support the *Kriegsministerium* and [foster] patriotic sentiment, then this is welcomed."[15] On the whole, the government's initial response to Keim's renewed propaganda was cautious, since it was eager to avoid a confrontation with Keim and the popular nationalists that might enhance their reputations as guardians of national virtue. While careful not to dissuade citizens from demonstrating their support for military expansion, the government tried to regain the initiative by insisting that the upcoming army bill was proof positive of the government's commitment to a strong army. When the league continued to use the weapon of nonpartisanship to attack its policy, the government responded by erecting its own shield, the *Reichsvereinsgesetz* (Imperial Law of Associations of 1908), to protect itself from the league's barbs.

At stake in February 1912 was the league's label as a "nonpartisan" association. As of early that month, the league had not registered itself in the *Vereinsregister* in Berlin, even though it was supposed to be an *eingetragene Verein* (e.v.). All political associations were required by the Law of Associations to register with the Berlin authorities, but the Army League considered itself to be nonpartisan and, therefore, maintained that registration was unnecessary. As Germany's most liberal associational law to date, the Imperial Law of Associations of 1908 had as its primary objective the containment of socialist and Polish associations, not the restriction of dissenting opinion from conservative or liberal ranks.[16] The wording of the law was left deliberately ambiguous so as to allow the government maximum or minimum application. According to its statutes, "every association which intended to have an influence on political matters" was to carry the political label and as such was liable to the following conditions. First, according to clause 3, a political association was required to have an executive committee (*Vorstand*) and a constitution. The executive committee was required to deliver to police authorities within two weeks of founding the membership list and constitution. Second, according to clause 5, the association was required to notify the local police a minimum of twenty-four hours in advance of its intention to hold a public meeting. The notion of "public meeting" was also not defined stringently but, according to legal interpretation, was meant to apply to a meeting in which the number of individuals in attendance exceeded the actual number of associational members. Clause 7 stipulated that public gatherings outdoors ("*unter freiem Himmel*") and processions through public streets required the consent of the authorities. Clause 10 maintained that every public meeting required the presence of a leader of the association who would be responsible for retaining order. All women and youth under eighteen were prohibited by clause 17 from joining such associations.[17] Active military personnel were also barred from membership in political associations by the 1908 law as well as by Article 49 of the *Reichsmilitärgesetz*.

If the government chose to define the Army League as a political association, not only would the image of nonpartisanship be destroyed, but the league's activities would be severely restricted and a lucrative source of potential members—military men and German youth associated with the Young Germany Movement—would be removed. It would also have major ramifications for all the patriotic societies. But would the government be willing to risk taking a step that could lead inevitably to greater discord? The act of labeling the Army League a political association would have been tantamount to a declaration of war on all of the nationalist societies. Several times in the past the government had considered placing the Navy League, the Eastern Marches Society, and the Imperial League against Social Democracy in this category.[18] In 1910, for example, bureaucrats scrutinized the activities of the Eastern Marches Society, reporting, "As far was can be determined only a handful of officers and military personnel are members . . . and these few for the most part are restricted to paying dues and here and there attending social activities."[19] In all likelihood, the government's purpose now in threatening the Army League's position was to remind patriotic zealots like Keim that the government would continue to direct policy, and that if he or any other popular nationalist got too far out of line, it would react swiftly and decisively.

In late February 1912 two nationalistic newspapers sympathetic to the Army League, the *Tägliche Rundschau* and *Berliner Neueste Nachrichten,* broke the news that the government was on the verge of declaring the league (and the other patriotic societies) political associations.[20] The government apparently could not come to a consensus on how to deal with the league and was sending mixed signals, which were in turn picked up by the nationalistic press to evoke sympathy for the league, whose status was in jeopardy. At times it seemed that the government's attitude vacillated daily, depending upon the severity of the league's current criticism. On 26

February, the day following the disclosures by the nationalist press, War Minister Heeringen acknowledged the league to be a nonpolitical association, noting that since it appealed to so many officers, any change in its status would force active military personnel to relinquish their membership.[21] The newspapers' contention had actually taken the government by surprise, and it declared the reports to be "completely superfluous [*vollkommen überflüssig*]."[22]

> Nothing is known in the Ministry of the Interior about the intention to treat the patriotic societies as political organizations. Previously . . . according to the circular of 4 May 1910 . . . the Minister of the Interior was inclined to concede that these organizations should not be considered as political organizations, at least not in the sense of provision 49 of the *Reichsmilitärgesetz* which prohibits *active* military personnel from participation in political organizations.[23]

Nevertheless, Heeringen was never favorably disposed toward the Army League nor its demands for substantial military reforms, and even he was prone to changing his mind, especially when the league stepped up its campaign for the Army Bill of 1912: "Owing to the criticism of the Army League, which is wide of the mark, utterly irresponsible and insulting in character, and which at the moment is aimed at measures which His Majesty has approved for the army, it is highly undesirable that active officers should have anything to do with the league in the interest both of the good name of the army and of its internal coherence."[24]

Given the differences of opinion within the government on this issue, the Ministry of the Interior chose to postpone its final decision until it could study the matter more carefully. A hasty decision might prove to be one it would regret. Wishing to appear impartial and responsive, the Ministry invited both General Keim and Rear Admiral Weber, president of the Navy League, to meet with its officials to discuss the "objectives" of their respective organizations. Keim, however, brusquely refused to cooperate, suspecting that the Ministry's offer was purely cosmetic.[25]

In mid-March, Prussian Minister of the Interior, Johann v. Dallwitz, clarified his stand on the Army League in a memo to the Chancellor. Comparing the league's position with that of the Navy League, Dallwitz pointed out that since Keim's departure in 1908, the Navy League had steered a less openly defiant antigovernmental course that allowed it to remain within the boundaries of an organization befitting the nonpolitical label. On the other hand, the Army League persisted (and even reveled) in its antigovernmental rhetoric. The problem with the Army League, the Secretary explained, did not lie with its goal of instructing the German public about the army—this, after all, was a worthy cause, and the Navy League's efforts had helped to raise the public's patriotic consciousness and enthusiasm for Germany's naval program. What worried Dallwitz most was the personality of the Army League president. With an explosive nature, fierce independence, and penchant for leveling sharp criticism, Keim clearly made even the most inflexible and cynical bureaucrat squirm. He was simply too unpredictable and thus potentially dangerous; the Army League under Keim's guidance was like a riderless horse.[26] Yet, removing Keim and his organization as threats would be difficult, Dallwitz reckoned. Any effort to apply the political label and make it stick to an organization that prided itself on its nonpartisan status would be problematic, given the Associations' Law's imprecise definition of the word "political." "The Imperial Associations' Law does not contain a specific definition of a political association," the Secretary moaned to Bethmann. "Any attempts to include a detailed definition . . . were abandoned because of the law's elasticity."[27] To declare the irritating league a political association would, therefore, simply invite further discord within the nationalist ranks and likely benefit the socialists, something that the government wished at all costs to avoid.

Keim took the government's threat seriously.[28] He insisted that Kiderlen-Wächter, the league's "mortal enemy," was behind the plot and was trying to punish the Pan-Germans for their relentless criticism of his Moroccan policy. If the government carried out its threat, Keim warned that it would have a "devastating effect [*verheerende Wirkung*]" on his league.[29] Class, to whom Keim confided his fears, tried to allay his friend's concern by maintaining that the government would likely take the path of least resistance, a prediction that proved accurate. The Ministry of the Interior ultimately decided to leave the league's nonpolitical status intact, perhaps in the hope that the active military personnel in it might be able to have a moderating effect.

This issue now resolved, the Army League's ability to perpetuate the image of nonpartisanship was nevertheless hampered by its own propaganda and actions, which were riddled with inconsistencies. General Keim's claim that the league recognized only patriotic Germans and not their political labels did not necessarily mesh with the political posturing within the league. National Liberals, Conservatives, and Agrarian Leaguers within the association maintained a tenuous truce at best. Nationalistic fervor could not disguise the antipathy that these politicians felt toward their rivals. Election-time alliances between these parties were often nothing more than marriages of convenience, a concerted effort to defeat a Socialist candidate, rather than a narrowing of their ideological differences or a demonstration of "nationalist unity." The Socialist gains in the Reichstag elections of 1912 underscored the tenuous accommodations between National Liberals, Conservatives, and Agrarians, and the reverberations were felt in the Army League.[30] A controversy erupted over Keim's choice of Hermann Paasche, a prominent National Liberal Reichstag deputy, as the league's first vice president.[31] The Agrarian League protested the selection of Paasche to this post, claiming that he was a friend of both Jews and socialists whose interests he had consistently supported in the Reichstag.[32] Keim apparently ignored the first manifestations of discontent until Class explained the gravity of the situation. Should Paasche be allowed to retain his vice presidency in the league, Keim would lose the support of the Agrarian League, especially in the critical Eastern Marches regions, where the Army League required its cooperation to recruit most effectively. On 2 April 1912 Class urged Keim to request Paasche's resignation immediately, lest relations between the Agrarians and Army League deteriorate or be broken off completely. Paasche's presence, Class warned, was like a "red flag [*rotes Tuch*]."[33] One month later the *Berliner Neueste Nachrichten* reported a story in which one of the Agrarian League's leading functionaries and president of its Posen provincial federation, retired major Ernst August v. Endell, criticized Paasche:

Major v. Endell recently stated publicly in the *Deutsche Tageszeitung* that he could not associate himself with the Army League as long as *Geheimrat* Paasche, a man who supported publicly the move to allow Jews in the officer corps, who played such a vital role in a party, the majority of whose representatives voted Bebel and Scheidemann to the presidency of the Reichstag, and who took no action to prevent this election from occurring, remained in the Executive Council.[34]

Precisely one week following this exchange, the *Berliner Neueste Nachrichten* announced that Paasche had resigned his vice presidency, ostensibly because of "parliamentary responsibilities."[35] Following closely upon the heels of Paasche's resignation was that of Otto v. Dewitz, Free Conservative member of the Prussian House and the Army League's second vice president, who attributed his departure to his "busy schedule." The truth was that both Paasche and Dewitz were pawns sacrificed to the Agrarian League because Keim required its cooperation in the Marches. The league's figures seem to bear this out. In early 1912 the Army League claimed 1,400 members in its Posen branches; one year later that number had tripled to 4,600 individual and 1,500 corporate members dispersed throughout nineteen branches.[36] Partisan bickering knew no boundaries. Keim, in the interest of expanding his association and maintaining at least an outward semblance of harmony, was not above cutting a political deal, if the price was right. In order to avoid future embarrassment and controversy, Keim tried to ensure that no "controversial" member of a political party could hold office in the league.[37]

In addition to projecting a nonpartisan image, the league sought to present itself as a "classless" association, accessible to all regardless of social background or gender. Following the precedent established by the Navy League, it maintained membership dues at a minimum of one mark to stimulate public participation and achieve its goal of a million members. Nonrestricted membership reinforced the impression that nationalism was the panacea for the nation's social ills, but the league bore a Janus face. The league's symbol, the Teutonic knight who prevailed upon a hill top and guarded the fertile valley below while the farmer tilled the earth, represented its efforts to protect the German nation and its values.[38] Rural solitude, hard work, sacrifice, and military virtues emphasized a desire to recapture the simplicity and morality of the past. Germans, the league argued, had become too complacent; life, of course, was difficult and unfair, but through vigilance and determination, it could become more tolerable. It invoked Bismarck's words that, "If one wants to live peacefully, one must also carry burdens, [and] pay taxes; without that it simply cannot be done."[39] Underlying its apotheosis of social order was the league's advocacy of militarism, domesticity, morality, and temperance, and its aversion to socialism.

### The Ideology of National Regeneration

*Deutscher Michel, erwach!* (Awake!) and *Vogel-Strauss Politik* (ostrich politics) were two key slogans incanted by the league to conjure up the image of a Germany ill prepared for an impending national struggle. The term *Deutscher Michel*, a reference to Michael, the patron saint of Germans and a manifestation of the *Volk* (nation), first came to be used during the Reformation and was subsequently adopted by later political movements, the league included, to rally Germans into action.[40] Michael was generally depicted as a good-hearted, sleepy-eyed country bumpkin, clad in breeches and a peaked night cap, who remained oblivious to the dangers posed by lurking foes. He represented the German nation that needed to be roused from its indifference and forced into preparing for the armageddon. Likewise, the ostrich that habitually buries its head in the sand suggested a similar imagery. The government's willful ignorance of the dangerous forces present within German society and those that hovered on its borders threatened to destroy the nation. The Army League's responsibility was to convince the government and the public that the remedy for the nation's ills lay with the concept of a "nation in arms." As one German nationalist expressed it, "What safeguards our peace is not flexibility, agreements (and) understandings, but only our good German sword and the feeling that we are hoping to look up to a government which will not allow this sword to rust when the appropriate time has come."[41] Decisive action, not promises, was required to protect the German state and German culture. As its constitution stated, the Army League served a dual purpose—to fortify the Germany army and to strengthen Germans' patriotic consciousness. As the "school of the nation," the army acted as a physical deterrent to Germany's enemies and as a source of spiritual inspiration and cultural rejuvenation.[42] It protected the nation from foreign and domestic foes alike, from those who sought to plunder its territory and pillage its industrial wealth as well as from those who were eager to debase its rich cultural heritage. Whereas the army's greatest foes, aside from France, England, and Russia, were socialism and pacifism, its most sacred ally was war.

War, its inevitability and its function as a purifying and integrative factor, was to some extent part and parcel of late nineteenth- and early twentieth-century European culture. Even in liberal England it manifested itself in invasion scares and in the propaganda of the National Service League and Imperial Maritime League. British invasion-scare novels found a receptive audience, especially Erskine Childers' *Riddle of the Sands* (1902), which told of the serendipitous discovery in the Frisian islands of clandestine German preparations to invade England, and William Le Quex's *The Invasion of 1910*.[43] Newspapermen like Lord Northcliffe sought to capitalize on the popular appetite for these stories: when Le Quex's novel was serialized in the *Daily Mail,* the German invasion route was changed to include those towns in which the paper's circulation figures were sagging.[44] Although Northcliffe retained Lord Roberts, former commander of British forces in the Boer War and president of the National Service League, as technical advisor, he readily sacrificed accuracy for greater publicity and increased sales. There could be no doubt that sensationalism sold newspapers. Meanwhile, Britain's corresponding militarist organizations, the Navy League and the National Service League, subscribed to the likelihood of war with Germany and contributed to the susceptibility of British society to naval scares.[45]

But this war fever, while evident in Europe, was pronounced in Germany. Spy scares were common in the popular press. The Army League, convinced that spying against Germany was increasing, advocated stiffer penalties for espionage and demanded higher rates of conviction.[46] Another favorite propaganda ploy used by the league to engender fear in the hearts of fellow Germans was to claim that the French would use their Black Colonial troops to invade Germany (the *"Schwarze Gefahr"*).[47] The possibility of mixed or black races overrunning pure, Aryan Germany made Keim's blood boil, and the league purposely tried to play on Germans' ignorance about and fears of other races to galvanize them into action. Lecture/slide shows on the African colonies and black natives were quite popular at league meetings. One demonstration, which dealt with the Herrero Conflict of 1904–5 (in Southwest Africa), depicted the dangers that German colonists supposedly encountered daily from the heathen blacks.

Steeped in Social Darwinistic doctrines, the writings of General Colmar von der Goltz, Friedrich v. Bernhardi, and Otto Schmidt-Gibichenfels (the latter an Army League member), left an indelible mark on the league's ideology.[48] They glorified war and encouraged sacrifice for the Fatherland; they stressed that war had been a part of man's natural development from the beginning of time and would remain so until the end. War was a "necessary element in the life of nations . . . an indispensable factor of culture, in which a true civilized nation finds the highest expression, . . . a biological necessity of the first importance, a regulative element in the life of mankind which cannot be dispensed with."[49] The seriousness with which these theorists and the Army League viewed war is evident in phrases like *"Krieg ums Dasein* [war of survival]," and *"Vernichtungskrieg* [fight to the finish]."[50] The truly great civilized nations of the world were those that recognized the value of war and whose citizens, skilled in its art, managed to thrive, while those nations, who like "Michel" or the ostrich ignored war's greatness, were doomed to decline and obscurity. Hegel's proclamation that "war prevents men from 'going soft' [*versumpfen*] and 'ossifying' [*verknöchern*]," and General Moltke's assertion that "without war the world would fall into laziness and become lost in materialism" were cited often with approval in the league's monthly journal and organizational lifeline, *Die Wehr*.[51] War, the league and its prophets insisted, purged society of decadence; it protected "the highest and most valuable interests of the nation," and any attempt to interfere with war's natural progression was viewed as a "criminal transgression."[52] Adjectives like "natural" and "healthy" were used frequently in its propaganda to reinforce the biological function of war: "Only if the *Volk*'s soul is healthy [*gesund*] does it have a future, does it merit a future," stressed the league's journal, and it added, "Occasional wars are not only desirable for the continued health of the individual and of society as a whole, but also necessary."[53]

Socialism and pacifism, with their deleterious emphasis on international cooperation, became targets of the Army League's propaganda warfare. Because these movements deemphasized the uniqueness of German culture and condemned war as an evil, the league directed the brunt of its propaganda against them. According to the association, socialists and pacifists belonged to the decadent classes who used peace as a "weapon of domination" to protect their interests.[54] They lulled Germans into a false sense of security, the Army League charged; they advocated cooperation and solidarity and failed to recognize the inherent differences among the races, appealed to individualism rather than obedience to the state, and willingly ignored the motives of revenge that relentlessly inspired Germany's enemies to engage it in a battle for its survival.[55] General Keim stood firm in his conviction that "a nation that has national pride can be defeated but never destroyed," and that pacifists and socialists alike were utopians who had failed to heed the lesson of history that only those nations that prepared for war were able to avoid it.[56]

The league's president was particularly incensed by the Left's attack on him and his association and became unhinged when he was publicly denounced as a *Landesverräter,* a traitor to the nation, and a "patriotic fanatic."[57] Trying to restore his and the league's good name, the general quipped that if he was a traitor, then so were His Majesty and the Chancellor because they, too, were committed to Germany's defense. He added that the Army League performed a great service to the German nation by protecting it against the revanchist policies of France and the destructive tendencies of left-wing radicals. The general maintained that pacifists and socialists, in their appeal for peaceful coexistence, did the nation a terrible injustice by advocating improved relations with France, which indoctrinated children with Germanophobic nursery rhymes and taught them that Alsace-Lorraine rightfully belonged to France, not Germany.[58] Keim assured the public that the Army League would actively combat antimilitarist and Germanophobic sentiments.

While trying to discredit the pacifist movement in Alsace-Lorraine, Keim became embroiled in a particularly nasty altercation, which was brought to national attention by the press, involving the Center Party Reichstag deputy for the region and outspoken Alsatian nationalist, the Abbé Emile-Wetterlé.[59] Keim's reputation for being a *Feuerkopf* was magnified by articles he published in *Tägliche Rundschau* and *Der Tag,* in which he denounced the Abbé as a scoundrel, bastard, and traitor to the German nation.[60] Though a man of the cloth, the Abbé was no stranger to such vituperation, having previously been tried and convicted for anti-German declarations.[61] He promptly responded in kind by charging the volatile general with slander. The case went to court in Strassburg (in Alsace-Lorraine), where the defendant availed himself of the services of his good friend, lawyer Heinrich Class, as legal counsel. While technically Keim himself was on trial, in a sense the Army League and popular nationalism were also under indictment. The articulate Class resorted to every device to vindicate the general, but the court ruled in favor of the Abbé and fined Keim the sum of 200 marks.[62]

Legal decisions aside, the league did not change its tactics and continued to insist that the army was the linchpin that brought Germans together as a community. The army instructed Germans in the art of warfare and educated them to recognize spiritual decay and to reject anything that threatened the very fabric of the German state. It also functioned as a role model for Germany's youth as well as for the working class. Keim's preoccupation with the issue of the military preparedness of the nation's youth, which had resulted in 1910 in the stillborn *Deutscher Jugendverband,* led him in 1912 to make an attempt to resurrect his goal of creating a "*Freiwillige Jugendwehr* [voluntary youth militia]" through the auspices of the Army League. Young men between the ages of fifteen and nineteen were to undergo rigorous but stimulating military exercise for a minimum of an hour every Saturday under the supervision of active reserve or militia officers.[63] In this way Germany's youth would be exposed to the rigors of army life in a limited and less potent dose. Participants were to wear caps and pelerines and carry knapsacks in imitation of military fatigues and gear. The intent of this instruction, however, was far from harmless or even playful; it did not aim at mere conviviality. In seeking to establish these groups, the league had a dual purpose in mind: to upgrade the youth's physical condition through exercise and drill and to inculcate them with what the league considered among the highest virtues—honor and obedience to the Fatherland. Since discipline demanded self-restraint, the Army League forced its youthful participants to abide by a moral code of abstinence from alcohol and tobacco while participating in their exercises. "There are things far more important and more manly than visiting/drinking in pubs, flirting, and smoking cigarettes," the league maintained.[64] Restoring morality among Germans was as much its intention as was improving the youth's physical stature. And what better way to revitalize what the league considered to be a spiritually and physically moribund society than to begin with shaping the impressionable minds of Germany's youth.

This was precisely the message that Richard Nordhausen trumpeted in his book, *Zwischen 14 und 18,* on which Keim's youth program was in part modeled.[65] Nordhausen portrayed Germany as a decaying nation and its youth, upon which its future rested, as having strayed from the path of righteousness. The adolescent years were characterized by youthful insubordination, willfulness, and lust, which triumphed over order and reason. Young men's fancies, Nordhausen continued, turned to wine, women, and song and to reading deplorable literature (*Schundliteratur*) like Nick Carter, Nat Pinkerton, and Sherlock Holmes stories.[66] Like his colleagues, Nordhausen blamed the degeneration of Germany's youth on industrialization, which destroyed the fabric of the family.[67] His solution included replacing pulp literature with more traditional books along the lines of Gottfried Keller and Goethe.[68] He also advocated a program of compulsory military education for all boys between the capricious ages of fourteen and eighteen, which would instill in them the rigors of military drill and discipline. With such training, "there would not be any more problems."[69]

But Keim and his followers were equally concerned with the older generation, which appeared lost to socialism. Because it considered workers easy prey for socialism, the league redoubled its effort to tout the benefits of army life. The more workers the league could recruit for the army, the greater the opportunity to render workers immune to socialist ideology and to increase the army's numerical strength.[70] Moral and physical rejuvenation were the keynote of military life. Its tedious rituals of drills and parades built character and muscles. The league stressed as well that in the army workers could find a temporary reprieve from their harsh existence in Germany's urban centers. The army offered working-class recruits exercise in the fresh country air followed by the consumption of generous portions of healthy food, neither of which, the league claimed, were attainable in the stale, sordid environment of the city and factory. Young workers would expect to gain additional weight and thus increase their chances for survival.[71] The Army League's message resounded like an advertisement for a modern-day health spa where workers could check in for a brief and beneficial interruption from their normal routine and leave refreshed in body and spirit. Urbanization was a double-edged sword: while urban factories stimulated Germany's economic growth and provided the necessary funds for the nation's defense, they also bred socialism and crime. Industrial smokestacks belched out impurities into the atmosphere, forcing city dwellers to inhale potentially harmful air, while urban overcrowding led to the spread of immorality in the home and in the streets, and an increase in crime and prostitution. All in turn had an adverse effect upon the size of Germany's population. "There is hardly a family in Berlin which survives beyond three generations," Nordhausen pointed out.[72] By demonstrating to the worker the positive aspects of army life, the Army League hoped to encourage him to return to civilian life as a productive member of the community with a renewed sense of self-worth and with a higher set of values to guide him.

As with Germany's youth, the league's reeducation program stressed the importance of abstaining from alcohol. The emphasis on abstinence was not new; middle-class temperance movements had been guided by the belief that the worker wasted most of his income on drink. League propaganda also warned against the dangers of excessive drinking, reminding workers that drunkenness undermined their productivity, created familial tension, and jeopardized Germany's industrial expansion. One *Die Wehr* article proposed that workers follow the example set by some soldiers who had sworn off alcohol completely and formed a club, the Association of Abstinent Soldiers, to spread the word about the evils of drinking.[73] It also applauded the work of the German Association for the Prevention of Alcohol Abuse (*Deutscher Verein gegen den Missbrauch geistiger Getränke*) in attempting to reduce excessive alcohol consumption.[74] In fact, the Army League and the German Association for the Prevention of Alcohol Abuse had much in common: each considered itself nonpartisan, favored Germany's industrial growth, criticized the selfish interests of the agrarian Junkers (the Junkers produced the grain for liquor and thus had an interest in alcohol consumption), and drew its members from the middle classes.[75] The Association's "fundamental purpose was to create a more harmonious and therefore more efficient industrial society, to ensure Germany's success in an increasingly competitive world economy, and to disseminate their own moral and cultural values": precisely the objective of the Army League.[76] This message resounded like the Protestant, middle-class work ethic: hard work, thrift, and sobriety would reward the worker with a better life, and the community would also reap benefits through his increased productivity. By appealing for sobriety, the league was also seeking to disarm complaints of workers who charged that they could not afford to pay more taxes for a larger military. The Navy League took the same approach with workers who blamed poverty, not a lack of patriotism, for their reluctance to finance the fleet.[77]

The Army League's argument for sobriety, while strident, fell on deaf ears. The SPD, for example, tried but failed to counter the allure of alcohol among the working class with its Schnapps boycott of 1909.[78] The boycott was viewed as both a moral and political initiative, for while it was concerned with the persistent problem of working-class alcoholic abuse, it was also directed against the continued economic and political domination of the Junkers who controlled the Schnapps trade and continued to block financial reform. By 1912 the leaders of the boycott were forced to admit that it had failed to reduce working-class alcoholic consumption or engage the sympathies and political energies of its members.[79] Since the consumption of alcohol, especially beer and wine, was as popular with most Germans as were associations, it is unlikely that the Army League's appeal to the individual's moral restraint in the face of alcoholic temptation achieved much, particularly in the army where drinking functioned as an aspect of military etiquette and as a release valve. Interestingly, the league did not choose to direct its antidrinking message to officers, nor did it abstain from serving alcoholic beverages at league functions. In fact, local Army League branches openly advertised that beer and wine would be plentiful at festivals and meetings, and indeed it would be difficult to imagine a *Stammtisch* without them. No doubt some Army League members (especially Keim) regarded the Junkers as purveyors of immorality and perpetuators of their own selfish economic interests, who avoided contributing toward the maintenance of the army by refusing to pay direct taxes. Yet nowhere in the league's moral propaganda does one find a sustained attack on the Junkers. With agrarians composing a considerable portion of the league's membership in its eastern branches, the league may have consciously resolved to avoid alienating them with a sustained public anti-Junker campaign.

Although the Army League undertook the responsibility of trying to improve the workers' existence through exercise and sobriety, its middle-class compassion for their plight had definite limits. Of utmost importance was combatting the spread of socialism among workers, not removing them from their abysmal environment or substantially improving their economic condition. Adolf Wagner, an old *Katheder-socialist* and Army League member, exemplified the league's position when he proclaimed that working standards in Germany were far better than in any of the other European nations and that German workers resided in "nice" living quarters that were "more satisfactory than the dwellings of workers in foreign countries."[80] Workers' lives were certainly not comfortable, as German historians have demonstrated, and their existence was shaped by many factors that they could not control.[81] The Army League sang the same paternalistic refrain as the workers' employers, whose concern for the working class generally depended upon the extent to which their own needs were served. For the league those needs were improving and staffing the army and halting socialist encroachment. In its pamphlet entitled "A Recruit's Letter to His Mother," an anonymous soldier complained about the woeful lack of spirit among Germans and praised the efforts of the Army League and the Imperial League against Social Democracy in helping to actively combat the spread of socialism.[82] The Army League tried to convince the working class of the importance of a strong defense by claiming that Ferdinand Lassalle, the founding father of the German workers' movement, had been a devotee of a strong army.[83] Yet, despite the quantity of propaganda the league produced, its anti-Socialist campaign failed to attract more than a handful of workers to its ranks.

Women also became a focus of the league's moralistic and nationalistic campaign. The largest of the German women's organizations, the *Bund deutscher Frauenverein* (the Federation of German Women's Associations) under the leadership of Marie Stritt (1902–8), had until 1908 endorsed suffrage for women, equality for women in marriage, and reform of the laws regarding child custody cases and the education of women. Thereafter, under its new leader, Gertrud Bäumer, the Federation "abandoned the idea of equality of the sexes and adopted the view that women were fundamentally different in character and abilities from men."[84] Like other German women's groups, the Federation increasingly steered a rightward course and accepted the notion of "domesticity," which assigned men and women to separate spheres and defined the woman's role as that of homemaker, childbearer, churchgoer, and instructor of morality (i.e., *Kinder, Küche, Kirche*). This role was welcomed enthusiastically by the Army League's leaders, some of whom were devout antifeminists and activists in the League for the Prevention of Emancipation of Women (*Deutscher Bund zur Bekämpfung der Frauenemanzipation,* founded in 1912). The Army League received the active support of the *Deutscher Frauenbund* (German Women's League), which was founded in 1909 as the women's offshoot of the Imperial League against Social Democracy, and its president and founder, Marie v. Alten, who had the distinction of being the only woman to grace Keim's *Ausschuss* (executive committee).[85]

Women were encouraged to join the Army League (and could legally do so by the 1908 Imperial Associations Law), but only a minority ever sat on executive boards of local branches, and those who did were most often wives of military officers or other league officials. For example, a Frau Lieutenant Colonel Hamann served as treasurer of the Cottbus chapter for 1912–13, two women were included in the steering committee of the Wiesbaden affiliate in 1913, and a Frau bank president Frief was elected to Hersfeld's executive committee in April 1913.[86] Of the fifteen women on the *Gesamtvorstand* (general council), which consisted of upwards of a hundred individuals in 1914, seven were the spouses of the leading executives who themselves sat on the council—Frau Keim, Frau *Oberregierungsrat* Perrin, Frau *Oberzollpräsident* Carthaus, Frau *Oberregierungsrat* Galleiske, Frau General Taubert, Frau *Landmesser* Jacobshagen, and Frau *Obergeneralarzt* Demuth.[87] As a rule, women were not recruited by the national organization as circuit lecturers but occasionally spoke before a local branch meeting, usually on festive occasions and on the topic of the "patriotic duty of women." Unlike the Navy League and the Colonial Society, which organized separate women's affiliates, the Army League saw no need for this division. Because its officials considered women incapable of understanding political matters, the league did not feel obligated to create a women's auxiliary, which in any case would necessitate both a keen interest in political issues and a thorough knowledge of managing an association. The league certainly did not want to have to worry that women might stray from its objectives or, even worse, demonstrate their independence by challenging established programs.

Within the Army League itself, women could be particularly useful as role models by perpetuating the values of motherhood, patriotism, and morality. Women were supposed to be protected from the evils produced by urbanization. "Woman is weaker than man," Nordhausen emphasized, ". . . and yet upon her rests the incredible burden of motherhood. With particular care we must shield her from the destructive haste and agony of contemporary work fever."[88] Those of the fairer sex who were infected with the work ethic and tempted by modern materialism would be incapable of producing "healthy" offspring. Nordhausen's definition of health went beyond mere physical fitness to incorporate a proper frame of mind as well, namely a receptivity to traditional German values.[89] As women were generally perceived to be more religious than their spouses, they were to serve as "high priestesses" who would proselytize their families on the virtues of having faith in religion and of sacrificing themselves to the cause of the Fatherland. They were to prepare their husbands and sons for the inevitable war by providing them with a sense of dignity and courage and by giving them moral support. To encourage women to accept this role, the league published stories in *Die Wehr* on the deeds of other patriotic women. Women were to offer their bodies consentingly for the purpose of procreating and suckling Germany's future warriors and giving them the spiritual encouragement necessary to defeat the enemies of the nation. There was a kind of immaculate conception quality attributed to the woman's role as well, as one article revealed: "The little wife must grow and transform herself into a full-fledged wife: pure and like crystal, profound and warm, like the vibrating sound of the viola; . . . radiant like the morning sun, full of vigor, like the glow of midday; childlike . . . ; maternal . . . and inexhaustible and steady like a mountain. . . . Inspiration produces heroes!"[90] The league depicted woman as a rock of ages, capable of exhibiting strength and courage and demonstrating emotions at the appropriate moment. As one female member put it: "All of us women are the nerves of the great . . . and industrious woman known as Germany."[91] Another traditional gender role exploited by the league was that of nurse. During actual combat German women, married and single, were to be instructed in the importance of caring for patients and of maintaining sanitation. The league suggested that women enroll in courses in first aid, which it provided, and form a *Sanitätsverein* (Sanitation Club) that would keep them abreast of the latest methods on keeping the wounded and their own children protected from infection.[92]

This concern for cleanliness was a feature that the middle classes believed distinguished themselves from the poverty-stricken, socialist working masses. It also dovetailed neatly with the association's concern for the purity of the German culture, language, and race. The league shared with the Pan-German League and the German Language Association (*Allgemeiner Deutscher Sprachverein*) a fervent devotion to the glorification of German culture and the protection of the German language from bastardization by an influx of foreign words and phrases.[93] Immigrants who refused to abandon their native traditions and language threatened to undermine the purity of German customs by perpetuating inferior traditions and refusing to be absorbed into a superior German culture. The obvious targets here were Jews and Poles residing in the Eastern Marches who, to the consternation of German officials and popular nationalists, chose to retain their cultural independence. Equally disturbing were native Germans who deflowered their own language by substituting foreign, especially French, words for proper German ones.[94] Lurking just beneath the surface of all this was a racist and anti-Semitic ideology articulated by certain league members like Otto Schmidt-Gibichenfels, the editor of the notoriously racist monthly journal, *Politisch Anthropologische Revue;* publisher J. F. Lehmann; aristocrat and Army League official Kurd v. Strantz; neoromantic poet Börries v. Münchhausen; and retired generals (and Army League stalwarts) Karl Litzmann and Eduard v. Liebert.[95] Racist and anti-Semitic overtones could be detected in the league's propaganda from its inception, but it was not really until after the First World War that they became central to the Army League's message.

## The Propaganda Machine

Of course, the league's ability to disseminate its message depended upon two primary factors: the efficiency of its propaganda machine and the indispensable journalistic expertise of those individuals charged with keeping it well oiled. Keim created two distinct yet complementary agencies that were commissioned with the responsibility of ensuring the maximum return on the league's propaganda: the Business Office (*Geschäftsstelle*) and the Press Department (*Presse Abteilung*). In just two years, between 1912 and 1914, the affairs of the Business Office were handled by three different men in succession, Theodore Bassler (1912), retired captain Hering (1913), and Mayor Thiele (1914), amply confirming suggestions that Keim's incessant demands for perfection might eventually repel even the most ardent supporter. The Business Office dispensed *Die Wehr,* recruited prominent speakers to serve as circuit lecturers, and distributed as well as sold propaganda materials such as postcards and other memorabilia. The Press Department, on the other hand, oversaw the publication of *Die Wehr,* the weekly *Nachrichten,* and assorted pamphlets and circulars, as well as the release of official statements to the press; it enjoyed a more stable existence under the guidance of its chief, Hermann Müller-Brandenburg (1912–14), and Heinrich Rippler and Richard Nordhausen.[96] At age twenty-seven, the youngest of the officials, Hermann Müller-Brandenburg brought with him not only journalistic experience but most importantly, as far as Keim was concerned, intense ambition and determination. He actively contributed to several major league publications, including *Die Wehr* and the *Wehrkalender,* as well as to pamphlets entitled, "The Peace Movement and its Dangers for the German Nation," and "The Others and We," and he frequented the lecture circuit until military service intervened in 1914.[97] Heinrich Rippler was well acquainted with the instruments of propaganda, serving as editor of the *Tägliche Rundschau,* while Richard Nordhausen also dabbled in journalism under the pseudonym of "Caliban." Equally advantageous for the Press Department's ability to disseminate propaganda was the cooperation of newspaper entrepreneur and league treasurer, George v. Büxenstein, whose holding included the *Tägliche Rundschau, Die Post,* the *Berliner Neueste Nachrichten,* and the publishing conglomerate *Deutscher Verlag.*[98]

Under the auspices of both divisions, hundreds of thousands of pamphlets, song sheets, postcards, and other memorabilia were produced and sold. *Die Wehr* increased its circulation from 60,000 issues in 1912 to 90,000 by April 1913 to approximately 108,000 during the First World War. Members received the monthly journal gratis and individual issues could be purchased by nonmembers at twenty-five pfennigs a piece. Weekly copies of the *Nachrichten* cost five marks, and as of April 1913 it had nearly 2,700 subscribers.[99] The *Wehrkalender* (1914) cost one mark for nonmembers and seventy-five pfennigs for members, while the ten-pamphlet Army League series (*Schriften des Deutschen Wehrvereins*) ranged from twenty-five to fifty pfennigs each. Postcards, song sheets (the league even had its own song composed by Gottfried Schwab), and commemorative medals generally did not exceed ten pfennigs and were extremely profitable; in two months' time in 1913 the league's special commemorative 1813–1913 postcard reportedly sold

200,000 copies. Another popular item was the postcard depicting the league's emblem, the medieval knight. Although most of the propaganda was produced and distributed by the central office in Berlin, some of its more established branches churned out their own literature, ranging from reproductions of special lectures (in late 1912 the Württemberg Provincial Federation manufactured 30,000 copies of a lecture by Lieutenant General v. Schmitt, which sold for twenty-five pfennigs, and which was printed free of charge by a Stuttgart publishing company) to annual reviews of branch activities (the Söllingen branch published "Our First Year in the Army League"), none of which, unfortunately, has survived.

In many respects, the Army League's propaganda machine resembled, but did not necessarily rival, that of its sister organization, the Navy League. In 1912, for example, the Navy League's organ, *Die Flotte,* had a readership of about 360,000, and it *Kalender,* published in 1913, sold 500,000 copies.[100] In addition, it too printed postcards and stamps (one mark for 100), pamphlets (usually one mark), pictures of His and Her Majesty, the Crown Prince of Prussia, and maneuvers of the German High Sea Fleet, which were suitable for framing. It also published *Mitteilungen des Deutschen Flottenvereins,* albeit on an "infrequent basis [*im zwangloser Folge*]."[101] On the whole, the Navy League had greater funds at its disposal to produce and distribute its propaganda than did the Army League.[102] Between January 1912 and June 1913 the Army League spent 46,833.75 marks on propaganda and an additional 25,072.28 marks on the publication and distribution of *Die Wehr,* so three-quarters of its operating budget (95,886.53 marks) went toward creating its image. But for the same period its income was 99,428.51 marks (95 percent of which came from membership dues), indicating that it was spending close to the brink of its resources.[103] Although the league's approach to propaganda was probably not different from that of its rival associations, it simply lacked the funding (whether from special funds like those of the Navy League or from sufficient membership dues) to support its ambitious efforts.

Following the examples set by the Pan-German and Navy leagues, the Army League etched out a prominent national profile. A Berliner perusing his daily editions of local newspapers could expect to encounter full-length accounts of its assault on "nonpatriotic" government officials who hesitated or refused to abide by its ultimatums. The Army League was only one of many patriotic societies that operated its national headquarters out of the capital. Since these societies' objectives as well as membership overlapped, the Army League, in order to emerge from the pack as the front runner, needed to be even more aggressive. To ensure its survival among the competition and to vie for the public's affections, the league at all times had to foster the impression that it was a highly dedicated and intensely driven organization at the forefront of the nationalist crusade. But how long could the league continue to maintain the furious pace of propaganda? And how extensive was its patriotic appeal beyond the parameters of the capital and the militaristic Prussian state? An undue concentration on the league's efforts in Berlin, therefore, would result in a grossly misleading picture. As Geoff Eley adroitly pointed out (but neglected to fulfill) in his book on the Radical Right, the historian should refrain from concentrating solely on "high politics" and instead focus upon "the internal relations between leaders and led, Berlin and the branches, the centre and the periphery."[104] After all, the label "popular nationalism" would seem to imply a broadly based nationalist appeal beyond the narrow confines of Berlin and the intimate circle of league officials. Thus, in order to put popular nationalism to the litmus test, one must try to account for the plethora of local and regional factors that may have figured into the Army League's supposed popularity, as well as into the breadth and depth of its members' commitment to the cause. The next two chapters will flesh out the contours of associational life that have often been obscured by a Prussocentric focus.

## CHAPTER 4

# "More Prussian than the Prussians": The Army League in the Liberal Southwest

That a militaristic organization like the Army League should have been inaugurated in Württemberg rather than in Prussia might, upon reflection, seem curious.[1] If Prussia could conjure up vivid images of militarism, bureaucracy, and Junkerdom, Württemberg suggested constitutionalism and a more liberal ethos. Politically, socially, and economically, Württemberg's development bore little resemblance to that of the Prussian state. Lacking a counterpart to Prussia's landowning Junkers, Württemberg consisted of small- to middle-sized holdings owned by peasants and noblemen alike. Thus, without substantial landholdings, the state's nobility were unable to exert the same degree of control over the local population and regional affairs. Another factor responsible for the state's deviation from what is commonly considered the Prussian norm was French influence, which shaped in part Württemberg's liberal proclivity.

Indeed, liberalism flourished in this southwestern state throughout *Vormärz* and beyond, despite occasional setbacks.[2] Threatened by the repression that immediately followed in 1848, liberals cooperated with each other, despite ideological differences, to revive the movement's fortunes by founding the *Fortschrittspartei,* or Progressive Party, in the early 1860s. But the very same issues that had divided liberals in 1848—the questions of suffrage (*Wahlrechtsfrage*) and German unification—resurfaced quickly, revealing the fragility of any liberal compromise. Rather than serving to cement a permanent broader liberal alliance, the events of 1863 and 1864 (i.e., the granting of 1863 of a general amnesty by the King of Württemberg for all political exiles of 1848, followed by the repeal in 1864 of the oppressive Law of Associations of 1852) drove a further wedge into the movement. Returning political exiles like "democrats" Karl Mayer and Ludwig Pfau, finding aspects of the Progressive Party too restrictive and not wishing their ideas to be compromised, capitalized on the easing of associational restrictions by establishing a separate liberal organization, the *Deutsche Volkspartei* (German People's Party), to champion the antiaristocratic, anti-Prussian, and antimilitaristic sentiments of rural, small-town Protestant, lower-middle-class Württemberg.[3] Alarmed by this reemergence of left-wing liberalism and committed to principles that the People's Party opposed—German unification under Prussia, limited suffrage, and military expansion—the right wing of the movement, under the leadership of Julius Hölder, announced the formation of its own party, the *Deutsche Partei* (German Party), in 1866.[4]

Throughout the Bismarckian decades the two liberal parties, the German Party and the German People's Party, found themselves competing for the affections of voters in both local and national elections.[5] The incessant and often petty rivalries that characterized their relationship during the first two decades of the new Reich threatened to undermine the liberal movement's ability to expand its electorate after 1890. Disturbed by the liberals' political bickering and dissatisfied with the inability of the corresponding national parties to address their needs, an ever-increasing number of former liberal voters sought alternatives. The repeal of the anti-Socialist Laws and the relative absence of religious tension when compared with the Prussian experience paved the way for the rise of the Social Democratic and the Catholic Center parties, on the one hand, and the emergence of popular agrarianism (the *Bauernbund*) on the other.[6] These new parties potentially offered former liberal voters the attention that it seemed neither liberal party could provide. The Social Democratic Party (SPD) sought to focus on the political demands of Württemberg's neglected working class; the Center provided political, social, and even economic refuge for the state's ignored Catholic minority; while the Agrarian League promised to address the needs of the economically depressed farming community.[7] The once-predominant liberal movement in Württemberg was by the turn of the century being squeezed by the emergent forces of the political Left and Right and forced to compete with them for a limited pool of middle-class voters. This increasing polarization and fragmentation of Württemberg politics was also reflected in the proliferation of the patriotic societies in the state. Many prominent nationalistic associations—the Pan-German League, Colonial Society, Navy League, and Imperial League against Social Democracy—began to infiltrate the state's local network of sociability beginning in the 1890s.[8]

Symptomatic of the widening chasm between the political Left and Right was the founding in Stuttgart on 20 January 1912 of the Army League's first branch. Neither Keim's memoirs nor league documents explain why Stuttgart was chosen to inaugurate the league's campaign, but one might speculate upon two possible motives. First, as the site of the national headquarters for its bête noir, the German Peace Society (*Deutsche Friedensgesellschaft*), Stuttgart offered the Army League a convenient platform from which to denounce the forces of pacifism and international cooperation.[9] The Württemberg federation of the Peace Society comprised more than one-quarter of the association's total membership as well as over one-half of its national branches in 1913, prompting Stuttgart pastor and national vice president of the Peace Society, Otto Umfrid, to observe that "without the activity of those of us in Stuttgart the German Peace Movement would probably have disappeared."[10] The Army League's second motive for choosing Stuttgart was the fact that the Peace movement's "natural allies," the Social Democrats, also enjoyed a relatively comfortable position within the city. Electoral cooperation between the SPD and liberals in city run-off elections and the publication of the highly acclaimed *Schwäbische Tagwacht* made Stuttgart a target for ultanationalists. By founding its first branch in Stuttgart, the Army League hoped to kill two birds with one stone.

Seventy-three individuals from the greater Stuttgart area assembled on 20 January, a full week prior to the association's official national founding in Berlin, to provide an impetus for the founding of the first branch.[11] Not until two weeks later, on 5 February, was the Stuttgart branch officially established with the drafting of a constitution. At that time, as with the preliminary meeting on 20 January, those men who attended did so by private invitation only.[12] The branch's constitution provided for an executive committee (*Vorstand*), which consisted of one acting and two honorary presidents, two secretaries, one acting and one honorary treasurer, and twenty other members.[13] Theoretically, the executive committee numbered twenty-seven, but the constitution also provided for the incorporation of new members by means of a by-election, thereby guarding against sudden death, resignation, or removal of one or more of its executives. The president and secretary were to be chosen from and by the executive committee, and the executive committee itself was to be elected for a three-year term by the general members who attended the annual meeting (*Hauptversammlung*). Membership dues were set at one mark minimum, although wealthier members were urged to contribute more generously.

Of the twenty-eight men who served on the branch's executive committee between 1912 and 1914, the majority came from three occupations: military officers (8), bureaucrats (8), and businessmen (7).[14] A handful of educators and professionals filled out the remainder. Within these broad occupational categories, the executive committee members tended to be men of considerable status and were often local *Honoratioren*. Each bureaucrat was university-trained (*akademische Beamten*), bearing titles of *Oberverwaltungsgerichtsrat, Oberregierungsrat, Ministerialrat,* and *Geheimer Hofrat.* Of the eight military men, five were retired from active duty and held the rank of general, while a *Präzeptor* and professor represented the educational ranks. Five *Fabrikanten,* a newspaper magnate, and a purveyor to the court comprised the business community. In an effort to avoid the obvious appearance of being an elitist association, the Stuttgart executive committee pledged itself to recruiting an artisan and a worker to its ranks in the future. Noting the committee's intentions, the socialist organ *Schwäbische Tagwacht* commented wryly: "If one [worker] should be found, then we implore [one] to photograph him . . . because a worker, who comes to the Army League and allows himself to be elected to the Executive Committee, is a noteworthy sight."[15]

Since many of these executives were well-known figures in their communities, some were likely to have known each other prior to their Army League duties, having circulated in the same social circles or served together on other associational boards. To take two examples, *Präzeptor* Friedrich Bassler and Professor Emil Hüzel, the two educators on the executive committee, were colleagues in the city's *Realgymnasium,* while the branch's treasurer, banker and consul Max Dörtenbach, and Lieutenant General v. Schmitt devoted themselves to upper-class man's best friend by patronizing the Association for the Breeding of Pure Racing Hounds (*Verein zur Züchtung reiner Jagdhunderassen für Württemberg*), which was sponsored by the King of Württemberg.[16] Such personal contacts were also exploited as a primary vehicle by which to establish new branches throughout the state. An organizing committee would meet with an unspecified number of "appropriate [*geeignete*]" individuals to pave the way for the foundation of additional branches.[17] *Vertrauensmänner* (organizers) were to "convince a number of influential individuals of [the branch's] necessity. Once there is a convinced nucleus, then it is imperative to attract an even larger gathering to a lecture at which the founding can take place. These people must be invited by private means only."[18] This "old boy network" approach (*Honoratiorenpolitik*) allowed league officials to contact well-known and respected local or regional figures who themselves might be persuaded to found a branch or who in turn might suggest the names of other friends or colleagues as likely organizers. It could also save officials the time and trouble of seeking out capable or willing leaders and occasionally perhaps spare them the embarrassment of being stuck with someone less worthy for the demands of the position.

Once the Stuttgart branch had been set into motion, its executives turned to the task of launching chapters throughout the state. To create the proper patriotic atmosphere within which to launch these new branches, the national headquarters in Berlin supplemented local efforts by dispatching circuit lecturers like *Oberstleutnant* z.D. Hüber of Riesa (Saxony), who delivered a speech entitled "French rearmament and the necessity of the Army League" in numerous locations between 17 and 30 January 1912.[19] Hübner's efforts were not misplaced, for twelve of the sites he visited subsequently established their own Army League branches. Once branches were founded, executive committees were appointed in accordance with the constitution of Stuttgart. The minimum number of individuals required to establish a local branch was twenty individuals or fewer, if necessary.[20]

By the fall of 1912, however, it was apparent to Württemberg's executives that reinvigorating the already established branches and spurring the formation of new ones would require a "bigger gun" from the national association. General Keim volunteered himself for this purpose, firing the opening salvo in the state's autumn campaign and lecturing throughout November on his favorite topic in the hope of stimulating new interest in his beloved organization. On the twenty-seventh of the month General Keim addressed the founding of the Tübingen branch, which would become one of the state's largest, and wound up his grand tour on the twenty-ninth in Stuttgart. Claiming that "Germany can find peace only if it is defended by a strong army" and that "only in the offensive can victory be ours," Keim warned his audiences against the belief that diplomacy could prevent war.[21] World history was not fashioned by diplomats, the general explained, but by the desire of the people. France wanted the Rhineland again; England sought to eliminate its German business rivals; Russia also looked covetously at Germany's possessions. If all nations demanded something, then the one in the middle (i.e., Germany) would receive nothing.[22] To prevent the rape of Germany, the general suggested that Germans work with the Army League for the passage of the forthcoming army bill.

On 7 May, with the league's recruitment program in full swing, a Provincial Federation (*Landesverband*) of Württemberg was created to give order and direction to the rapidly expanding network of local branches. The Stuttgart executive committee figured prominently in the Federation's establishment, laid the framework for the other newly founded branches, and provided the Federation with a few of its own executives and more prominent members, including His Excellency, Lieutenant General Franz Freiherr v. Soden (president); retired *Finanzrat* Ludwig Klüpfel and *Fabrikant* Artur Vetter (honorary presidents); *Verlagsbuchhändler* Dr. Sproesser and *Gerichtsassessor* Marquardt (secretaries); and consul and banker Max Dörtenbach (treasurer).[23] As they did in the Stuttgart executive committee, bureaucrats, military officials, and businessmen figures prominently in the Federation's executive board (representing a total of 13 of the 16 committeemen). Moreover, the bureaucrats were academically trained, while the officers held the rank of general or higher. The social makeup of the Federation's executive committee appears to have been even more restrictive than that of Stuttgart's. The three remaining committeemen were from the educational and legal professions and the nobility.

Two days before the celebration of Otto v. Bismarck's birthday, on 29 March 1912, the Stuttgart branch held its first public meeting, a lecture evening (*Vortragsabend*) in the concert hall of the Liederhalle, which featured two speakers, His Excellency Lieutenant General v. Schmitt and Prof. Dr. Gustav Jäger. Presiding over the meeting was branch president Johannes Haller, who opened the festivities by reminding his audience of the importance of the league's goal of fortifying the army to ensure the nation's security. Military matters, Haller maintained, were a concern of everyone, regardless of political affiliation, and the Army League's function was to ensure the army be kept in prime condition, a goal the Navy League had sought with regard to Germany's fleet.[24] Next, Lieutenant General v. Schmitt offered his professional opinion in a lecture entitled "On the Army Bill: Comparisons between the German and French Armies," in which he echoed Keim's warning that the French army in 1912 was better equipped and staffed than its German counterpart and that something must be done immediately to redress this woeful imbalance. So critical did the Stuttgart branch deem v. Schmitt's speech that it ordered 25,000 copies reproduced for distribution to the public. The concluding speaker of the evening was Professor Jäger who, with the aid of slides, discussed the correlation between military strength and labor productivity, arguing that vigorous military training for Germany's workers would improve their productivity in the factories as well as their performance in the field.[25]

Five weeks later five hundred people crowded the Bürgermuseum in Stuttgart on 8 May to attend the branch's second public meeting.[26] This time the main attraction was a colorful and well-respected local figure, *Oberstudienrat* Gottlob Egelhaaf, who spoke on the subject of "Germany and the State of World Affairs."[27] Egelhaaf's lecture, like v. Schmitt's, summarized the league's specific demands upon the government in Berlin for the rejuvenation of the army. These included actual fulfillment of compulsory military service, an increase in the army's peacetime strength, and its greater receptivity to the use of new technology. Egelhaaf invoked the maxims of Frederick the Great to lend historical justification to the league's cause: "Germany's abundance of able-bodied men must be fully utilized so that, in any event, we must assure ourselves of going into battle with overwhelming military superiority. In the offensive lies the guarantee of victory."[28] Convinced that a successful war could be waged only through the deployment of every available highly trained young man, Egelhaaf insisted that Germany's youth be required by the government to undergo military instruction from an early age. His second demand, an increase in the army's peacetime strength, he believed, would facilitate smoother, more rapid mobilization for war. Using the same statistics employed by Keim in previous speeches, he argued that the German army's peacetime strength in 1911 stood at 0.78 percent of the nation's population, whereas the French equivalent was much higher, at 1.40 percent. This meant that Germany was not taking full advantage of its larger population. Furthermore, if the army was to achieve its maximum potential, its leaders, he maintained, would have to recognize the importance of utilizing the airplane and automobile. Germany's position in the heart of the European continent, surrounded by vengeful enemies, demanded the immediate overhaul of its army.[29] In the patriotic atmosphere of the impending one hundredth anniversary of the Battle of Leipzig, the Army League and Egelhaaf hoped the nation would be receptive to their call for a new army bill.

With the arrival of summer, the traditional vacation time, the Württemberg Federation could not maintain the momentum of the spring. Branch activities were temporarily suspended until the coming autumn; only four new branches were founded during the summer, and these in name only. On the surface, at least for some members, politics seemed to have taken a back seat to the frivolities of warm summer days. For the league's executives, however, summer was a time for reflecting on the events of the recent past (the establishment of thirteen branches with an approximate total membership of two thousand) and deciding the strategy for the autumn.

November 1912 marked a turning point in Württemberg. As of October the league had established thirteen branches in a space of approximately ten months; between November 1912 and April 1913 a total of forty-five new branches were founded at a rate of 7.5 foundings per month as opposed to only 1.3 for the preceding period (see Figure 1). From the late autumn of 1912 until early spring 1913 the league more than doubled its individual membership, from 2,361 in November to 5,657 by April.[30] Certainly Keim's persuasiveness and persistence helped to get the ball rolling, but the general's speeches could not alone account for the sudden expansion. Rather, a combination of factors were responsible for this dramatic associational growth. First, the Army League had begun by the fall to iron out some of the bugs inherent in the formative period, in which branches were coordinated and ideas systematized by the recent establishment of the Provincial Federation. Second, the branches courted the support of the local press to publicize their message to the wider public. Newspaper editors sympathetic to the league's goal often offered its activities greater exposure, as was the case with Dr. Karl Elben, member of the Stuttgart branch's executive committee and simultaneously editor-in-chief of the prominent National Liberal *Schwäbische Merkur*. Third, the outbreak of the Balkans War in October 1912 seemed to justify for some Germans the Army League's advocacy of a larger and technically superior Germany army. And fourth, the announcement by the government of discussion on a new army bill

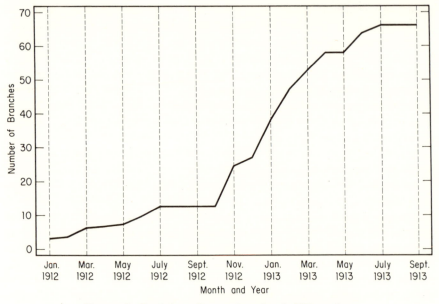

FIGURE 1. Total Army League branches in Württemberg.

for 1913 galvanized the league into intensifying its propaganda campaign and membership drive. By April 1913, then, the Provincial Federation counted fifty-eight branches with only ten districts in the state beyond its reach.[31] All four of Württemberg's regions, the overwhelmingly Protestant Neckar and the Schwarzwald (with its pockets of Catholics from Oberndorf to Spaichingen in the southeast and Horb to Rottenburg in the middle) to the Jagst and the Donau (with the predominantly Catholic southern regions), were represented.[32] On the surface, at least, neither religion nor politics appeared to affect the emergence of branches, but upon closer examination, two important trends can be detected.

First, many of the branches founded were in garrison towns. As noted in Chapter 1, the Army League's nonpolitical status enabled military men to join, and the league's commitment to improving the opportunities for promotion and retirement benefits also provided an incentive for military participation. Second, over 70 percent of the fifty-eight branches were established in towns with overwhelmingly Protestant populations. In the twelve branches founded in predominantly Catholic districts, the Protestant minority probably provided the bulk of the support. Although one cannot discount altogether the participation of some Catholics (despite Keim's reputation as a rabid anti-Catholic), both of the clearest cases of Catholic support occurred under unusual circumstances. For example, the Tettnang branch, located in the far southern tip of the Donau region renowned for its succulent white asparagus, was organized by a Catholic landowner and Center Party outcast, *Gutsbesitzer* Adorno. Adorno's neutrality toward the Center harmonized with the Army League's professed nonpartisan, classless, and ecumenical outlook. The league was optimistic that Adorno could attract other nationally minded Catholics who might otherwise be apprehensive of Keim's prejudice. Adorno's indifference toward Centrist politics is best illustrated in the following:

> *Gutsbesitzer* Adorno-Kaltenberg (Tettnang) cannot be designated as a Center candidate because he had never committed himself politically and therefore cannot warrant what is demanded of him by the Center's electorate. The consensus in the Tettnang district is that Adorno, to those who know him, is not the right man for the vacancy. The Upper Swabian Center must appoint someone who has been active in the party. Adorno's attitude even at best gives the impression of benevolent neutrality towards the Center.[33]

In the case of Tettnang, the strong bond between the Center Party and Catholics hampered Adorno's ability to recruit more than thirty-two members to his nonpartisan cause.[34]

A second example of Catholic participation was in the town of Hohenstadt, where 381 of its 387 residents were Catholics. Located in the Aalen district of the Jagst region, it had been founded five hundred years earlier by the Catholic von Adelmannsfelden family.[35] In July 1912, one of its descendants, *Rittergüter, Württembergischer Kammerherr, Königlicher Bayerische Rittmeister* a.D. Gustav Graf v. Adelmannsfelden, established a local branch and served as its president.[36] Gustav simultaneously was an executive in both the Württemberg Provincial Federation and the General Council. Unlike his brother Wilhelm, who had served as a Centrist Reichstag representative from October 1881 until June 1893, Gustav apparently never dabbled openly in politics and thus reflected the Army League's prescribed refrain of being "above the parties."

Like Adorno's Tettnang branch, v. Adelmannsfelden's group was relatively small, numbering only twenty members between its founding in July 1912 and November 1912. Paralleling the growth of the other Württemberg branches, Hohenstadt's membership doubled to forty between November 1912 and April 1913. Thereafter, however, the branch was unable to recruit more than an additional five supporters. While 45 members out of a possible 387 may seem insignificant, in reality this represented 11.6 percent of the townspeople. When one takes into account that nearly one-third of Germany's population were children under the age of eighteen, the branch's ability to mobilize local Catholics looks more impressive.[37] Even so, v. Adelmannsfelden's stature and nonpartisan image (like that of Adorno) could not overcome entirely the uneasiness that his local Catholic brethren continued to feel toward the league.[38]

The Army League's appeal in Protestant districts likewise depended upon a variety of variables, foremost among them the personality, enthusiasm, and influence of the chapter president or other executive members. For example, the Tübingen branch, one of the earlier and larger of the local affiliates, boasting a membership of 242 individual and 200 corporate (including 9 university corps) members, was led by Professor Dr. Gustav v. Schleich. A professor of ophthalmology in the medical faculty and member of the university senate, v. Schleich was simultaneously active in the local National Liberal organization and sat on the Army League's national *Gesamtvorstand.*[39] That a considerable portion of Tübingen's

membership was made up of students, and of these, many studied medicine, may
testify to v. Schleich's influence and prestige within the university community. On
the other hand, personality sometimes had just the opposite effect on a branch's
ability to recruit, as the case of Leonberg demonstrates. An overwhelmingly Protestant town of nearly 2,800 (according to the 1910 census) located just to the west of
Stuttgart in the Neckar region, Leonberg joined the Army League bandwagon in
February 1913 under the guidance of its president and founder, Jonathan Roth. A
local citizen who had made good, Roth (born in 1873) was an intensely driven
young lawyer actively committed to the local *Bund der Landwirte* organization. In
the two years during which he served as president, he failed to recruit more than
seventeen members, despite his reputation as a devout nationalist (he simultaneously served as the president of the local Navy League branch). Since Roth was
elected to the Reichstag in January 1912 as a *Bund der Landwirte* deputy, he may
have been too occupied with his parliamentary responsibilities to his district to have
devoted enough time to reverse the sagging fortunes of his Leonberg Army League
branch.[40]

By the spring of 1913 the executives of Württemberg's Provincial Federation
undertook a massive effort to extend the network or branches and stimulate new
interest in the association. The Federation demanded, "The existing branches must
continue to expand. We must work arduously to prevent branches from stagnating
and even dissolving. This danger exists more today than it did one year ago. It has
been claimed that with the passage of the Army Bill the need for an Army League
has disappeared. . . . Such indifference must be combatted in every way."[41]
Provincial Federation president Franz Freiherr v. Soden echoed this sentiment,
writing his cousin, Julius Freiherr v. Soden, ex-minister of state for Württemberg,
"It will certainly be difficult to expand or even maintain the organization at the
present state once the Army Bill has been passed."[42] The Federation's executive
committee agreed with v. Soden's assessment and concluded that infusing the Army
League with new energy and members would be extremely difficult in light of the
pervasiveness of associational boredom (*Vereinsmüdigkeit*). Another manifestation
of the problem was the lack of dedicated, energetic branch officers, which inevitably resulted in branches "falling asleep [*einschlafen*]" or "disintegrating [*zerfal-
len*]."

Intent on reversing the trend toward apathy, the Provincial Federation developed
new strategies by which branches could counteract declining interest.[43] Above all,
it recommended that local branches use slide shows (*Lichtbilder*) to accompany
lectures. Slide shows were generally inexpensive to fund and always attracted large
audiences who enjoyed marveling at slides of exotic places (especially the German
colonies), whereas before they could only read about such places. For this purpose
special lecturers were placed at the branches' disposal. Professor Dr. Fetzer of
Schwäbisch Gmünd and *Schulrat* Dr. Haller of Ludwigsburg toured the circuit most
frequently, armed with slides made available to them from the Benzinger Slide
Institute in Stuttgart. Between 19 and 30 April 1913, nine new league branches were
established following a slide/lecture presentation by national circuit lecturer Dr.
Wiese (Berlin).[44] In addition to slide shows, it was suggested that branches increase
the number of patriotic celebrations and family entertainment evenings. Festivities

marking the Kaiser's and Bismarck's birthdays and the battles of Sedan and Leipzig tended to attract larger crowds, and joint celebrations with other patriotic societies also were useful in recruiting the public. Women were thought to be particularly valuable in helping branches organize these festive occasions, the implication being that they were somehow naturally predisposed to arranging social affairs. A third means by which new members could be recruited was through the increased distribution of the league's journal, *Die Wehr,* and other pertinent pamphlets, particularly Lieutenant General v. Schmitt's lecture on the French and German armies and the league's pamphlet no. 6, *"Wer die Wehrvorlage verwirft ist ein Volksfeind."*[45] Branches were also requested to leave copies of propaganda in places frequented by veterans, military men, and teachers. "The membership of officers on active duty is desired. Naturally, they should play no active role. So long as the propaganda is pertinent and presented in a reasonable fashion, we will not have problems."[46] What word of mouth could not achieve, it was hoped printed material could. To ensure maximum publicity, it was suggested that the local branch develop a symbiotic relationship with the press. And finally, the Provincial Federation reminded the branches to make every possible effort to dispel the notion that the league was an "opposition party" by stressing that it was a "national association, which freely speaks its peace and distances itself from any partisan politics, agitation, and propaganda."[47]

What was behind the Federation's concerted drive to recruit new members? After all, by July 1914 Württemberg numbered sixty-five branches whose combined individual and corporate membership exceeded 16,000, lending the impression of a thriving association. Although the Federation increased at a steady and impressive rate from January until April 1913, thereafter its expansion, for all intents and purposes, ground to a halt. If one looks at Table 1, this trend becomes evident. Twenty-eight branches (43 percent) stagnated after their establishment, twenty-one (32.3 percent) grew initially but stagnated thereafter, ten (15.4 percent) exhibited erratic behavior, four (6.2 percent) declined, and two (3.1 percent) could not be assessed because they were founded so late that only one set of membership figures was available. This stagnation, which characterized a majority of Württemberg's branches, was not disclosed in the pages of *Die Wehr;* it emerges only in the apprehensive correspondence of local Army League leaders. With few exceptions, the league chose not to publish more than one membership figure for any branch, but even in some cases where it did, the trend was again apparent. Aside from the fierce competition of other nationalistic societies for the affections of the local populace, the Federation blamed its stagnation on a lack of inspirational leading personalities whose enthusiasm and organizational skills were essential to maintaining the necessary high level of enthusiasm and commitment.[48] (See Table 2.)

Dwindling finances were a further indication of flagging interest. In 1913 the Provincial Federation observed that its "financial situation is far from favorable and this is primarily due to numerous [*zahlreichende*] outstanding membership dues."[49] It warned ominously that if individuals continued to be delinquent with their dues, it would be forced to increase the minimum dues. The Federation pointed out that of the 6,000 marks it was required to send to national headquarters in Berlin for 1912–13, it received a supporting grant of only 800 marks in return from Berlin, a sum

TABLE 1. Membership of Württemberg Branches, 1912–14

| Branch | Nov. 1912 | 1 April 1913 | 1 Jan. 1914 | 1 July 1914 |
|---|---|---|---|---|
| Stuttgart | 860 | 970 | 1018/3000 | 1000/2900 |
| Riedlingen | 100 | 105 | 100 | 94 |
| Ludwigsburg | 485 | 570 | 625 | 620 |
| Nagold | 44 | 68 | 66 | 62 |
| Heidenheim | 50 | 50 | 110/500 | 110/530 |
| Schrozberg | 38 | 38 | 40/130 | 40/130 |
| Ulm | 415 | 535/1300 | 530/1300 | 525/1300 |
| Gmünd | 85 | 180/550 | 200/600 | 160/700 |
| Heilbronn | 56 | 118 | 148/250 | 148/250 |
| Bietigheim | 32 | 62 | 60 | 58 |
| Hohenstadt | 20 | 40/269 | 45/270 | 45/270 |
| Altshausen | 27 | 30 | 28 | 25 |
| Besigheim | 21 | 26 | 26 | 26 |
| Aalen | 26 | 43/300 | 44/300 | 49/300 |
| Münsingen | 14 | 18 | 18 | 20 |
| Weingarten | 36 | 80 | 80 | 71 |
| Ravensburg | 22 | 130 | 140 | 122 |
| Maulbronn | 30 | 42 | 46 | 48 |
| Sulz | | 34 | 30 | 30 |
| Bopfingen | | 38 | 37 | 32 |
| Pfullingen | | 29 | 30 | 30 |
| Langenburg | | 75 | 71 | 75 |
| Tübingen | | 242/200 | 202/160 | 163/180 |
| Neckarsulm | | 32 | 32 | 28 |
| Waiblingen | | 38/145 | 41/140 | 43/130 |
| Gaildorf | | 31 | 29 | 30 |
| Nürtingen | | 100 | 67 | 76 |
| Neuenbürg | | 67 | 56 | 60 |
| Calw | | 92 | 100 | 100 |
| Böblingen | | 29 | 29 | 29 |
| Rottweil | | 140 | 145/400 | 149/400 |
| Kirchheim u. T. | | 168/153 | 165/153 | 171/153 |
| Friedrichshafen | | 120 | 105 | 125 |
| Esslingen | | 75 | 91/615 | 98/650 |
| Geislingen a. St. | | 303/625 | 402/605 | 361/670 |
| Herrenberg | | 133 | 133 | 127 |
| Isny | | 49 | 49 | 49 |
| Ellwangen | | 62/503 | 57/548 | 70/550 |
| Waldsee | | 70 | 110 | 101 |
| Hohenheim | | 180 | 200 | 171 |
| Korntal | | 28 | 78 | 78 |
| Hall | | 32 | 35 | 35 |
| Altensteig | | 60/120 | 62/135 | 51/150 |
| Reutlingen | | 30 | 64/300 | 65/510 |
| Leutkirch | | 83 | 81 | 55 |
| Metzingen | | 20/340 | 20/340 | 20/340 |
| Leonberg | | 17 | 17 | 16 |
| Schöntal-Künzelsau | | 5/56 | 9/55 | 10/50 |
| Vaihingen | | 12 | 11 | 11 |
| Crailsheim | | 61 | 70 | 58 |
| Biberach | | 20 | 22 | 22 |

TABLE 1. (Continued)

| Branch | Nov. 1912 | 1 April 1913 | 1 Jan. 1914 | 1 July 1914 |
|---|---|---|---|---|
| Brackenheim | | 25/344 | 84/344 | 84 |
| Freudenstadt | 8 | | 34 | 37 |
| Mergentheim | 44 | | 62 | 64 |
| Künzelsau | | | 32 | 24 |
| Oberndorf | | | 11 | 11 |
| Göppingen | | | 150/460 | 161/470 |
| Tettnang | | | 32 | 32 |
| Dornstetten | | | 16 | 38 |
| Calmbach | | | 11 | 10 |
| Welzheim | | | 22 | 20 |
| Marbach | | | 29 | 23 |
| Mochenwagen | | | 19 | 44 |
| Murrhardt | | | | 24 |
| Urach | | | | 8/1300 |

*Sources:* For list of November 1912, *Die Wehr*, Heft 1 (1913). Remainder compiled from: MAS M 1/3 Bd. 54; HSAS, E14 Bü 1389, Protokoll über die zweite Gesamtvorstandssitzung am 5. April 1913, and Verzeichnis der Ortsgruppen bez. Berzirksgruppen: Landesverband Württemberg, 31 December 1913. Branches are listed in the order of their founding from January 1912 throught March 1914. Figures refer to number of individual/corporate members.

TABLE 2. Membership of Württemberg Branches of the Army League and Navy League on 1 April 1913

| Branch | Army League | Navy League |
|---|---|---|
| Aalen | 43 | 75 |
| Altensteig | 60 | 33 |
| Altshausen | 30 | 38 |
| Besigheim | 26 | 53 |
| Biberach | 20 | — |
| Bietigheim | 62 | 88 |
| Böblingen | 29 | 125 |
| Bopfingen | 38 | 41 |
| Brackenheim | 25 | 46 |
| Calmbach | — | 12 |
| Calw | 92 | 60 |
| Crailsheim | 61 | 71 |
| Dornstetten | — | 44 |
| Ellwangen | 62 | 38 |
| Esslingen | 75 | 450 |
| Freudenstadt | 8 | 194 |
| Friedrichshafen | 120 | 115 |
| Gaildorf | 31 | 61 |
| Geislingen a. St. | 303 | 162 |
| Gmünd | 180 | 220 |
| Göppingen | — | 140 |
| Hall | 32 | 80 |
| Heidenheim | 50 | 95 |

(Continued)

TABLE 2. (Continued)

| Branch | Army League | Navy League |
|--------|-------------|-------------|
| Heilbronn | 118 | 352 |
| Herrenberg | 133 | — |
| Hohenheim | 180 | 20 |
| Hohenstadt | 40 | — |
| Isny | 49 | 68 |
| Kirchheim u. T. | 168 | 113 |
| Korntal | 28 | — |
| Künzelsau | — | 33 |
| Langenburg | 75 | 39 |
| Leonberg | 17 | 39 |
| Leutkirch | 83 | 73 |
| Ludwigsburg | 570 | 368 |
| Marbach | — | 32 |
| Maulbronn | 42 | 37 |
| Mergentheim | 44 | 114 |
| Metzingen | 20 | 40 |
| Mochenwagen | — | — |
| Münsingen | 18 | 53 |
| Murrhardt | — | 26 |
| Nagold | 68 | 72 |
| Neckarsulm | 32 | 66 |
| Neuenbürg | 67 | 76 |
| Nürtingen | 100 | 162 |
| Oberndorf | — | 79 |
| Pfullingen | 29 | 61 |
| Ravensburg | 130 | 137 |
| Reutlingen | 30 | 175 |
| Riedlingen | 105 | 28 |
| Rottweil | 140 | 171 |
| Schöntal-Künzelsau | 5 | 36 |
| Schrozberg | 38 | 10 |
| Stuttgart | 970 | 2300 |
| Sulz | 34 | 45 |
| Tettnang | — | 53 |
| Tübingen | 242 | 290 |
| Ulm | 535 | 915 |
| Urach | — | 80 |
| Vaihingen | 12 | 31 |
| Waiblingen | 38 | 49 |
| Waldsee | 70 | 62 |
| Weingarten | 80 | 70 |
| Welzheim | — | 30 |
| Total | 5657 | 8646[a] |

[a]The Navy League maintained an additional 110 branches with 3,055 members throughout Württemberg in 1913.

Sources: MAS, M 1/3 Bd. 54; HSAS, E14 Bü 1389, Protokoll über die zweite Gesamtvorstandssitzung am 5. April 1913, and Verzeichnis der Ortsgruppen bez. Bezirksgruppen: Landesverband Württemberg, 31 December 1913; HSAS, E14 Bü 1345, Deutscher Flottenverein, Rechenschaftsbericht für das Jahr 1913.

that was "not enough for the Federation to exist upon."[50] Any further discussion of the Federation's financial situation, however, is complicated by the fact that the only figures for 1912–13 available refer to the Stuttgart branch, which was one of the state's healthiest. By the end of 1912 the Stuttgart branch had recorded an intake of 3,044 marks in dues and a balance after expenditure for the year of 1,149 marks.[51] By themselves these figures are meaningless unless they are compared with those for 1913. In December 1913 Stuttgart received 3,589.45 marks in dues and additional revenue from donations (30 marks) and the interest (171.56 marks) on its bank deposits, for an annual income of 3,791 marks. With the surplus from 1912 of 1,149 marks, the league could dispose of 4,940.01 marks. In 1913, then, 94.7 percent of its annual income came from membership dues. Thus in 1913 dues for Stuttgart rose by 17.9 percent while membership increased 18.3 percent over that of 1912. This would seem to indicate that in both 1912 and 1913 the same proportion of members were paying dues (but not everyone necessarily paid his or her share) and that increased activity entailed a larger cash outlay as evidenced by the minuscule balance remaining at the end of 1913 (only 45 pfennigs). In its annual report of 1913 the branch pleaded for new members (and with them more dues) and further generous individual donations from patriotic individuals, such as one wealthy member who in November 1912 contributed 1,000 marks.[52] Granted that, as Keim had put it, the league was not a "savings association," the branch, and indeed as we shall see, the association as a whole, operated on a financial shoestring, at odds with the public image it wished to present, and just barely a step above bankruptcy.[53]

The most frequent criticism of local studies is that their focus on local peculiarities neglects the degree to which the locality under study reflects any broader (and presumably more significant) national trends. This stricture cannot be applied to the case of the Army League in Württemberg. Rather than representing an isolated or aberrant example, the pattern of the league's development in that state— characterized by rapid expansion followed soon thereafter by stagnation—was replicated in nearly all of the Army League's other regional organizations between January 1912 and August 1914. The following chapter will examine the intricacies of associational life in Army League branches throughout the Reich.

## CHAPTER 5

# The Anatomy of a Patriotic Society

Founding an association like the Army League demanded careful planning and coordination; maintaining it over a period of time as an influential association was another matter. The Army League's commitment to securing a larger and more efficient army was apparent in the relentless crusade it waged for the passage of the 1912 and 1913 army bills. Its effectiveness as an association, however, cannot be judged solely by the adoption of these measures. To survive it had to balance the attainment of its goals with the maintenance of a relatively consistent degree of participation and interest in those goals. Accordingly, associations such as the Army League sought to establish a broad and durable network of branches as the medium of popular participation, and to supplement ideological appeals with a variety of social or economic incentives. This chapter, therefore, will explore the interrelationship between the strength of its structural framework, the geographic breadth of its appeal, the administrative ability of its national and local executives, the cooperation of its members, and the stability of its finances. As such, this chapter offers a revealing look at the anatomy of a patriotic society.

## Structure and Geographic Strength

The Army League's constitution, which resembled that of other patriotic societies, provided for two executive bodies: the *Ausschuss* (Executive Council) and the *Gesamtvorstand* (General Council). The more authoritative of these, the *Ausschuss,* consisted of the league's officers—the president, two honorary vice presidents, a secretary and honorary secretary, a treasurer and honorary treasurer, the Business Manager, and Press Chief—as well as several other influential individuals, totaling a maximum of twenty-one.[1] Its members, who were elected for a three-year term by those league members present at the annual meeting (*Hauptversammlung*), were responsible for formulating league policies and ensuring their implementation. Meetings of the *Ausschuss* were not necessarily held at regular intervals but were convened when deemed necessary by its members. The *Gesamtvorstand,* on the other hand, was a considerably larger council that included the members of the *Ausschuss,* the presidents of the various provincial federations, and other "deserving" individuals who were also elected for three years' service by the *Hauptversammlung.* Although the constitution did not provide a specific function for this executive body, it appears to have been a sounding board for *Ausschuss* policies and a forum in which local and regional representatives might find the opportunity to express their interests. Furthermore, judging from the individuals who participated, it seems likely that selection to the *Gesamtvorstand* was often intended to reward members who had contributed in a particular way to the organization, whether by shouldering the burden of inaugurating local branches, setting an appropriate example of fervent patriotic participation, or contributing toward the funds necessary to maintain an active local branch or regional federation.[2] Like the *Ausschuss,* the *Gesamtvorstand* had no set meeting schedule but could be called into session only by the *Ausschuss* when appropriate. Members of both councils fulfilled their positions on a voluntary basis; salaried employees (the constitution did not specify the positions to which this applied) were appointed by the president upon the approval of the *Ausschuss.*

Paragraph 2 of the constitution stipulated the fundamental goals of the league: "The Army League seeks the strengthening of the patriotic consciousness as well as the preservation of a manly spirit in the German people. It especially seeks to fortify the German army inwardly as well as numerically so that it is indisputably maintained to safeguard the Empire and its status as a world power."[3] Any changes in its stated objectives required the approval of three-quarters of the *Hauptversammlung,* which met annually any time during the first six months of the year (the league generally held its meetings in May), and fourteen days prior written notice (thereby making any alterations very unlikely).

Local branches adhered to the general guidelines of the national constitution but were allowed to introduce modest variations so long as these did not conflict with the overall thrust of the national organization.[4] For example, the Essen affiliate molded its own constitution after its particular needs. While adhering to most of the dictates of the national constitution, it provided for an executive committee (*Vorstand*) to consist of a maximum of nine members, including a president, an honorary president, a secretary, a treasurer, and five *Beisitzer,* (executive members) who were elected by the *Hauptversammlung* for terms of three years, but in a staggered manner so that every year one or two officers would step down from office and be replaced with a newly elected candidate. Annual meetings were required to be held in either March or April, at which time the officers were to present members with a detailed annual report of the league's activities as well as a program for the upcoming year's events. Membership dues (no minimum was given) were to be delivered to the branch treasurer, an undisclosed portion of which would be forwarded to the national organization in Berlin. To ensure the complete honesty of the treasurer, the constitution provided for his figures to be verified by two members who were not associated with the officers of the *Vorstand.*

Patriotic societies like the Army League required at the very minimum a firm constitutional structure that could serve to coordinate the vast number of local branches springing up from the *Reichsland* to East Prussia and Schleswig-Holstein to Bavaria. More than five hundred Army League branches were established between January 1912 and August 1914, accounting for approximately 100,000 individual and 250,000 corporate members (see Table 3). Within three months of its founding the Army League had managed to surpass in size the Pan-German League, which at its zenith in 1900–1901 counted nearly 21,000 adherents.[5] In the first few months of 1912 the branches comprising the Hanseatic Cities and Brandenburg registered the largest gains with over 4,000 members each, followed by the federations of Württemberg, Silesia, and the Kingdom of Saxony with approximately 1,700 apiece, Posen with 1,400, Pomerania with 1,200, and Hanover 1,000. As of May 1912, however, only 18,942 members belonged to a regional federation and the remaining 15,000 or so individuals remained independent.[6] The league fared less satisfactorily in Bavaria, Baden, Hesse, East Prussia, and the Rhineland. Between August 1912 and May 1913 the Army League registered its most impressive gains with individual membership doubling and corporate figures increasing nearly twentyfold. Corporate figures, in particular, boosted the league's image and combined membership. When an organization joined in a corporate capacity, all the existing members of a particular local branch of, say, the *Jungdeutschlandbund* or a *Kriegerverein,* would thus automatically be added to the Army League's total membership rolls. The result was a rapid infusion, on paper at least, of additional adherents, and of additional funds as well, for local branches of affiliating organizations often pledged upwards of ten marks when seeking formal corporate affiliation with the Army League. But such corporate affiliation did not necessarily mean that local *Jungdeutschland* members now participated enthusiastically in their local Army League chapter as well; in a sense, they were simply names transferred from one ledger to another. And in some cases there was further duplication of membership with misleading implications that the Army League often lacked the inclination to investigate or reveal. For example, many individual members were simultaneously individual members of similar local patriotic societies which, when those societies opted for corporate affiliation with the Army League, could lead to those individual's being counted both as original individual members and new corporate members. In such cases, it would depend on the vigilance and energy of the local secretary to catch such discrepancies and on the integrity of the local executive to reduce their advertised total membership to levels that more accurately reflected the number of active members. By May 1913 the Army League's combined membership exceeded that of the Colonial Society, the Eastern Marches Society, and the Society for Germandom Abroad.[7]

In reality, however, only a handful of provincial federations and local branches were responsible for the league's impressive membership figures. Brandenburg, the

TABLE 3. Army League Membership Figures

|              | Individual | Corporate | Branches |
|--------------|-----------:|----------:|---------:|
| May 1912     | 33,000     | 10,000    | 250      |
| August 1912  | 37,000     | 100,000   | 284      |
| January 1913 | 55,000     | 150,000   | 450      |
| May 1913     | 78,000     | 190,000   | 440      |
| May 1914     | 90,000     | 260,000   | 500      |

Kingdom of Saxony, the Hanseatic Cities, Thuringia, and Württemberg accounted for the lion's share, and interestingly (with the exception of Württemberg), these regions also constituted the strongest pockets of the Pan-German League and Navy League membership.[8] Although most of the Army League's branches were established in towns with populations of between 2,000 and 10,000, the largest number of members came from chapters in the large cities of these provinces, suggesting perhaps that the league recruited best where the Protestant bourgeoisie perceived the threat of socialism to be the greatest, and where other patriotic associations were already active. Nowhere was this more evident than in Berlin and its environs. Brandenburg appeared to be the most vigorous of the league's federations. It comprised fifty-one branches by the First World War, seventeen of which were clustered around the capital. In early 1912 these Berlin branches formed the independent Provincial Federation Berlin-Brandenburg. By June 1913 that Federation had well over 9,000 members, some of whom were recruited from the Technical Academy (*Technische Hochschule*) in Charlottenburg, the Royal Central Cadet School in Lichterfelde, large military workshops in Spandau, and the University of Berlin[9] (see Table 4).

The remaining thirty-four branches of the Brandenburg Provincial Federation were scattered throughout the province's twenty-six electoral districts. Their activities, unlike those of the Berlin-Brandenburg Provincial Federation, by and large went unreported in *Die Wehr*. The silence reflected the fact that there was relatively little to report. An exception was the league's focus upon its Cottbus branch, a garrison town that was established in December 1912 and had a membership of 125 as of January 1913, including a woman treasurer, Frau *Oberstleutnant* Hamann. On the whole, however, like the Württemberg Federation, the Brandenburg branches (at least 57 percent of them) stagnated (or even lost membership) during the course of 1913.

Reservoirs of Army League support were found in both the Kingdom and Province of Saxony, with twenty and twenty-four branches respectively.[10] Three cities in each accounted for a majority of members: in the Province of Saxony, Halle a.S. (1,721), Magdeburg (over 1,000), and Görlitz (over 300); in the Kingdom of

TABLE 4. Membership of Provincial Federation Berlin-Brandenburg

| Branch | 1912 | 1913 | 1914 | 1915 | 1916 |
|--------|------|------|------|------|------|
| Forst | 375 | —[a] | — | — | — |
| Friedenau | — | 560 | — | 810 | — |
| Friedrichshagen | 288 | 300 | 395 | — | 400 |
| Halensee | — | 120 | — | — | — |
| Neukölln | — | 94 | — | — | — |
| Pankow | — | 40 | — | — | — |
| Spandau | 190 | 640 | 667 | 446 | 412 |
| Tegel | — | 136 | — | — | — |
| Weisensee | — | 20 | — | — | — |
| Wilmersdorf | 200 | 266 | — | — | — |
| Gross Berlin | — | 3180 | — | — | — |

[a]Indicates no figures available.

*Source: Die Wehr*, passim. No figures were available for the remaining six branches.

Saxony, Dresden, Leipzig, and Chemnitz had well over 1,000 each.[11] With the exception of Görlitz, whose population was 85,000 in 1910, each city had over 100,000 inhabitants and active socialist movements. Thuringia, too, proved fertile soil for the league; as of spring 1913 it had thirty branches with 4,000 individual and 2,800 corporate members. The same could be said of the Hanseatic Cities of Hamburg and Lübeck. *Die Wehr* often claimed that meetings in Hamburg attracted upwards of two thousand people, while Lübeck also maintained a special university chapter for its students.

Unfortunately, insufficient membership data vitiate any further attempt to provide a detailed account of the league's strength throughout the remainder of the Reich. In some cases one finds contradictory figures that only obfuscate matters. For example, the Posen Federation was reported in *Die Wehr* to have had nineteen branches, whereas my own count revealed seventy-nine! Only upon one occasion in 1914 were the figures for Provincial Federation Hesse-Nassau revealed (thirteen branches with 2,000 members), while the Braunschweig Federation was acknowledged twice, revealing a membership of 1,257 individuals and 5,100 corporate members in early 1913 and 1,834 individuals and 6,648 corporate adherents in twenty-five branches one year later.[12] Surprising, too, is the absence of information regarding the Rhineland and Westphalian chapters, despite references to "huge" branches in Cologne, Düsseldorf, Essen, and Dortmund. The only specific mention of the Cologne branch's size appeared in private correspondence between Heinrich Class and Dr. Hofmeister, an ardent Pan-German, president of the Pan-German League's branch in the city, and local organizer of the Army League, in which Hofmeister claimed had a membership of over seven hundred as of February 1913.[13]

Like the Pan-German League, Colonial Society, and Navy League, the Army League established a network of chapters around the globe, although they appear not to have been either as active or as large as their patriotic society counterparts.[14] The port city of Bari (Italy), Mexico City (Mexico), Jaunde (Cameroon), Tsingtao (China), and Singapore had relatively small branches (generally between twenty-five and thirty members). Mexico City, though, claimed one hundred supporters at the time of its founding in October 1913, most of whom were businessmen, navy personnel or merchant seamen, and consular staff. For these men the league offered an opportunity to keep abreast of events in the Fatherland, to socialize with other Germans far from home, and to help strengthen Germany's commercial and imperial links.

The fact that the Army League recruited especially well in urban areas, where the socialist challenge appeared imminent, is suggestive, but it does not by itself prescribe the kinds of people who were active in the league, or what had prompted them to join. This next section pursues these issues by reconstructing the league's social profile according to its hierarchical structure, from the small coterie in positions of national responsibility down to the general membership.

### Social Profile

Meeting the Army League's administrative requirements was a formidable task. Keim's fiery and irreverent personality acted as a double-edged sword, for while it proved useful for nationalistic demagoguery in electrifying audiences and rallying them around the league, it also promoted discord. Even the most dedicated nationalist, secure in his independence of mind, would have been unable to tolerate the general's company for too long. Among Keim's inner circle, primarily those individuals who sat on the league's *Ausschuss,* were some of the most fiercely independent nationalistic thinkers of the Wilhelmine era: Dietrich Schäfer, Richard Nordhausen, Heinrich Rippler, Eduard v. Liebert, Kurd v. Strantz, Karl Litzmann, and Hans v. Wrochem.[15] One can imagine the intensity of the *Ausschuss* meetings, given the highly emotive nature of the nationalist issue. These men all brought with them a variety of skills, honed by their previous associational ventures, from which the league could benefit. Just as politics was a theater in which politicians could display their thespian talents, so, too, was the Army League a stage upon which the associational leadership could perform, demonstrating their ability to speak to the needs of the *Volk* and to recruit them for the cause of the Fatherland.[16]

Calling himself one of the founding fathers of the Army League, Dietrich Schäfer, professor of history, served as an honorary vice president and had the distinction of being the only academic in the inner circle.[17] Born in Bremen in 1845, Schäfer, the son of a granary worker, lived a good part of his youth in squalor with his family in a cramped, dimly lit basement apartment. His father, a son of a shoemaker from the province of Oldenburg, suffered from numerous work-related afflictions and died at the age of forty-one. Young Dietrich and his mother, who already had experienced the premature deaths of three other children, were left to fend for themselves. His mother obtained a position as a maid for an upper-class household and, as a result, was rarely at home to care for her son. Despite these hardships, Schäfer later insisted that he never developed any hostility toward those individuals who were more fortunate than he. "I was always in high spirits . . ., and even today I look upon my childhood days with pleasure. . . . How terribly unfortunate are those children who become embittered in their youth out of envy for those more fortunate than they."[18]

From an early age Schäfer had decided to pursue a career in teaching, and since he was a particularly gifted student, he was able to attend university to fulfill his professional goal. After spending a year touring England in 1867, he returned to Germany to begin his studies at the University of Jena in 1868. One year later, Schäfer left Jena to participate in a historical seminar in Heidelberg led by the famous historian Heinrich v. Treitschke. It was Treitschke who cast a spell over the young, impressionable Schäfer, who henceforth dedicated himself to realizing Treitschke's vision of a united German state.[19] Study in Heidelberg was interrupted by the Franco-Prussian War, for which he enlisted, even though, as he explained, he was no longer "of draftable age." His service in the military and Germany's subsequent unification were among the high points of his life, reinforcing his commitment to a "strong and battle-ready army" for Germany.[20] Upon finishing his tour of duty, Schäfer resumed his career in higher education at the University of Göttingen, from which he graduated, and in 1872 he accepted a teaching position in his native Bremen. In 1877 he left the port city to assume a teaching post at the University of Jena, and in subsequent years served on the faculties of the universities of Breslau, Tübingen, Heidelberg, and Berlin.

During his military and university days, Schäfer began to develop a keen political and national awareness that led to his joining the National Liberal Party while he taught in Breslau. There Schäfer supported National Liberal candidates in the Reichstag elections of 1881 and 1884 and occasionally lectured on behalf of the party on subjects of national and historical interest.[21] Although in sympathy with the National Liberal platform, Schäfer showed little inclination, as he put it, toward "political engagement."[22] By the time he arrived in Heidelberg in 1896, however, he had moved more closely to what he called *"praktike Politik."*[23] Throughout the 1890s, Schäfer, now middle-aged and basking in his reputation as a prominent historian, immersed himself wholeheartedly in pursuit of the "national interest." In 1892 his national inclinations were given additional impetus by his tête-à-tête with the man whom he (and so many other nationalists) idolized as "the greatest of our contemporaries," recently retired chancellor Otto v. Bismarck.[24]

Participation in associational life was another means by which Schäfer demonstrated his commitment to the German nation. Already as a student in the 1870s Schäfer had joined several associations, a trend that continued unabated after 1890. Although best known for his activities in the patriotic societies—the Navy League, the Eastern Marches Society, and the Pan-German League—he also devoted himself to a variety of cultural associations.[25] To them he brought a concern for the effect of German industrialization. His experiences in large cities such as Breslau and Berlin left him with the conviction that Germany's urban areas were breeding grounds for socialism. The sense of hopelessness and misery that prevailed among the working class facilitated the work of Socialist agitators who sought to recruit workers for the destruction of the bourgeois system. Large cities, he argued, encouraged the spread of immorality and disease, given the unsanitary conditions and restricted living quarters they offered.[26] Of course, Schäfer had been all too familiar with these conditions as a youth. But he had beaten the odds and now subconsciously saw himself as a model for workers to overcome their unfortunate circumstances without succumbing to socialism. In addition, the historian was a strong advocate of the army and navy, maintaining that their budgets must remain independent of parliamentary scrutiny.[27]

Although Schäfer left a detailed memoir, unfortunately some of his other colleagues did not. Hermann Paasche (1851–1925), a *Geheimer Regierungsrat* and *Gutsbesitzer* in Wahlfrieden bei Hochzeit, chose to express his national commitment by serving as a deputy for the National Liberals in the Reichstag (1893–98; 1898–1918) and as vice president of the Colonial Society, while Otto v. Dewitz (born in 1850 in Zachow, Kreis Regenwalde) was a retired army officer and *Landrat* who represented the eighteenth electoral district of Schleswig-Holstein as a Free Conservative in the Prussian House of Representatives.[28] Richard Nordhausen (secretary), Henrich Rippler (honorary secretary), and Hermann Müller-Brandenburg (press chief) constituted a younger cohort in the league's inner circle. Nordhausen's life has remained shrouded in obscurity, save for his birthdate (1868) and his occupation (a writer). Rippler, who was born in Kempten in 1866, attended gymnasium and subsequently the University of Munich.[29] In 1891, at the age of twenty-five, he migrated to Berlin to dabble in freelance journalism and in 1892 found himself as an assistant editor of the *Tägliche Rundschau*. Four years later he was appointed its editor-in-chief. At some point between 1891 and 1896 Rippler joined the Pan-German League and the Navy League and considered himself a true "man of the people."[30] At age twenty-seven, Hermann Müller-Brandenburg was the youngest member of the league's executives. The son of a businessman from Elberfeld, Müller-Brandenburg attended *Realgymnasium* and *Oberrealschule*. In 1906 he enlisted in the army as a one-year volunteer but chose to reenlist. By 1910 he turned to penning articles on the military for *Die Post*.[31] George v. Büxenstein, newspaper entrepreneur, *Kommerzienrat,* and Pan-German sympathizer (born in Berlin in 1857), held the position of treasurer and was, with the possible exception of Kurd v. Strantz, the most aristocratic of the inner circle. In 1908 Büxenstein was approached by the Conservative Party to supervise the various organs of the Conservative press, including the *Deutsche Zeitung, Berliner Neueste Nachrichten, Tägliche Rundschau,* and *Die Post* as well as the publishing firm *Deutscher Verlag.*[32]

The league's first vice president, Gisbert A. A. Pilgrim v. Baltazzi, born in 1864, was the son of a retired *Regierungspräsident* and *Wirklicher Geheimer Rat* and the descendant of an old ennobled Prussian bureaucratic family from Wesphalia.[33] Upon the death of his mother in 1866, young Gisbert was sent to live with his uncle in Paris because the responsibilities of his father's position left him no time to care for his son. Until the age of fourteen he was schooled by a private tutor but later was allowed to attend gymnasium. Between 1883 and 1886 he matriculated at the universities of Paris and Berlin, taking a degree in law and subsequently entering the Prussian Civil Service in the tradition of his family. He served the Foreign Office in Berlin, Paris, and London as an attaché and in various other capacities, and traveled extensively. In 1910 he became a governmental minister, but one year later poor health required him to resign his post. In the spring of 1912, however, he replaced Hermann Paasche in the position of the league's first vice president. Given Keim's antipathy toward the system, this appointment is puzzling. Simply put, nothing in v. Baltazzi's background or experience conformed to the popular nationalist pattern; he did not appear to have been a member of any patriotic society, nor had he been dismissed from any position or taken issue with bureaucratic policies. Was then v. Baltazzi a straw man whom Keim used to create an image of the league as moderate in order to allay the misgivings of government officials who worried about the Army League's course in light of the general's previous track record in the Navy League? Unfortunately, without the benefit of memoirs or personal papers, the question must remain unanswered.

Perhaps the most eccentric and controversial of Keim's circle was Thuringian aristocrat, former *Assessor* and retired cavalry captain Kurd v. Strantz, *Freier und Edler Herr v. Tüllstedt.* Born in Erfurt in 1863, v. Strantz attended gymnasium and received a degree in law.[34] Choosing to forgo a career in the bureaucracy, v. Strantz instead pursued the route of the patriotic societies, where as polemicist extraordinaire he was able to put his talents to use. Given his volatile temperament and his appetite for German territorial acquisitions, the realm of popular nationalism was far more suitable for him than the staid bureaucracy. Von Strantz claimed to be a cofounder of the Imperial League against Social Democracy, an executive member of the Navy League, and an active supporter of the Pan-German League and Keim's General German Writing Association.

Also included among Keim's closest confidants were three professional military men: Eduard v. Liebert, Karl Litzmann, and Johannes (Hans) v. Wrochem, each of whom served in the *Ausschuss*. The son of an officer from Silesia, v. Liebert was born in Rendsburg, Holstein, in 1850. The premature death of his father in 1853 at the age of forty-seven nearly devastated his family. His mother, who at the time of her husband's death was only twenty-four years old and the mother of two young children, was left almost penniless. Although the state provided her with a widow's pension for the service her husband had rendered to the military, v. Liebert recalled that it was insufficient to cover even basic expenses. The tragedy of his father's death coupled with his mother's despair embittered v. Liebert toward the state for its lack of respect for his father, who had served the army with great diligence and selflessness.[35] As a result of her husband's death, v. Liebert's mother was forced to move in with her parents to support her family.

Von Liebert's recollections of life with his grandparents were not particularly pleasant ones. His grandfather, whom he described as a "strong patriarch of the old school," was responsible for his education and showed little patience for his grandson's slow educational development. On one occasion his grandfather became so infuriated by v. Liebert's inability to learn that he dragged the boy to his mother and exclaimed: "You take charge of your son; I can't do anything with him!"[36] In 1856 the family moved to Halle in Saxony, then a university town of forty thousand. Life in the big city, however, did not suit v. Liebert, who proclaimed in his memoirs that industrialization had "sapped the German people of their soul . . . [and] . . . demoralized [them]. It was tantamount to the devil himself."[37] Large cities, he added, were no longer populated by "pure Germans" but were infested by the "international horde."[38]

At age eleven v. Liebert entered the cadet corps, determined to follow in his father's footsteps and eager to escape the wrath of his grandfather. With the army undertaking the cost of his military education, his mother was freed of any further monetary obligations to her son. The cadet corps served as a substitute family for v. Liebert; it enabled him to cultivate a sense of self-satisfaction, "love for the Fatherland, ambition, courage, bravery and responsibility."[39] Like Schäfer, he considered his participation in the Wars of Unification and the subsequent achievement of German statehood the highlights of his life. In 1872, eager to pursue a permanent military career, he entered the War Academy where he studied Russian and military tactics, his favorite subject. Perhaps owing to his Silesian heritage, he maintained a keen interest in the eastern regions of the Reich, which led to his employment in the General Staff's Russian Division between 1881 and 1890. During these years v. Liebert signed on as a correspondent for the *Tägliche Rundschau,* penning articles on the military and reminiscing on his war experiences for the public.[40] An assignment to cover colonial issues for the newspaper in 1884 piqued his interest in colonialism and led to his joining the Colonial Society.[41] Intrigued by the colonies, in the late 1880s he requested and eventually received permission for a transfer from his duties in the General Staff to a bureaucratic post in the colonies with the Foreign Office. From 1896 until 1900 the German colony of East Africa fell under his jurisdiction; the brevity of his governorship was the result of an altercation with colonial officials over the construction of a railway for the colony. The government refused to fund the project, and v. Liebert's steadfast refusal to bow to his superior's viewpoint on the matter resulted in his recall to Berlin in 1900 and his reassignment as a commander of an army division. Devotion brought only demotion. Bitterly disappointed, v. Liebert returned home, convinced that the bureaucratic state had once again proven impervious to his needs.[42] In December 1902 the ex–colonial governor became embroiled in a dispute with army officials. This time, however, he was not reassigned but rather given the "blue slip" ("*blauer Brief*") at the age of fifty-two.[43]

Forced early retirement meant that he could now devote full time to his political inclinations (v. Liebert maintained that he was one of a handful of officers of the old school who willingly and actively engaged in politics).[44] Now as a retired officer he was free to accept an offer by members of the Conservative Party to run as their candidate in the 1903 Reichstag elections for the electoral district of Brandenburg. The election resulted in a run-off between v. Liebert and the Social Democratic challenger, who won by ninety-nine votes.[45] Dismayed by the outcome, the unsuccessful Conservative candidate sought consolation in the patriotic societies—the Pan-German League, Colonial Society, and Navy League—in which he served in executive capacities and as circuit lecturer. His loss, too, convinced him that something had to be done to stop the socialists from increasing their presence in the Reichstag. With this in mind, he founded in May 1904 the Imperial League against Social Democracy, which sought to strengthen German nationalism by aiding the election of bourgeois candidates.[46] Eager to try his hand in another election, two years later v. Liebert accepted a second offer to run as a compromise candidate of the bourgeois parties for the Reichstag district of Borgnau-Pegau in Saxony. Once again, the election resulted in a run-off with the Socialist opponent. This time, however, v. Liebert claimed victory.[47] In the Reichstag he chose to affiliate with the *Reichspartei,* whose spokesman he became on military and colonial matters. In 1912 he won reelection, but an official protest from the SPD to the Reichstag election commission concerning "electoral discrepancies" forced him into another election, in which he was unseated by his Socialist challenger.[48] Von Liebert was not only a rabid anti-Socialist but a notorious anti-Semite who considered Jews an inferior race.[49]

Another native of the northeastern reaches of the Empire was Karl Litzmann, born in 1850 in Neuglobsow, the descendent of patricians from Neuruppin. His father, who had studied law, was forced by the unexpected death of Karl's grandfather to forgo his career to manage the family's estate and glass factory. Young Litzmann idolized his father, whom he described as a gentle man and a philosophical soul who enjoyed classical music (Beethoven was his favorite composer), literature, and mathematics, and who was also responsible for his son's early education. His mother, the daughter of an officer, was also described by her son in the most endearing terms. In 1861 Litzmann's parents sent him to Berlin to attend *Realgymnasium,* and it was in the bustling capital that he developed an immediate and intense dislike for large cities, Socialists, and Jews.[50] At age seventeen he became a *Fahnenjunker* and enrolled in the War School in Potsdam, and in 1870 he fought in the Franco-Prussian War. German unification left him spiritually rejuvenated, and he entered the War Academy where he became acquainted with v.

Liebert. Litzmann's euphoria, however, was short-lived; the bankruptcy of his father in the early 1870s left him angry, embarrassed, and financially unstable.[51] The pleasure he experienced from his support of Bismarck's suppression of the so-called enemies of the Reich—Catholics and Socialists—may have been his way of compensating for the indignities inflicted on him by his father's bankruptcy.

In 1876 Litzmann joined the General Staff, and in 1887 was promoted to the rank of major at the age of thirty-seven. Bismarck's dismissal by Kaiser Wilhelm in 1890 forced Litzmann to reassess his attitude toward his beloved monarch, who had affronted the "Father" of the German nation. In 1902 the army offered Litzmann the post of director of the prestigious War Academy, an honor he accepted, but not without some reservation, since this meant exchanging his field duty for a desk position. For three years he remained in the position until a disagreement over the structure of the Academy resulted in his early retirement from the army in 1905.[52] For eight years thereafter he wrote for the *Tägliche Rundschau* on the military and the Socialist and Jewish menace, and in 1912 served the Army League in the capacity of a circuit lecturer as well as *Ausschuss* member.[53]

About Johannes (Hans) v. Wrochem's background little is known. He served with the German East Asian Army corps, departing in 1890 for duty in China and the Boxer Rebellion and touring much of the Asian continent.[54] After retiring from the army, he served as deputy governor of East Africa under v. Liebert, until he, too, became disillusioned with bureaucratic intransigence and resigned his post. In 1908 v. Wrochem joined the Pan-German League, serving in its *Vorstand* and offering his expertise on military matters and the French Foreign Legion.[55] Although he held no official post in the Army League, he nevertheless was present at the annual meetings and a frequent circuit lecturer.

Of noble Thuringian heritage, like v. Strantz, Prof. Reinhold Freiherr O.H.E. v. Lichtenberg was born in 1865 in Croatia.[56] His father served in the military and his mother was either of American or English lineage. Upon taking his degrees in law, art history, and archaeology, v. Lichtenberg traveled extensively in the Middle East and Asia in search of archaeological artifacts. He considered himself a conservative, and when not involved in field research, he participated in the *Richard Wagner-Verein,* the racist *Gobineau Vereinigung,* Keim's *Vaterländische Schriftenverband* and *Allgemeiner Deutsche Schriftenverein,* and the Pan-German League. Karl v. Böhlendorf-Kölpin also boasted impeccable credentials as former conservative deputy of the Reichstag, *Rittergutsbesitzer,* and retired major from Stettin (Posen).[57] His father was a *Regierungs Assessor* in Stettin and his mother belonged to the famous v. Puttkamer family. Following his Gymnasium studies, he entered the cadet corps in Potsdam and in 1889 married Gräfin Hildegard v. Moltke, the daughter of *Rittmeister* Graf Waldemar v. Moltke. Between 1883 and 1886 he attended the War Academy and in 1898 was elected as a Conservative to the Prussian *Landtag.* From 1903 until 1906 he served in the Reichstag, and in 1905 and 1906 toured the German African colonies as well as most of the Far East on a fact-finding mission for the Reichstag. He won reelection as a Conservative in 1912.

A revealing picture emerges from these biographical sketches. Nearly all of the men stemmed from middle-class or aristocratic Protestant households with roots in the eastern or northeastern reaches of the Reich; were well educated (having received gymnasium, university, or military school training) and generally experienced travelers who had toured the European, Asian, and African continents; and were aged fifty or older in 1912.[58] Moreover, a good portion had served in the Wars of Unification or were old enough to recall them, and had testified to the significance of these events in their future endeavors. One might suggest that a generational factor played a role in shaping their nationalistic attitudes and outlook upon the bureaucratic state. For them unification was a model against which Germany's future developments were measured. At that time law, order and military might had prevailed under Chancellor Bismarck, while the present smacked of international anarchism. These men exhibited a fanatic admiration for the Iron Chancellor, elevating him to mythical proportions after his dismissal in 1890, and especially after his death in 1898, as Litzmann attested: "We are all sworn devotees of Bismarck."[59] Bismarck's departure from office revealed the fragility of the sociopolitical consensus that the Chancellor had managed to construct over the course of two decades. It also shattered their opinion of the Kaiser, a figure whom they had also held to embody authority and wisdom. Von Liebert wrote in his memoirs that he once had considered his breakfast meeting with Kaiser Wilhelm on 8 February 1890 to have been one of the highlights of his life, but when the Kaiser dismissed Bismarck, he revised his opinion of the monarch.[60] This resentment toward Wilhelm II may have been reflected in the fact that the league avoided making him (or any other patrician) a patron, as, for example, the Navy League had done. The Kaiser, therefore, came to signify the bureaucratic incompetence and intransigence that Army League officials so often lamented.

Aside from the broader nationalistic vision to which they all subscribed, the members of the inner circle also shared a compulsion for journalism. Indeed, many had become acquainted with each other through their journalistic ventures, during military education or service, or in the realm of the patriotic societies. Keim, Rippler, Nordhausen, Müller-Brandenburg, v. Liebert, and Litzmann all wrote for some of the leading nationalistic newspapers, including the *Tägliche Rundschau*. The War Academy brought Keim, v. Liebert, and Litzmann together, while v. Wrochem and v. Liebert cooperated in their bureaucratic posts in Africa. And, of course, these bonds were reinforced by their participation in the Navy League and Pan-German League. Not only did the league's executives share certain values, outlooks, and social backgrounds, but their devotion was fueled by a combination of intense nationalistic zeal and "will to power." But did these very same characteristics and attitudes apply to the league's broader membership?

Assigning members to broad occupational categories for the purpose of analyzing the social basis of the league is fraught with pitfalls. Often the terms current in Imperial Germany no longer have contemporary equivalents; or, frequently, they do not fit easily into one particular category. For example, what is one to make of an *Ackerbürger?* Likewise, lawyers, doctors, or businessmen who held the title of *Rat* or *Staatsanwalt* defy simple categorization. They could be defined as professionals and businessmen, or, on the basis of their title, as bureaucratic officials. In such instances, because of the importance of their official affiliations, I have chosen to regard such individuals as members of the bureaucracy. The category of businessmen, to take another elastic grouping, includes a broad spectrum of occupational designations—*Kaufmann, Besitzer, Fabrikant, Manufaktur*—which were not always employed by the league consistently. There were instances when an individual was described as a *Kaufmann* at one point, only to be labeled as a *Manufaktur* at a subsequent point. These caveats, however, are only to warn against a spurious sense of precision in using social categories and not to deter one from the critical task of investigating and analyzing the broader patterns of membership within the Army League.

A composite sketch of the league suggests a preponderance of bureaucrats, military men, educators, businessmen, and professionals, often described by historians (or by themselves) as "custodians of patriotism."[61] While regional variations do indeed exist, on the whole these individuals (especially those who held office) tended to be men of *Bildung,* having been university-trained or, as with the case of the military, having obtained the rank of major or higher. They also displayed impressive credentials and were considered local *Honoratioren,* highly respected and influential citizens. At least 60 percent of the bureaucrats who served in executive capacities were academically trained (*akademische Beamten*), to which their title of *Assessor, Landgerichtsrat,* and *Regierungsrat* testified, while a majority of the educators were *Oberlehrer,* professors or principals of secondary schools. Businessmen were just as likely to be upstanding, long-time members of the community who had served on local city councils and who were eager to demonstrate their patriotism. Lawyers, doctors, pharmacists, and architects also felt compelled to sacrifice their spare time to the league's cause (see Tables 5, 6, and 7).

It is difficult to explain precisely why these groups figured prominently, not only in the Army League, but in the other patriotic societies as well. Bureaucrats' fierce patriotism has long been acknowledged as part and parcel of their unique relationship to the state. Participation in the patriotic societies was simply something that naturally accompanied the job, almost a habit of mind acquired in state service.[62] Army League branches in the Eastern Marches recorded a higher than average proportion of bureaucrats, educators, and landed elites and a lower proportion of military men, professionals, and businessmen. This concentration of bureaucrats can be explained by Posen's pivotal position as an Eastern March buffer state between Germans and Poles, where the provincial government encouraged the settlement of *Reichsdeutsche* to offset the rapidly expanding Polish Catholic population.[63] This process of redistribution was carried out by Posen's largest and most influential group, the German bureaucracy, and supported by the local landed elite. In the city of Posen the honorary secretary and treasurer of the local Army League branch were secretaries in the settlement commission (*Ansiedlungskommissarsekretär*), the honorary treasurer a *Landeskanzleibeamter,* and four of the five *Beisitzer* worked for the customs department.[64] William Hagen observed precisely the same pattern regarding bureaucratic patronization of the Eastern Marches Society.[65] Whether as executives or rank and file members, bureaucrats saw the Army League and the other patriotic societies as an extension of their governmental domain in which they could gain enormous satisfaction as well as prestige from helping to fortify the Fatherland and its remote outposts against culturally and socially inferior peoples.

Military enthusiasm for the league is somewhat easier to determine. Of course

TABLE 5. Composition of National *Gesamtvorstand* and *Ausschuss*

| | Gesamtvorstand | | | | | | Ausschuss | | | | | |
|---|---|---|---|---|---|---|---|---|---|---|---|---|
| | 1912 | | 1913 | | 1914 | | 1912 | | 1913 | | 1914 | |
| Occupation | No. | Percent | No. | Percent | No. | Percent | No. | Percent | No. | Percent | No. | Percent |
| Military personnel | 17 | 29.3 | 30 | 27.0 | 40 | 25.5 | 3 | 18.8 | 3 | 15.0 | 4 | 18.2 |
| Bureaucrats | 12 | 20.7 | 25 | 22.5 | 37 | 23.6 | 4 | 25.0 | 5 | 25.0 | 5 | 22.7 |
| Educators | 12 | 20.7 | 19 | 17.1 | 22 | 14.0 | 3 | 18.8 | 2 | 10.0 | 2 | 9.1 |
| Businessmen | 5 | 8.6 | 9 | 8.1 | 12 | 7.6 | 1 | 6.3 | 2 | 10.0 | 2 | 9.1 |
| Professionals | 2 | 3.4 | 8 | 7.2 | 10 | 6.4 | — | — | — | — | — | — |
| White-collar employees | — | — | 3 | 2.7 | 4 | 2.5 | — | — | — | — | — | — |
| Landed elites | 2 | 3.4 | 4 | 3.6 | 4 | 2.5 | 2 | 12.5 | — | — | 1 | 4.5 |
| Nonacademic intellectuals | — | — | — | — | 1 | 0.6 | — | — | 3 | 15.0 | 3 | 13.6 |
| Clergymen | — | — | 3 | 2.7 | 3 | 1.9 | 2 | 12.5 | — | — | — | — |
| Politicians | — | — | — | — | — | — | 2 | 12.5 | 4 | 20.0 | 4 | 18.2 |
| Women | — | — | 1 | 0.9 | 15 | 9.6 | 1 | 6.3 | 1 | 5.0 | 1 | 4.5 |
| Unknown | 8 | 13.8 | 9 | 8.1 | 9 | 5.7 | — | — | — | — | — | — |
| Total | 58 | | 111 | | 157 | | 16 | | 20 | | 22[a] | |

[a]Despite the constitution's provision for a maximum of 21, this figure is correct.

Source: *Die Wehr*, 1912–14. Figures are rounded to the nearest one-tenth of a percent.

TABLE 6. Rank and File According to Region

| Occupation | Composite | | Brandenburg | | Rhineland | | Saxony | | Schleswig-Holstein | | Württemberg | |
|---|---|---|---|---|---|---|---|---|---|---|---|---|
| | No. | Percent | No. | Percent | No. | Percent | No. | Percent | No. | Percent | No. | Percent |
| Military personnel | 408 | 29.4 | 109 | 30.0 | 65 | 38.5 | 23 | 33.3 | 13 | 11.4 | 19 | 26.0 |
| Bureaucrats | 225 | 16.2 | 55 | 15.2 | 16 | 9.5 | 9 | 13.0 | 21 | 18.4 | 18 | 24.7 |
| Educators | 158 | 11.4 | 51 | 14.0 | 15 | 8.9 | — | — | 12 | 10.5 | 7 | 9.6 |
| Businessmen | 107 | 7.7 | 25 | 6.9 | 22 | 13.0 | 3 | 4.3 | 19 | 16.7 | 8 | 11.0 |
| Professionals | 124 | 8.9 | 27 | 7.4 | 17 | 10.1 | 6 | 8.7 | 6 | 5.3 | 10 | 13.7 |
| White-collar employees | 91 | 6.5 | 17 | 4.7 | 21 | 12.4 | 2 | 2.9 | 11 | 9.6 | — | — |
| Landed elites | 33 | 2.4 | 21 | 5.8 | 1 | 0.6 | 1 | 1.4 | 1 | 0.9 | 1 | 1.4 |
| Nonacademic intellectuals | 8 | 0.6 | — | — | — | — | 1 | 1.4 | — | — | — | — |
| Clergymen | 26 | 1.9 | 7 | 1.9 | — | — | — | — | 1 | 0.9 | 3 | 4.1 |
| Artisans | 14 | 1.0 | 8 | 2.2 | 3 | 1.8 | — | — | 1 | 0.9 | 2 | 2.7 |
| Workers | 15 | 1.1 | 3 | 0.8 | 1 | 0.6 | 1 | 1.4 | 1 | 0.9 | — | — |
| Innkeepers | 5 | 0.4 | — | — | — | — | — | — | — | — | — | — |
| Retired | 4 | 0.3 | 2 | 0.6 | 2 | 1.2 | — | — | — | — | — | — |
| Doctors w/o ID | 15 | 1.1 | 6 | 1.7 | — | — | — | — | 1 | 0.9 | 2 | 2.7 |
| Directors w/o ID | 6 | 0.4 | — | — | 1 | 0.6 | — | — | — | — | — | — |
| Women | 53 | 3.8 | 11 | 3.0 | 3 | 1.8 | 1 | 1.4 | 2 | 1.8 | 3 | 4.1 |
| Unknown | 98 | 7.1 | 21 | 5.8 | 2 | 1.2 | 23 | 33.3 | 25 | 21.9 | — | — |
| Total | 1390 | | 363 | | 169 | | 69 | | 114 | | 73 | |

Source: Die Wehr, Ehrentafel 1914–18. Figures are rounded to the nearest one-tenth of a percent. The term Doctors w/o ID and Directors w/o ID refer to those for whom no information was given that would have enabled me to place them in a specific category (i.e., professionals, educators, businessmen, or white collar employees).

TABLE 7. Rank and File According to City

| Occupation | Gross-Berlin No. | Gross-Berlin Percent | Spandau No. | Spandau Percent | Leipzig No. | Leipzig Percent | Hersfeld No. | Hersfeld Percent | Dessau No. | Dessau Percent |
|---|---|---|---|---|---|---|---|---|---|---|
| Military personnel | 13 | 26.5 | 47 | 56.7 | 15 | 34.1 | 18 | 56.3 | 4 | 8.8 |
| Bureaucrats | 7 | 14.3 | 6 | 7.2 | 7 | 15.9 | 3 | 9.4 | 16 | 35.5 |
| Educators | 5 | 10.2 | 13 | 15.7 | 4 | 9.1 | 6 | 18.8 | 3 | 6.6 |
| Businessmen | 2 | 4.1 | 2 | 2.4 | 7 | 15.9 | — | — | 4 | 8.8 |
| Professionals | 2 | 4.1 | 3 | 3.6 | 9 | 20.5 | 4 | 12.5 | 10 | 22.2 |
| White-collar employees | 7 | 14.3 | 6 | 7.2 | 2 | 4.5 | — | — | 4 | 8.8 |
| Landed elites | — | — | — | — | — | — | — | — | — | — |
| Clergymen | — | — | 3 | 3.6 | — | — | 1 | 3.1 | 1 | 2.2 |
| Artisans | 1 | 2.0 | — | — | — | — | — | — | — | — |
| Students | 4 | 8.2 | — | — | — | — | — | — | — | — |
| Directors w/o ID | 2 | 4.1 | — | — | — | — | — | — | — | — |
| Unknown | 6 | 12.2 | 3 | 3.6 | — | — | — | — | — | — |
| Total | 49 | | 83 | | 44 | | 32 | | 42 | |

| Occupation | Clausthal No. | Clausthal Percent | Königsberg No. | Königsberg Percent | Regensburg No. | Regensburg Percent | Friedrichshafen No. | Friedrichshafen Percent | Soest No. | Soest Percent |
|---|---|---|---|---|---|---|---|---|---|---|
| Military personnel | — | — | 13 | 46.4 | 30 | 100.0 | 3 | 15.0 | 12 | 32.4 |
| Bureaucrats | 13 | 48.1 | 10 | 35.7 | — | — | 7 | 35.0 | 8 | 17.7 |
| Educators | 3 | 11.1 | 1 | 3.6 | — | — | — | — | 4 | 10.8 |
| Businessmen | 1 | 3.7 | 3 | 10.7 | — | — | 3 | 15.0 | 4 | 10.8 |
| Professionals | 2 | 7.4 | 1 | 3.6 | — | — | 4 | 20.0 | 3 | 8.1 |
| White-collar employees | 5 | 18.5 | — | — | — | — | — | — | — | — |
| Landed elites | 1 | 3.7 | — | — | — | — | 1 | 5.0 | 3 | 8.1 |
| Artisans | 2 | 7.4 | — | — | — | — | 1 | 5.0 | — | — |
| Workers | — | — | — | — | — | — | 1 | 5.0 | — | — |
| Clergymen | — | — | — | — | — | — | — | — | 3 | 8.1 |
| Total | 27 | | 28 | | 30 | | 20 | | 37 | |

Source: Die Wehr, Ehrentafel 1914–18. Figures are rounded to nearest one-tenth of a percent.

soldiers and officers were naturally sympathetic toward an organization that sought to strengthen the military's position; yet there was more to their participation than simply that. A sense of self-preservation drove many to the league, which campaigned for substantial improvements in the status of the *Unteroffizier*, or NCO, and the *Unteroffizieranwärter*. Low pay and poor opportunities for advancement resulted in the disillusionment of many NCOs and NCO candidates, and they often resigned from the army to seek more lucrative civilian employment.[66] Both groups, which were recruited almost exclusively from the lower middle class, were viewed by Army League officials as bastions against the Socialist menace; they were, to use Keim's metaphor, "the cement which fortifies the internal structure of the armed forces."[67] By demanding that their plight be redressed, the Army League hoped that in return for better pay and conditions NCOs would bind themselves more closely to the "school of the nation" and thus to bourgeois values as well. Officers, too, had reason to join the league because it supported their livelihood and values, as well as sought technological improvements such as the use of airplanes and newer weaponry and the implementation of more flexible formations and intensive training of recruits, which in the long run would make their job less onerous. League branches in which nearly all of either the executives or rank and file were military men were not uncommon.[68] In Hersfeld (Hesse-Nassau), the *Kriegschule* with its military candidates, officers, and teaching staff comprised 75 percent of the chapter's membership; in Leipzig, headquarters for the Nineteenth Army Corps, the military provided well over one-third of the members; in Königsberg (East Prussia) over 80 percent came from the ranks of the military and bureaucracy in a city that served as the headquarters of the First Army Corps and as the center of provincial government; in Friedrichshafen am Bodensee the Zeppelin airship factory offered the local chapter a ready-made pool of military personnel or contractors, while an astonishing 100 percent of Regensburg Army League members belonged to the army.[69] The military also comprised a respectable portion of the Bonn branch. Of the league's eighteen regional federations, eight were presided over by high-ranking military officials: *Oberst* a.D. Hering (Thuringia), *Exzellenz, Generalleutnant* a.D. Franz Freiherr v. Soden (Württemberg), *Oberstleutnant* z.D. Zeiss (Bavaria), *Exzellenz, Generalleutnant* v. Schmidt (Hanover), *Oberstleutnant* z.D. Abbes (East Prussia), *Exzellenz, Generalleutnant* Bauer (Rhineland), Major a.D. Raffauf (Province of Saxony), and *Oberst* Keppler (Westphalia).[70]

Educators, like bureaucrats, displayed an unusually high level of nationalistic enthusiasm and considered themselves as "guardians of German culture."[71] This kind of pedagogical intensity anticipates Remarque's classic portrait of the zealous Gymnasium teacher, Kantorek, whose devotion to the Reich, bordering on the obsessive, was transmitted to his naively patriotic students who eagerly enlisted for the First World War. Dietrich Schäfer's memoirs also testify to the magnetic pull that his history professor Heinrich v. Treitschke had upon him.[72] Imbued with an overwhelming sense of patriotic commitment, Schäfer undertook the task of proselytizing his own students as to the virtues of nationalism. *Studienrat* Gottlob Egelhaaf, a National Liberal and Army League member, recalled the indelible imprint his teachers at the University of Tübingen had left upon him; the enthusiasm and authority with which historians Reinhold Pauli and Julius Weizsäcker lectured left him spiritually rejuvenated and compelled him to pursue a career in teaching.[73] To teachers who prized the opportunity to mold impressionable minds, the Army League offered an extended classroom, a wider field for the propagation of their patriotic catechism. In Ahrensböl near Lübeck teachers comprised the entire executive council, and in Wierschleben all but one of the league's local officers belonged to the teaching profession.[74] An academic branch was inaugurated in the port city of Kiel in the spring of 1913 under the auspices of the preexisting local chapter, so that students and pedagogues could pay homage to the league. According to *Die Wehr,* this academic affiliate attracted 130 individuals and 12 corporate members in 1913.[75] Yet the example of Kiel evidently did not inspire similar academic branches in university towns such as Heidelberg or Göttingen, although the Tübingen chapter, led by university Professor v. Schleich, consisted of a considerable number of students and faculty members as well as individuals from other social groups.

A number of professionals and businessmen figured prominently in league circles. Many of them were veterans of the Wars of Unification, while others in their spare time continued to serve in the militia or reserve. Without wishing to question their patriotic commitment, we can indeed speculate that in some cases these individuals were also attracted to the Army League because of the attention it called to the plight of the veteran. League officials accused the government of spending money on refurbishing government buildings when it should have increased veterans' pensions, and they urged bureaucrats to treat those who had served their country diligently with greater respect and compassion.[76] For others, participation ensured a greater public prominence. The local branch in the city of Oberhausen was led by two respected individuals—Carl Schäfer, a civil engineer and retired *Oberleutnant,* and *Fabrikbesitzer* and local veterans' association president Carl Becker.[77] As the city's chief engineer, Schäfer was responsible for the rebuilding of Oberhausen's railway station in 1913–14, which became a source of pride for the community.[78] A manufacturer and owner of the Oberhausen *Glasfabrik,* Carl Becker was a much beloved personality. The fourth of five children from a Protestant family originally from Mülheim a.R., Becker attended *Volks-* and *Realschule,* and in 1894 began an apprenticeship in the Oberhausen *Glasfabrik,* owned by a friend of his father's, Herr Funcke. After ten years of loyal service and upon the death of the company's owner, Becker purchased the factory and turned what had once been a small concern into a large, lucrative operation. For his dedication to the community and his work in a number of patriotic societies and other voluntary associations, Becker received the title of Senator.[79]

The membership of the Hamburg branch read like a *Who's Who* of the business field. Its president, Edmund J. A. Siemers, ran a prosperous business (*Fabrik G. H. J. Siemers and Co.*) and served in the local Senate; vice president Cornelius Berenberg-Gossler co-owned and operated the banking house of Johannes Berenberg-Gossler and Co.; and Warner Poelchau, director of the Deutsche Bank branch in Hamburg and member of the Hamburg Senate (1902–10), served as secretary/treasurer.[80] Other prominent business supporters included Gustav J. S. Witt, honorary president of the Advisory Council of the Hamburg-America Shipping Line; Albert Ballin, also with the Hamburg-America Shipping Line; Rudolf Crasemann, president of the Hamburg branch of the *Hansabund;* F. A. Schwarz, president of the Hamburg Vereinsbank; and Hermann Heye, co-owner of the H. Heye *Glasfabrik*.[81] Another prominent Hamburg businessman and Army League member, Senator John v. Berenberg-Gossler, displayed his commitment to aristocratic codes of honor as well. In the autumn of 1912 he received a three-month prison sentence for having engaged in a pistol duel with Graf Königsmarck. The incident made local headlines not only because the Reichstag had passed legislation making duelling illegal, but also because he was the eldest son of the famous banking family and the older brother of Cornelius v. Berenberg-Gossler, the local Army League vice president.[82] In Hagen three hundred members of the local *Gewerbeverein* joined the Army League chapter in a corporate capacity.[83] In nearby Essen two architects and an engineer predominated on the league's executive council, while chemists from local factories were found in the Berlin chapters.[84]

There were, of course, branches whose composition was more diverse (see Table 8). For example, the Gollnow (Pomerania) chapter's executive board boasted a pharmacist, a clergyman, a teacher, two artisans, and a white-collar worker.[85] The Bad Liebenstein (Saxe-Meiningen) included two businessmen, one the owner of a publishing company, and an aristocrat, with the remaining council composed of two artisans, a pharmacist, a pit foreman, and a factory owner.[86] The appointment of women to office was indeed a rarity. In one case, the wife of *Oberstleutnant* Hamann received the office of treasurer of the Cottbus affiliate, whereas in Wiesbaden, two women graced the executive council of the local chapter.[87] Otherwise, women were excluded from the daily administration because they were presumed to be lacking both in political acumen and managerial skills. The league, however, encouraged women's general participation and often took great pains to point out that women were among its members, though it persistently avoided providing any specific figures as to its gender mix. Branches even offered appealing incentives including discounts at department stores in the hope of luring women into joining.[88] By and large, though, those women who pledged their support were either the wives, daughters, or close relatives of other league members. Occasionally, a few women showed their appreciation to the league by making rather substantial donations, as did Frau Gräfin Lüttschau, who gave the Liegnitz branch 100 marks.[89] Judging from the regional figures presented in Table 6, somewhere between 3 and 4 percent of the league's members were women.

The participation of workers is even more difficult to document. Of course the league insisted that it welcomed workers into its ranks, and preached that its gospel was of direct relevance to the individual worker's life—all Germans, regardless of social class, were affected by the issue of national security, and all Germans would benefit from the physical and moral regeneration at which the league aimed. From a working-class perspective, however, the Army League's programs seemed designed to perpetuate bourgeois hegemony (witness the exclusion of workers from any significant administrative role in the organization) and ensure that proletarian blood, not that of the comfortable *Bürgertum,* would be spilled first to preserve the country's military position. Table 6, calculated from the notices of league members who had given their lives on the battlefield, indicates that perhaps 1 percent of the league was drawn from the working class. Likewise, in heavily industrialized areas such as Oberhausen or Sterkrade, where the league directed particular attention to workers

TABLE 8. Executives According to City

| Occupation | Hordel b. Bochum | | Enger i. Westphalia | | Landsberg a. Warthe (Brandenburg) | | Forst i. Brandenburg | | Wierschleben | |
|---|---|---|---|---|---|---|---|---|---|---|
| | No. | Percent | No. | Percent | No. | Percent | No. | Percent | No. | Percent |
| Military personnel | — | — | — | — | 3 | 14.3 | — | — | — | — |
| Bureacrats | 1 | 14.3 | 2 | 40.0 | 6 | 28.6 | 4 | 28.6 | 7 | 58.3 |
| Educators | — | — | — | — | 1 | 4.8 | 2 | 14.3 | 3 | 25.0 |
| Businessmen | 1 | 14.3 | 1 | 20.0 | 2 | 9.5 | 2 | 14.3 | 1 | 8.3 |
| Professionals | 1 | 14.3 | — | — | 4 | 19.0 | 1 | 7.1 | — | — |
| White-collar employees | 3 | 42.9 | — | — | 1 | 4.8 | 1 | 7.1 | — | — |
| Landed elites | — | — | — | — | 2 | 9.5 | — | — | — | — |
| Clergymen | — | — | 1 | 20.0 | — | — | — | — | — | — |
| Artisans | 1 | 14.3 | 1 | 20.0 | 2 | 9.5 | 2 | 14.3 | — | — |
| Students | — | — | — | — | — | — | — | — | — | — |
| Directors w/o ID | — | — | — | — | — | — | — | — | — | — |
| Workers | — | — | — | — | — | — | 1 | 8.3 | — | — |
| Agricultural workers | — | — | — | — | — | — | 1 | 8.3 | 1 | 8.3 |
| Total | 7 | | 5 | | 21 | | 14 | | 12 | |

Source: Die Wehr, passim.

(as in its campaign against the French Foreign Legion), a majority of those attracted were drawn from local *Angestellten* rather than the working class.[90] The Social Democrats had suggested as much when they urged that workers participating in the Army League be photographed so as to provide documentary proof for so improbable an occurrence.[91]

"Honored Army League member" (*Ehrenwarten*) was a title bestowed upon those individuals who had served the league in some significant way, perhaps by recruiting additional members, volunteering extra time for activities, or especially donating money. Lists of these individuals were published routinely in *Die Wehr* so other league members throughout the Reich could learn of their dedication to the association and, it was hoped, emulate their example. The league also publicized the names of those members who donated to special funds such as that for the relief of flood victims in the Eastern Marches. For those members with large egos, regardless of their social backgrounds, the practice of public citation for service must have been one of the league's more attractive incentives.

While a variety of factors shaped Germans' decisions to join the Army League, its membership tended to be drawn largely from the educated middle classes. Executive boards, especially, teemed with local notables—highly respected citizens of the community ranging from independent businessmen to professionals and bureaucrats. The lower middle class of white-collar employees, artisans, and low-ranking bureaucrats were more evident in the rank and file but did not exclusively compose the league's general membership. Of course, regional factors also affected the composition of the league, contributing to higher (or lower) concentrations of various social groups. Women and workers, nonetheless, accounted for a negligible proportion of the league.

Another interesting feature of the league was its generational structure. Individuals for whom ages could be discerned were either members of local executive councils or other prominent supporters. Yet even without precise birth dates, certain occupations offer clues as to the age of the member. For example, bureaucrats who held the title of *Rat* were men of the highest distinction in their respective professions and were generally middle-aged or older. Likewise, over one-half of the military men accounted for were retired (thus they were likely to be in their fifties or older, as in the cases of v. Liebert, Litzmann, and Keim), and those who were veterans of the Wars of Unification were naturally sixty years or older. Professors, too, were likely to be at least middle-aged as a result of the length of time required to achieve that position. A prosopographical analysis of 195 league members bears out these generalizations. The average age of this group was 53.5 years and the median age 58 years. Just under 10 percent (9.7 percent) were 40 or younger, 41.6 percent were between the ages of 41 and 59, and 48.7 percent were 60 or older. The military and landed elites comprised the oldest groups, with average ages of 59.9 and 61.5 years respectively (the median age was 62 years for both groups). Bureaucrats followed with an average age of 56.5 years and a median age of 59, then businessmen with an average age of 55.7 and a median age of 55, clergy with an average age of 55.6 and a median age of 53, and educators with an average age of 55.2 and a median age of 55. Professionals and intellectuals represented the youngest of this composite group with average ages of 51.6 and 49.6 and median ages of

51 and 52, respectively. The results are similar for the members of the 1912 *Ausschuss*, where the average age was slightly higher at 58.2 years, while the median age was 58.[92]

These statistics suggest the Army League's attractiveness to middle-aged (or older) respectable middle-class Germans. With an average age of nearly 54, most of these men were born before 1860 and thus likely to remember the Wars of Unification. Their membership in the Army League, therefore, may be seen to represent a political generation whose formative years were capped by the heady military triumphs under Bismarck. The same pattern can be discerned in the Pan-German League, where nearly three-quarters of the association's executives were born prior to 1860.[93] Although no comparable statistics exist for the Navy League, it would not be unfair to suggest that, given the high degree of overlapping membership in these organizations, a fair proportion of its executives were of the same generational cohort. What, then, were the implications of this "greying effect"? For the Army League (and, indeed, for the patriotic societies as well), survival depended upon its ability to recruit younger members. Keim and his executives exhibited great interest in the condition of Germany's youth—especially its physical and mental condition—yet the league seemed unable to increase the number of its younger members and was perhaps unwilling to groom them for positions of responsibility. Even in the Pan-German League only approximately 1 percent of its local leaders were students, while the figure stood somewhat higher for the Eastern Marches Society at around 3 percent.[94] The Liberal parties, too, were particularly concerned about the generational gap and how this would affect their ability to recruit voters in the future; hence the formation between 1898 and 1904 of the Young Liberal movements in both the left and right wings of the Liberal organizations.[95] Without an infusion of new talent, the Army League would eventually falter (as would any other organization). If Army League members formed a generational cohort, was it not possible that they shared a predilection for similar associations?

## Overlapping Membership

There are countless examples at the local, regional, and national level to support the assertion that the Army League recruited to a considerable extent (as was most apparent among its executives) from individuals who were simultaneously members of one or several other patriotic societies. Although this may not be a surprising revelation given individuals' tendencies to promote associations with similar causes, the significant fact here is that the league was recruiting primarily from a relatively narrow segment of the population.

Within the league's highest executive council, the *Ausschuss*, virtually all belonged to at least one other patriotic association if not several. Eduard v. Liebert and Dietrich Schäfer boasted memberships in the Pan-German and Navy leagues, the Eastern Marches Society, the Imperial League against Social Democracy, and the Colonial Society. Keim, too, at one point or another, was active in the Navy League, Pan-German League, and the Imperial League against Social Democracy, among others. Heinrich Rippler, Karl Litzmann, and Kurd v. Strantz patronized the Pan-German League, Navy League, and Eastern Marches Society, and Professor Reinhold Freiherr v. Lichtenberg belonged to the Pan-German League in addition to the *Richard Wagner-Verein* and the racist *Gobineau Vereinigung*.

At the local and regional level the pattern was duplicated. In Württemberg, the following members of the Federation council and local executive boards were also active in the Württemberg Navy League: Karl Elben, *Hofrat* J. J. Hoppe, Lieutenant General v. Berger, Franz Freiherr v. Soden, Major General Freiherr v. Hügel, *Kaufmann* Karl Pfeilsticker, Professor Goppelt.[96] *Geheimer Hofrat* Dr. v. Sieglin belonged to the local Colonial Society, as did *Oberstleutnant* a.D. Stein, while Gottlob Egelhaaf supported the Pan-German League and Colonial Society.[97] The presidents of the Army League chapters in Sulz (Dr. Hermann) and Esslingen (*Gaswerkdirektor* Fischer) participated in the local chapters of the Pan-German League.[98] In Hamburg, H. E. Bohlen, *Rechtsanwalt* Dr. W. A. Burchard, Dr. Johannes Lappenberg, Dr. R. Mönckeberg, Senator Refardt, Mayor Dr. Schroeder, *Regierungsrat* Dr. Merck, and bank director Kurt v. Sydow patronized the Navy League, and Mayor O'Swald, F. F. Eiffe, F. C. Paul Sachse, and F. A. Poppenhausen were active in the Colonial Society.[99] In the Rhineland, *Baurat* Lucius of Mainz listed himself as a Pan-German League member, as did Düsseldorf supporters Friedrich Majefsky, Ferdinand Duncker, and Wilhelm Wenk.[100] These individuals are but a few of the best examples of overlapping membership.

Overlapping membership, which perhaps accounted at least in part for the Army League's impressive figures, also raises some questions about the commitment of those individuals who pledged themselves to several organizations simultaneously.[101] Did these people represent a devout group of patriotic activists upon whose participation the Army League (and the other patriotic societies) depended for survival? Or were some of them simply compulsive joiners who did so for the prestige attached to the act of joining? Or were they individuals for whom multiple membership suggested active participation in one organization and limited responsibilities in the rest? All three of these possibilities were indeed likely. To argue then that the Army League recruited from a broad spectrum of fiercely patriotic Germans would be misleading. A relatively small segment of the population (less than 1 percent) joined it, and an even smaller percentage were "activists" in the sense that they were willing to sacrifice whatever was required of them to sustain the momentum of the association. One might argue that the Army League (and perhaps the other patriotic societies as well) had what might be called a maximum recruitment potential. Theoretically, the league could seek the support of any German, but, in more practical terms, it could expect the dedication of a far smaller group who could combine the necessary leisure, financial resources, and the nationalist spirit and/or desire for social prominence.

With regard to overlapping membership (and to the general membership as well), at what point and to what extent did the phenomenon of *Vereinsmüdigkeit* (associational boredom), a trend which the league executives acknowledged in their reports, affect the operations of the association? (see Table 9). In the Army League's case, 1913 was a turning point in its ability to recruit new members and to retain the interest of old ones. General Keim was puzzled and distressed by the sudden apathy that was plaguing his association, complaining: "I cannot understand how there are

TABLE 9. Membership of Patriotic Societies, 1902–14

| Year | Navy League | Pan-German | Eastern Marches | Colonial Society |
|------|-------------|------------|-----------------|------------------|
| 1902 | 236,793 | 22,300 | — | 32,161 |
| 1903 | 233,487 | 19,068 | 26,468 | 31,482 |
| 1904 | 248,004 | 19,111 | — | 31,985 |
| 1905 | 276,044 | 18,618 | — | 32,159 |
| 1906 | 315,430 | 18,500 | 39,000 | 32,787 |
| 1907 | 324,083 | — | 45,500 | 36,956 |
| 1908 | 307,884 | — | 48,800 | 38,509 |
| 1909 | 296,172 | — | 50,500 | 38,928 |
| 1910 | 291,426 | — | 53,000 | 39,025 |
| 1911 | 298,014 | — | 53,200 | 39,134 |
| 1912 | 320,464 | 17,000 | 54,100 | 41,163 |
| 1913 | 331,910 | — | 54,150 | 42,212 |
| 1914 | 331,493 | 18,000 | 53,656 | 42,018 |

Sources: Jahresbericht des Deutschen Flottenvereins für 1912; Eley, Reshaping the German Right, 366 (for Navy League figures for 1913 and 1914); Chickering, We Men Who Feel Most German, passim; Wertheimer, The Pan-German League, 54 (for figures for 1903–5; 1912); Galos, Gentzen, Jakóbczyk, Die Hakatisten; Tims, Germanizing Prussian Poland, 288 (for figures for 1903, 1906–8); Eley, Reshaping the German Right, 366.

people in the Army League who maintain that after the passage of the Army Bill the Army League no longer has a raison d'être. Whoever says this does not comprehend the essence of the Army League."[102] The league's journal also complained about *Vereinsmüdigkeit,* as in this later extract:

> The members of the *Nationale Verbände* do not consider their membership in these organizations as a vital necessity [*Lebensnotwendigkeit*], even more rarely as a necessity for the *Verein* itself. The great majority of members are driven to the *Verein* by nothing more than curiosity. Moreover, even the leading provincial and local personalities are seldom devoted to them . . . . In most towns branches are founded simply because "we must have one here too". . . . Today we see the *Nationale Verbände* from the standpoint that one can take them or leave them.[103]

While the initial years of any association can sometimes be erratic, as reflected in a rise and fall in membership figures, it is curious that as the last of the patriotic societies, the Army League could not capitalize upon the successes of its predecessors and avoid their shortcomings. Certainly Keim, Schäfer, and v. Liebert were seasoned patriotic zealots whose firsthand knowledge of these associations should have enabled them to ensure for the Army League a more auspicious second year. The league's trend toward stagnation was most likely a combination of mismanagement by its executives, growing indifference by its members (both active and passive), and the fact that the passage of the 1913 Army Bill had robbed the league of its raison d'être. This was not from a lack of effort on the part of the league, which constantly exhorted local branches to ever greater activity. But guidelines as formulated from above were often modified or reinterpreted when implemented in the popular arena of local branch activity.

## Sociability

Sociability served as a barometer of the league's ability to disseminate its broader nationalistic message to Germans. Its objective was not simply to proselytize them about the importance of the league's goals but to bring them together socially, thereby strengthening communal, cultural, and nationalistic values. In pursuit of its goal to recruit "every good German man and woman," the Army League strove to achieve a delicate balance between propaganda and sociability.[104] Circulars from the regional federations informed individual branches of the kinds of activities that would sustain interest in the league as well as attract potential members and suggested occasions suitable for celebration. Lectures, many of which were accompanied by slide shows, served as the primary means by which the league disseminated its propaganda. In this way, the league could lend credibility to its message by providing the audience with a more tangible (and perhaps more stimulating) medium than the lecture alone could offer. Lecture/slide presentations usually began at 8:00 or 8:30 P.M., lasted no longer than two hours, and were delivered either by prominent military officers or other aficionados on variations of the theme of national efficiency—"The Necessity of the Army League," "National or Partisan Politics?," "Will Universal Manhood Suffrage be Fulfilled?," "Michel, Awake!" or "World Politics and Disarmament." Such presentations were also acclaimed by the other patriotic societies; the Navy League's Essen chapter reported that festivals including such shows "were the most actively in demand; on occasion the crowd was so large that hundreds of people had to be turned back at the doors."[105] Navy League officials were eager to promote lecture/slide shows and boasted in the annual report for 1912 that the number of presentations had increased dramatically from 631 in 1910 to 841 in 1911 to a record high of 1,216 for all branches.[106] *Die Wehr* provided details whenever possible of its own slide shows, concentrating primarily on the overflowing crowds and their enthusiastic reception. A lecture by General Keim attracted over twelve hundred Germans to the Tivoli Hotel in Eisenach with "hundreds more left outside unable to claim a seat," and it brought the local branch one hundred new members who pledged following Keim's spellbinding speech.[107] Often lecture/slide shows were used to found new branches, as was the case in Altenburg (Saxony) where *Oberstleutnant* Hübner's talk on the "Results of French Military Maneuvers" heralded the creation of the nearby Gössnitz and Schmölln chapters.[108] To facilitate the use of slide shows, the Army League made arrangements with special slide vendors, such as the Benzinger company in Stuttgart.[109]

Although the Army League apparently did not maintain a speakers school to train its lecturers as did the Colonial Society, it occasionally shared lecturers with other patriotic societies. Since these lectures were often highly technical in content, discussing in considerable detail military maneuvers and troop formations, circuit lecturers tended to be drawn from a hard-core group of officers, reservists, militiamen, or simply aficionados. While women were never excluded from attending these sessions, they generally chose not to attend. Presuming their interests lay in more practical (i.e., domestic) spheres, the league instead offered lectures and courses for women on patriotic duty and hygiene. Knowing how to care for the wounded in the battlefields under less than optimum conditions and to safeguard the home front against the spread of disease and lice was the patriotic responsibility of all German women. While subject matter seemed to vary little, there were, nevertheless, none-too-subtle social gradations regarding the fees paid to circuit lecturers. Whereas postal workers and teachers received reimbursement for their travel expenses (as in the case of Postal Secretary Hüner of Breslau, who was paid nine pfennigs per kilometer by train) or a second-class train ticket, as well as possible small daily expenses befitting the status of a middle-ranking bureaucrat, higher-ranking military officials and prominent figures generally could expect as minimum payment a second-class train ticket and an honorarium of as much as sixty marks in addition to daily expenses.[110]

Serious lectures were followed by a more convivial atmosphere of drinking and discussion. The more beer that flowed, the more animated the discussion. Choral societies also demonstrated their vocal talents with renditions of "Deutschland über alles" and numerous other patriotic songs. Occasionally, the post-lecture activities were marred by discord, especially when members of the Peace Movement or Socialist Party planted themselves in the audience. The Hamburg branch thought it could prevent any heated exchanges between General Keim and antileague activists present for his speech by stipulating beforehand that absolutely no discussion would be tolerated following the general's lecture. As one might suspect, these precautionary measures failed to prevent socialist hecklers from interrupting Keim with boos and hisses several times during the course of his speech.[111]

Celebrations of patriotic festivals, beer and entertainment evenings, *Stammtische,* and excursions to battlefields or war memorials formed a web of sociability that helped reinforce the bonds within the league. Branches went to great lengths to celebrate every conceivable national event. The Kaiser's and Bismarck's birthdays and the founding of the Reich and Sedan Day were eagerly and dutifully commemorated. A single celebration of the anniversary of the founding of the Reich brought out fifteen hundred participants in Altenburg (Saxony), while Lübeck's comprehensive celebration of the Kaiser's birthday, his twenty-fifth jubilee as reigning monarch, the marriage of Princess Victoria Luisa, and the one hundredth anniversary of the Wars of Liberation attracted at least a thousand from the port city.[112] The larger the festivities, the league reasoned, the greater the opportunity to recruit potential members, and for this reason local branches were instructed to mark important patriotic dates with enormous festivities and to share them when possible with other local patriotic societies whose members might have a natural sympathy for the league's goals. Ensuring respectable attendance for such events meant that entrance fees were kept to a minimum, usually one mark per person, four marks per family, and fifty pfennigs for students. Federation Berlin-Brandenburg held an enormous festival (a *Volksfest*) which began at 7:00 P.M. with a lecture on the Wars of Liberation, followed by music by a military band and later a ball with dancing. At 10:00 P.M. a boat was made available for those who wished to travel to the *Erholungsheim Spinderfeld* for further activities. All of this entertainment cost individuals one mark, families three marks, and students fifty pfennigs, and was pronounced by Kurd v. Strantz, president of the federation, as a great success.[113] As the executive board of the Hagen branch put it, "nothing would be spared to ensure that the . . . *Familienunterhaltungsabend* would be downright pleasant, genial, and entertaining."[114] For single league members of either sex, these events may have served additionally as a kind of *Heiratsmarkt,* an opportunity to meet one's future spouse, since the workplace did not lend itself for this purpose.[115]

Another means of combining propaganda with *Geselligkeit* was organizing excursions to places of historical interest. These trips, however, were the brainchild of neither the Army League nor the other patriotic societies; they had been long a part of the *Vereinsleben* of the middle and working classes. Sometimes these excursions involved simply pleasure boat outings for the day; others involved more lengthy planning, such as trips to famous battlefields or monuments. The Army League benefited in particular from the completion in 1913 of the monument to the Wars of Liberation (*Völkerschlachtdenkmal*) in Leipzig and chose to hold its annual meeting there.[116] By and large, though, the Navy League appears to have offered far more in the way of longer and more exotic excursions than did the Army League, and it attracted greater numbers of members to participate in them. An examination of the participant list for a Navy League trip sponsored by the Württemberg Federation to Bremen, Heligoland, Kiel, and Hamburg indicates that several hundred members from local Württemberg branches took part.[117] Arranging shorter trips to see plays such as Böttcher's *Vaterland* were also part of the Army League's strategy to mix entertainment with ritualistic propaganda.

For some members the most satisfying event of the year was the annual meeting that generally took place in May. For three days members from every region of the Reich could congregate in a designated city to see old friends, make new ones, and discuss pressing issues. In 1913 the league chose the city of Leipzig as the site of its *Hauptversammlung,* to which hundreds of members thronged to see the newly completed and impressive monument to the Wars of Liberation conceived by Bruno Schmitz and erected between 1911 and 1914. "Sacrifice" was the motto of the convention, although judging from the league's schedule of events, participants were treated to all the comforts of a conventioneer.[118] On Friday, 16 May, members arrived at 8:00 P.M. to be welcomed by league officials; on 17 May the conference began in earnest with a meeting of the *Gesamtvorstand* from 11:30 A.M. until 3:00 P.M., followed by a communal dinner between 4:30 P.M. and 5:00 P.M. From 5:00 P.M. until 8:00 P.M. members attended a special exhibition on the Wars of Liberation, and at 9:00 P.M. they were treated to a get-together at Auerbachskeller, the place made famous by Goethe in *Faust,* where the beer flowed freely. At 10:00 A.M. on Sunday all participants were invited to attend the general meeting, at which time the league's executives spoke on various pressing issues, including the state of the association, and the treasurer delivered his report on the finances. Three and one-half hours later lunch was served, and at 4:00 P.M. all participants toured the war monument and had their photo taken as a group. A book and photograph exhibition awaited the conventioneers at 5:00 P.M., and at 6:30 P.M. they departed from the main train station after three days of business and pleasure.

## Finances

By way of introduction to his financial report for 1912 presented at the annual meeting in May 1913, honorary treasurer Baltz reminded members that the league's purpose was to channel funds into agitational activity rather than to sit by in silence, husbanding a surplus.[119] Certainly a brief glance at the league's balance sheets would testify to the validity of the honorary treasurer's statement. In 1912 the Army League's expenditure matched its income of nearly 100,000 marks; the treasurer's report for 1913, however, revealed a substantial decline in its total income, which was now 77,000 marks. Ninety-five percent of the league's income came from membership dues (94,130.90 marks of a total of 99,428.51 [see Table 10]), while 75 percent of it went toward defraying the cost of propaganda (including *Die Wehr*). Having to rely so heavily on membership dues for revenue and lacking any substantial outside funding meant the league was continually in financial jeopardy.

Nonpayment of membership fees was a persistent problem, one for which there was apparently no remedy. Appeals for the payment of dues frequently appeared in *Die Wehr*. The national association pleaded for them, the provincial federations begged branches to pay them, and the branches tried in vain to cajole members into giving the bare minimum of one mark, but to little avail. This delinquency might be attributed to some members' disillusionment or dissatisfaction with the association. As Württemberg Federation president Franz Freiherr v. Soden pointed out, some members believed the league's goal to have been accomplished with the passage of the Army Bill of 1913 and thus no longer saw a need for their continued support, whether financial or moral.[120] Still others might have reasoned that wealthier members could shoulder the financial burdens with increases in their contributions. Yet the Army League was not unique in its crisis regarding membership dues; the Eastern Marches Society complained bitterly about its members' disregard for financial responsibility. Annual dues of one mark never were paid in full on a regular schedule, and some branches refused to remit the prescribed portion of their dues to national headquarters. Its officers worried about the implications of this "lack of financial discipline."[121] The Pan-German League, too, experienced a similar phe-

TABLE 10. Army League Finances, 1912–13

| | |
|---|---|
| Total income | 99,428.51 M |
|   Income from membership dues | 94,130.90 M |
|   Miscellaneous small income | 296.61 M |
|   Loans | 5,000.00 M |
| Total expenditures | 99,428.51 M |
|   Cost of *Die Wehr* | 25,072.28 M |
|   Founding costs | 328.00 M |
|   Propaganda | 46,833.75 M |
|   Office equipment/furniture | 3,059.70 M |
|   Rent for offices | 1,600.00 M |
|   Cost of maintaining library | 533.03 M |
|   Salaries | 13,727.72 M |
|   Incidental expenses, utilities | 4,712.05 M |
| Bank credit (outstanding debts) | 1,166.62 M |
| Outstanding debts for postcheck account | 749.92 M |
| Ready cash | 1,625.44 M |
| Balance (sum of above) | 3,541.98 M |

*Source: Die Wehr*, Heft 6 (1913).

nomenon, and it was estimated that in 1907 only about 14,000 of a total of 18,500 members paid dues.[122]

The Army League's enormous expenditure on propaganda also paralleled that of the other patriotic societies; where these groups diverged, however, was in regard to the availability and use of special funds and gifts. The Navy League had an array of these, which were used for a variety of purposes: to cover expenses for the production of its journal, *Die Flotte;* to maintain its *Alters-und Invalidenheim;* and to support its propaganda machine. It also had special accounts for China and Southwest Africa, and the Alexander v. Pflaum'sche Stiftung established with the aid of the Württemberg Federation upon the death of its Federation president in 1911. In 1912 the Navy League appeared to be in good financial shape without having to resort to wealthy industrialists for major contributions.[123] The Pan-German League, by comparison, relied heavily on the support of such individuals after 1910. Between 1902 and 1909, however, its financial status resembled that of the Army League more than the Navy League. But with the aid of its executive members, who had contacts with Ruhr and Westphalian industrialists, "the Pan-German League's financial problems now vanished overnight . . . [and] by 1 July 1910 the League was not only free of debt but showed a surplus of close to 10,000 marks."[124] Before the First World War the Army League apparently did not receive the kind of financial backing from industrialists as did the Pan-German League. While the Pan-German League and Class made some funds available for the Army League initially, Class refused Keim's pleas for additional money from the lucrative *Wehrschatz,* which, as Class explained, was off-limits to the general's association.[125] And while the Pan-German League president tried to persuade his industrialist contacts to contribute to Keim's operation, few took the bait.[126] Thus, in the Army League's case, huge expenditures on propaganda may have produced the impression of the league as a robust, smooth-functioning unit, but it meant that without substantial outside funding to cover these expenses, the Army League would be existing on a financial shoestring that was ready to snap at any moment.

In an effort to prop up sagging fortunes, league officials groped about for a fresh issue. In the summer of 1914 the First World War presented the league with precisely that opportunity. With the outbreak of hostilities Keim justified the league's previous incessant demands for immediate military improvements and the concomitant expenditures, and he proclaimed that the Army League's job was by no means over—rather, it had just begun. The war not only reshaped the course of German politics and the face of German society, it also revealed the more disturbing elements which had always been present in the league but which until 1914 had lain dormant, lurking just beneath the surface—annexationist demands and racism.

August Keim (*Die Wehr*, Heft 3/4 [1915], p. 3).

Admiral Graf von Baudissin (*Die Wehr*, Heft 5 [1917], p. 1).

Participants of the Annual Meeting of the Army League of 18 May 1913 in front of the Memorial to the Battle of Leipzig of 1813 (*Die Wehr*, Heft 6 [1913], p. 9).

Members of the Executive and General Councils at the Annual Meeting in Posen (*Die Wehr*, Heft 6 [1914], p. 3).

Cover page of the Army League's journal, *Die Wehr*, 1912.

Cover page of the Army League's journal, *Die Wehr*, 1912.

Cover page of the Army League's journal, *Die Wehr*, 1914.

# CHAPTER 6

# Twilight of the Demagogues

Trachtet am ersten nach der Macht;
dann wird euch alles andere zufallen.
DIETRICH SCHÄFER (1917)

Prior to August 1914, the Army League had championed the necessity of infusing German society with properly martial and nationalist virtues in preparation for a war it felt to be inevitable. This emphasis on domestic readiness was then reinforced by the persistent Francophobic tone of league propaganda. Whether it was the desire to recover Alsace-Lorraine or to lure unsuspecting Germans to serve in the Foreign Legion, the persistence of French hostility was all too readily apparent. With the outbreak of the First World War, of course, these themes appeared to gain even greater relevance. As hostilities spread, the league's warnings were confirmed, its concerns vindicated, its methods validated. Nonetheless, given the scale and scope of the war, the Army League's prewar phobias were to be supplemented by a further set of public concerns that, although detectable in its prewar discourse, were now given far greater emphasis.

Whereas condemnation of British imperial strength, commercial might, and diplomatic obstinance had been evident but muted in comparison with anti-French pronouncements before the war, the idea of perfidious Albion now gained equal currency. With this came a clearer realization of the economic implications of national rivalry (as opposed to earlier warnings about intangible factors, such as French prestige and pride). In turn, the Army League began to direct much more attention to territorial questions, to the economic consequences of a major war. The conflict, then, seemed both to offer a challenge and to provide an opportunity to ensure the expansion of Germany as a world power.

Few, if any, Europeans in positions of responsibility in 1914 expected the war to be a long one. After the stabilization of the western front following the Battle of the Marne, and the failure of either Germany and Austria or Russia to secure a quick knockout blow in the east, efforts to formulate a suitable German response revolved around three particular themes: (1) the extension of German resources necessary to the war effort (even if this meant acquiring territory rich in vital minerals or ores); (2) the incorporation into the Empire of areas that were either ethnically or historically German (to restore the boundaries of the former "Old Reich"); and (3) the improvement of the actual prosecution of the war effort (through more efficient management techniques or institutions). Taken together, these concerns all pointed toward the need for German autarky, and here England shone as the example to be copied. That island nation's imperial possessions provided critical resources and a sense of Anglo-Saxon communality in the great struggle, the lesson being that economic and cultural considerations intertwined. A strong economy and a united community, efficiently led, would finally guarantee Germany's place in world affairs.

Shortly after its inception the Army League had already begun to gravitate toward this idea. Kurd v. Strantz, in a pamphlet entitled, *Ein starkes Volk—ein starkes Heer,* had condemned England as "the only 'super power' which on no occasion has allowed us to dine at its richly stocked table." In his view, "a conflict is unavoidable."[1] Moreover, in 1912 a league member from the northern port city of Lübeck, the entrepreneur Senator Emil Ludwig Possehl, developed the idea of a *Kriegswirtschaftsstab,* a Department of Wartime Economic Planning.[2] The obvious parallel was with the German General Staff; having attempted to militarize German society through martial values, the league now considered militarizing the economy as well. Possehl was simultaneously a member of the Pan-German League and approached Class with his ideas, but found the Pan-German president unreceptive.[3] Nevertheless, Class called Possehl to Keim's attention, emphasizing his "enthusiasm" for the Army League's goals. By the time the Army League convened its first annual meeting in the spring of 1912, Possehl, now a member of its *Ausschuss,* delivered an address on the state of the German economy.[4]

His remarks were not reassuring. Unless the nation entered war economically prepared, the likely results would be starvation and the collapse of industry. The call-up of some one million citizens to active duty would surely disrupt production without some prior preparation. Furthermore, because Germany relied heavily upon imports, it would be vulnerable to British naval action. A blockade of the North Sea, for example, would impair the shipment of iron ore from Sweden, while closure of the Dardenelles would restrict the transport of vital corn and grain.[5] But an Economic General Staff, composed of representatives from industry, commerce, and agriculture, could nullify these potential weaknesses by preparing a comprehensive plan for the wartime allocation of resources and the direction of industry. Possehl rejected the criticisms of those who sneered at his plans. Quite to the contrary, he contended, only those countries that did everything to prepare themselves for a future conflict would emerge both prosperous and victorious.[6]

Determined to see his idea of a *Kriegswirtschaftsstab* implemented by the government, Possehl conferred in 1912 with the Secretary of State for the Interior, Dr. Clemens v. Delbrück.[7] Delbrück was receptive and claimed that he himself had embraced the idea of economic mobilization ever since the Franco-Prussian war. He agreed in principle with Possehl about the absolute necessity of ensuring the uninterrupted flow of German agricultural and industrial goods in wartime. Delbrück readily conceded that translating such desires into an effective program of action was difficult, for if calculating and organizing the nation's requirements in peacetime was onerous, it would be far more difficult to plan for a war of unknown scope and uncertain duration.[8]

He was, nonetheless, a persuasive advocate, and Bethmann delegated to him responsibility for forming a Permanent Commission for Mobilization Affairs. Composed of representatives from the Prussian and Reich ministries, the Admiralty, and the General Staff, the commission's brief was to explore the feasibility of economic mobilization. Despite his reservations, Delbrück remained optimistic and anticipated that the committee's recommendations would eventually be adopted by the Reichstag. But Delbrück's faced considerable opposition. Bethmann and his Conservative supporters, sensitive to electoral considerations, were not enamored of the commission's investigation, which pointed to the desirability of extending the state's role in economic and social affairs and raising additional revenue through new taxes.[9] Believing that publication or support of either prospect would alienate voters, the government preferred to temporize. Moreover, to implement measures obviously designed both to facilitate wartime mobilization and frustrate the impact of an inevitable Allied blockade was to send a clear signal to other countries about Germany's intentions. In 1913, then, the commission repeated its efforts to secure governmental sanctions for its proposals, but again without success.

The following year did not produce any real progress on the issue, but in May 1914, when the commission met again, it acceded to the Army League's demand that representatives be included from outside governmental circles. Only "impartial" witnesses with the necessary perspective and independence, the Army League contended, could be relied upon for an accurate assessment of the situation. Delbrück invited Possehl to attend the May meetings. Another meeting was scheduled for 31 July 1914, at which the league's proposal for an Economic General Staff was to have been discussed, but it never occurred, owing to the imminent outbreak of the First World War.[10]

Once the First World War actually began, the government's reluctance to commit itself to the commission's and the Army League's plans for economic mobilization resulted in immediate shortages of raw materials and skilled labor. With the reality of the government's shortsightedness only too apparent, a group of civilians scrambled to create a department to ease the situation. The result, the KRA (*Kriegsrohstoff Abteilung*), proved relatively successful in coping with the distribution of raw materials, but it could not address the problems that erupted in other sectors.[11] Serious shortages of manpower, especially of skilled labor, threatened to curtail essential military production and prompted the formation of the AZA (*Abteilung für Ausfuhr, Einfuhr, und Zurückstellung*). This Exports and Exemption Office was responsible for establishing guidelines for labor exemptions and resolving wage and other job-related disputes.

Taken together, these measures may have amounted to a directed economy or *Zwangswirtschaft*, but to the Army League and other critics they appeared as haphazard and uncoordinated attempts, rather than the integrated, comprehensive approach that the situation dictated. The longer the stalemate at the front persisted, the greater the necessity for the home front to maintain production, morale, and a consistent overall strategy. Ironically, by 1915 Possehl's desire to revive his original project was impeded by his indictment for treason in the wake of reports that this supposed ultrapatriot's Russian factories were manufacturing ammunition for the Russian war effort. Although he was acquitted following a lengthy trial, the accusations of war profiteering shattered his reputation and his health. Possehl died in 1919.[12]

In his absence, it was left to Kurd v. Strantz to undertake the Army League's advocacy of an institution coordinating wartime economic measures. In 1915 v. Strantz drew upon Possehl's original draft to produce a new league memorandum urging the creation of a Department of Wartime Economics Planning. The antigovernmental thrust was implicit throughout. He introduced and justified his memorandum by contending that ever since the Franco-Prussian war, Germany had faced the probability of another war with France and, since 1907, the distinct possibility of war on two fronts against Russia and perhaps England too. But the government, v. Strantz contended, had underestimated the severity of the threats to Germany's security and its economic survival. To rectify the grievous lack of foresight by the bureaucracy and politicians, as well as to eliminate shameless price-gouging and scandalous shortages of food—all issues graver than even the great Bismarck had faced—he outlined the following program:[13]

We [the Army League] demand the establishment of a Department of Wartime Economics, which would combine a strong armaments program with a comprehensive economic plan. The one is indispensable to the other. . . . The duties of this staff must extend beyond the term of this war. It must become a permanent fixture. . . . This staff should consist of: (1) representatives of the following Imperial Ministries: General Staff, Naval Office, Departments of Interior, Commerce, Transportation, and Treasury; (2) the commercial circles and associations, among these from agriculture, trade, the crafts, business, and labor; (3) the fields of law; (4) large municipalities; (5) other reputable individuals. The primary function of the staff would be to coordinate the arrangements for vital economic and social measures necessary for the winning of the war:

### I. FOOD SUPPLIES

(1) The securing of sufficient foodstuffs for the citizenry and the army.
(2) The setting of proper selling prices for wholesale and retail producers as well as for consumers.
(3) Cheap bread (unaffected by rising prices).
(4) Fixed wages for millworkers so the price of bread will correspond to the price of wheat.
(5) Elimination of all superfluous intermediate trading and the elimination of price-gouging and usury.
(6) Improvement in the availability of food and consumer goods like petroleum, spirits, cotton, flax, hemp, and other fabrics.
(7) State warehouses for distribution of foodstuffs to citizens . . . at fair (regulated) prices.
(8) Scientific establishment of a minimal daily nutritional requirement.
(9) Education of the masses in nutritional value through schools, lectures, and pamphlets.
(10) Complete and efficient utilization of all goods.

Several of v. Strantz's emphases were especially important. He stipulated that this Department of Wartime Economics should remain a permanent fixture, presumably on the grounds that if the transition from civilian economy to a wartime one had been difficult, the reverse was likely to be as well. It presupposed a degree of state intervention—even if leaning toward corporatism—that before the war many politicians, especially among Left Liberals, would have found difficult to accept. The role of civilian experts and the stress upon scientific formulation of universal standards suggested a technocratic bent designed to limit the latitude once enjoyed by party politicians. In that regard, of course, freeing national affairs from the uncontested grip of the parties and the government itself had been a familiar theme of the patriotic societies' efforts.

Finally, v. Strantz's memorandum, like Possehl's earlier proposals, was a reaction to perceived vulnerability. Germany was vulnerable externally to a two-front war and to blockade, but internally as well. The absolute priority of wartime production would strain a civilian population used to a consumer economy, but more seriously, it would give greater leverage to the working class. The prospect of well-organized trade unions was enough to alarm many Army Leaguers, who perhaps automatically equated such organizations with antinationalist inclinations (i.e., socialism and pacifism). But the sight of those workers striking in wartime, crippling the war effort, was almost too terrible to contemplate. Thus the stress on wage and price controls, and an adequate food supply, was all to contain, so far as possible, the seeds of industrial conflict.

The league's demands were rejected. Yet it realized that even domestic reorganization would, by itself, prove insufficient. In other words, in Germany's external relations, as in its internal affairs, it was not enough to return to the status quo ante bellum. Indeed, the Army League insisted that Germany could not expect its enemies to agree to a "moderate" peace settlement that recognized legitimate German demands. France was "vengeful [rachsüchtige]," Russia "insatiable [unersättliche]," and England "materialistic [goldgierige]." All therefore had compelling reasons to use any negotiated settlement to profit at Germany's expense. The French would stoop to anything to recover Alsace-Lorraine, the Russians were desperate for additional territory to accommodate their teeming masses, while the British, now incapable of competing on an equitable basis, would seize any opportunity to cripple the German economy. These attitudes toward the likely motivations of other countries were embodied in a list of war aims deemed essential by the Army League and published early in 1917 in Die Wehr.[14] Although these aims were revealed in the wake of the broader public discussions of war aims in November 1916, they had been communicated in private to Chancellor Hollweg earlier the previous year.

Their basic thrust was simple and direct. The nation, the Army League argued, must emerge from the war with "more territory . . . and a stronger economy."[15] The two goals were inseparably linked, for the latter could not be achieved without the former. Their scope, however, was breathtaking. The league's objective was to extend the German Empire's boundaries westward to include Belgium as a vassal state, northward to the Baltic, southward into the Tirol, and eastward through Polish territory.

Of particular interest to the league was Belgium, and its interests there were overseen by none other than General Keim himself. In September 1914 the Army League president had been summoned to the headquarters of the new German Governor General of Belgium in Brussels. Keim successfully discharged his first assignment from his former colleague in the General Staff and the new Governor General, Freiherr von der Goltz. He was rewarded with the military governorship of the Belgian province of Limburg, effective 1 November 1914.[16] Keim would be responsible for control of the province's administration, including the police, the local press, and the judicial system.

Keim aspired to do more, though, than merely keep order behind the lines. Belgium was a cultural battleground, and the indigenous conflict was directly relevant to the league's plans for a greater German state. Both Keim and the Army League's officials back in Berlin (especially v. Strantz) recognized that friction between the predominantly Catholic, French-speaking Walloons and the Protestant Flemish (who spoke a Germanic dialect) offered an opportunity to eliminate French influence in the region and Germanize its inhabitants.[17] Accordingly, Keim sought to portray the German occupation as an effort to protect and promote the Flemish language and culture with whose struggle against the alien French all good German nationalists sympathized. A local Flemish paper, the *Limburger Koerier,* applauded Keim's efforts, noting that "Belgian Limburg has found in its German governor a man for whom one must feel sympathy." The paper continued: "With body and soul he has helped the Flemish language because he is convinced that in the future there can be no better protection of Flanders' unique culture against Gallicism than the consistent cultivation of the Flemish language. . . . He has always been concerned about restoring the rights of the Flemish language—not just with words but with action. Early this year he decreed . . . that Flemish become the official language in Limburg."[18]

For once, perhaps, Keim found himself in complete agreement with the government in Berlin. Bethmann concurred that German assistance to the Flemish national movement would, as he explained to Wilhelm in February 1917, "constitute, politically, the best real guarantee for the future development of our relationship with Belgium."[19] Not surprisingly, Keim encountered especially harsh criticism from the French press. In fact, his tenure as governor of Limburg was clouded by accusations of improprieties and mistreatment of civilians. An article in *Le Matin* charged that Keim and his troops had occupied the estate of an emigré Belgian nobleman, imbibed from the owner's magnificent wine collection, and engaged in orgies. Keim, of course, dismissed these assertions as fabrications of an Allied propaganda machine that desperately sought to destroy his reputation and impede his pro-Flemish policies.[20] More serious accusations were raised regarding Keim's use of capital punishment, though he later claimed that Limburg had been teeming with spies, which justified such draconian measures.

The same mixture of political and economic objectives with more broadly cultural ones was evident too in the Army League's efforts to mobilize pro-German sentiment overseas. In 1914 v. Strantz suggested that Germany could play the role of international arsonist ("*Brandstifter*") to ignite the forces of nationalism in Ireland, India, Egypt, and Canada against the British government.[21] The promotion of internal subversion as a means of warfare found acceptance among both popular nationalist and governmental circles. On the eve of the war the Kaiser had announced his hope that the Islamic world would unleash a *jihad,* or holy war, against its foreign oppressors (who happened to be Germany's enemies as well), namely England, France, and Russia.[22] The Kaiser's penchant for the melodramatic was also echoed by more staid high-ranking diplomats like Count Bernstorff, the German Ambassador to the United States, and the former Colonial Secretary, Bernhard Dernburg, both of whom sought to manipulate anti-English sentiment among Irish-Americans to persuade the American government to remain neutral. To v. Strantz, however, whose efforts sometimes involved the kind of espionage and intrigue usually reserved for best-selling thrillers, subversion in the new world should also encompass sowing the seeds of Pan-Germanism among the country's estimated 30 million German-Americans. "The era of subservient nationalities is past, and the German-American community will have recognized finally that it no longer has to remain the servant to an English minority." Moreover, v. Strantz argued, "with the help of the Irish [i.e., Irish-Americans], it will make its majority count and will assert the equality of our language or destroy the Union."[23]

The Army League assumed that the reality of English administration of Ireland, and the failure of efforts to secure Home Rule, would provide a reservoir of animosity toward England that could be tapped, whether in peace or war. Already in July 1914 there had been clandestine efforts by independent German arms dealers to provide weapons for the Irish Republican Army.[24] Whether the German government sanctioned these arms deals is unclear, but Berlin recognized that an insurrection in England's backyard would deal a severe blow to that country. Logic dictated that subversive efforts in the United States might also reap benefits.

Both v. Strantz and Bernstorff were anxious to mobilize the German and Irish communities in America. Seeking to acquaint German-Americans with the Army League's aims, v. Strantz ensured that pamphlets were distributed to American branches of the Pan-German League and the Society for Germandom Abroad, as well as to various German-American veterans' associations.[25] The Army League reportedly maintained a branch in New York City, from which it operated a clandestine war relief network. The contributions that the league was able to solicit from patriotic German-Americans were quite impressive. At least two hundred thousand marks had been collected from various associations and found their way into the Army League's Dresden bank account by 1916.[26] Donors were publicly assured that the money would be used only toward humanitarian aid (food, clothing, and hospital items). Yet some (if not all) of what was collected was redirected for military purposes.

Only months prior to the April 1916 uprising in Ireland, the Army League recruited a long-time friend of General Keim's, Eduard Fürst zu Salm-Horstmar, to serve as the league's financial intermediary. The league's New York president, Herr E. Erler, was apparently ill-suited for his role as a fund raiser, since he was unable to assure donors that their contributions were being used for humanitarian purposes. In an urgent telegram to the Army League office in Berlin, Bernstorff suggested that the operations in the United States were being jeopardized by Erler's incompetence. "Please advise Prince Eduard Salm-Horstmar . . . that practices Erler here very objectionable," the telegram read. "He makes discord among German-Americans. Promises decorations for donations, etc.," Bernstorff continued. "Whole war relief work gravely endangered by suspicion created about ultimate destination of collected funds. Therefore . . . I had to advise societies here not send money Deutschwehr Berlin until actual business relations with Erler severed."[27] One day before the Easter Uprising in Ireland, American agents raided the Wall Street office of a German agent, a certain v. Igel, where they discovered documents implicating the German embassy in espionage.[28] Ambassador Bernstorff tried without success to secure the return of the documents to his custody.[29] While the incident disrupted the Irish-German network, it nevertheless failed to prevent the Army League from pursuing other means by which to ensure American neutrality and the defeat of Britain.

Germans like v. Strantz tried to demonstrate that no special relationship existed between America and England or that, if it did, comparable special relationships existed between America's Irish and German communities and their mother countries. If the strength of these latter could be demonstrated, it would influence American policy makers. Yet whatever the attractions of subversion, the continuing stalemate and the effects of Britain's blockade persuaded some German military and Army League officials that unrestricted submarine warfare was Germany's best chance of securing a decisive victory. The renewal of submarine warfare was a risky decision, however, for it substantially increased the likelihood of American intervention. Accordingly, between August 1916 (when Bethmann's overtures to consider a negotiated peace aroused a storm of indignation in popular nationalist circles) and January 1917, the German government pondered the possible consequences of renewing unrestricted use of submarines with a view toward determining if the possible military benefits outweighed the obvious risks.

To v. Strantz the risks were less significant, because he badly underestimated America's military capacity and its resolve to fight if provoked. "I rather pity [the U.S.]," was his contemptuous assessment to v. Jagow, "because the Union's army and navy are worthless."[30] Moreover, v. Strantz was confident that Irish- and German-Americans would cripple Wilson's chances for reelection in November 1916 by voting en masse for his opponent.[31] Even if that failed, v. Strantz entertained delusions that the Irish and German communities would rebel against the American government's policy. Indeed, other Germans shared his optimism. Foreign Minister Arthur Zimmermann insisted that if the American government declared war on Germany, some five hundred thousand German-Americans would revolt, and, he suspected, that they could expect Mexican assistance as well.[32]

On 9 January 1917, then, the German government decided to resume unrestricted submarine warfare on 1 February in an attempt to bring Britain to its knees by July. In April, of course, the United States entered the war, thereby giving the weary Entente a much-needed psychological and military boost. The American decision prompted v. Strantz to vent his displeasure on the government for having failed to support fully his subversive fantasies. "I have always taken the view that our complacency toward North America would hurt us," he complained bitterly.[33]

At one time I seriously suggested to v. Jagow that the German and Irish Americans wanted to invade Canada and [would] buy only German weapons and ammunition for that purpose. Von Jagow informed me that we could not offer any help . . . [but] if the Japanese were to advance through Canada to Europe, he would support this [plan]. It seems to me that now is the time to make such an offer to the German and Irish Americans. Wilson is frightened of this and it would still be desirable if we could in some way strengthen this movement.

Recognizing the psychological impact of American intervention, the Army League was determined to demonstrate in no uncertain terms that Germany remained committed to waging war until it won a decisive victory. Reports that many Germans now supported a Scheidemann Peace (one without territorial annexation) rather than a more draconian Hindenburg Peace had to be countered as erroneous. Therefore June 1917 found the redoubtable v. Strantz in Scandinavia seeking to mobilize support among countries that, culturally if not always diplomatically, maintained links to the Germanic people. He timed his mission to coincide with the Stockholm Conference, a gathering in early June of the various Socialist parties to discuss the prospects of peace. While the Socialists wrestled with this issue, v. Strantz met with sympathetic Swedes and Danes to reassure them that, contrary to newspaper accounts, only a small percentage of Germany's population subscribed to the peace proposals of the Socialists, Progressives, and Centrists. Scheidemann's and Erzberger's propositions, which they defended as a peace which brought "no enforced repression of peoples and frontier areas," were, in the Army League's view, inadequate and inappropriate.[34]

He had particularly harsh words for the Swedish Minister Wallenberg and the prominent Swedish Socialist Branting. Both were Germanophobes who hindered the Army League's efforts to secure Swedish support for German policy, especially territorial annexation in the Baltic. In part this renewed attention to Sweden reflected the Army League's growing disenchantment with Germany's Austrian allies, whose incompetence, v. Strantz suggested, had hampered Germany's ability to capture Petersburg and the Åaland islands.[35] The mission to Sweden also demonstrated the way economic and cultural objectives intertwined in the league's attitude toward the Baltic. The entire area, including parts of the Ukraine, was, according to v. Strantz, distinctly underpopulated. It offered an ideal location for German colonization, with soil and climate more akin to that of the eastern part of the Reich itself. He calculated that an additional 15 million German settlers could live in these areas without difficulty, cultivating grain or engaging in trade and commerce (the port of Riga would prove especially valuable).[36] Some 3 million ethnic Germans living within Russian borders could be reunited with their kinfolk, thus strengthening the cultural ties of the German nation.[37] Problems of overcrowding in German cities could be cured, and new settlers living a hardy agrarian life would be less exposed to the fallacies preached by the SPD. The result would be a more homogeneous, prosperous, and stable German Empire.

Of course, the Army League had been interested in the Baltic before 1914. In this sense, as in so many others, the war accelerated existing trends and brought to the surface ones that had lain submerged. League branches had solicited donations from members for an *Ostseeanwohnerspende,* a fund that provided humanitarian relief to poorer German residents as well as to those whose property was damaged by flooding. At the league's third annual meeting, symbolically held in Posen, a keynote address highlighted the issue of German nationality in the Eastern Marches.[38] The league conveniently neglected to mention that only about 7 percent of the Baltic's population were ethnic Germans (the vast majority being Estonians and Letts), and that Germans there had since the eighteenth century enjoyed special privileges conferred upon them by the Russian tsars.[39] They were not, therefore, exactly the subservient nationality that the Army League portrayed them to be. Nonetheless, the league exploited the sentiments of some Baltic Germans who yearned for reconciliation with the Fatherland.

Grandiose annexationist schemes nevertheless failed to conceal the fissures within the league. The war did not prove to be a panacea for Germany's perceived ills—moral degeneration, the spread of pacifistic and socialist values, and the gradual weakening of the patriotic fibre. Nor did it serve as a catalyst for the propagation of the league's goals or the expansion of its membership. Rather, mounting casualties, labor unrest, and general war weariness undermined the league's influence. The war also altered the league's complexion, as Keim, v. Liebert, and Litzmann left their offices on the Bernburgerstrasse in Berlin for comfy posts on the western and eastern fronts. Dietrich Schäfer found new avenues for his nationalist endeavors in the *Unabhängiger Ausschuss für einen deutschen Frieden* (the Independent Committee for a German Peace, 1916), which he founded and served as president, as well as in the *Deutsche Vaterlandspartei* (the German Fatherland Party, 1917).

In the absence of these officials, the league's activities were coordinated by a group of dedicated members who had served the association in various other capacities. Upon Keim's departure to Belgium in September 1914, vice president v. Baltazzi assumed the general's presidential responsibilities, assisted by v. Strantz and league secretary Gustav Horst Sieber, an American-trained physician.[40] From September 1915 until December 1916 v. Strantz, along with *Geheime Räte* Georg Zacher and Friedrich Schwartz, administered the league's daily operations. Imperial Admiral Graf Friedrich A. A. v. Baudissin, former commander of North Sea naval operations and of the Kaiser's private yacht, the *Hohenzollern,* tended to the league's affairs from January 1917 until the war's conclusion.[41]

The war wreaked havoc as well upon the *Gesamtausschuss* and local executive boards, whose members often succumbed to enemy bullets or, in some cases, hardening arteries. To offset the losses, new members were added. Like their predecessors, they tended to be men of some stature: Carl Röchling, a steel magnate and National Liberal, Dr. K. Oskar Poensgen, chairman of the Oberbilk Steel Works and a member of the Young Liberals, and Wilhelm Schwaner, the editor of the racist journal *Deutscher Erzieher.*[42] It was easier, however, to comb the country for a handful of willing notables than to recruit the hundreds of individuals necessary to staff the many local executive boards. These local branches, often the hardest hit by deaths, resignations, or departures, experienced growing difficulties in conducting branch affairs. The Munich branch, for example, tried but failed to replace seven of its ten board officials, while in East Prussia a critical shortage of leaders led to the dissolution of many branches. And it was upon these men that the league really depended to exercise influence beyond Berlin. The damage was readily apparent, even in Berlin itself. One of the most active and populous chapters, that in Berlin-Friedenau, could not overcome the toll exacted by casualties and indifference. In 1916 that branch reported that at least 160 of its 810 original members "could no longer be persuaded to maintain their membership in the association."[43] Moreover, these figures did not include the indefinite number of other members killed, captured, invalided, or simply out of touch.

Yet the league's national executive urged branches to carry on in the face of adversity in the best Prussian tradition. Despite mounting evidence of staggering casualties and inefficient prosecution of the war effort, the league continued to advocate festivities celebrating Bismarck's and the Kaiser's birthdays and commemorating Sedan Day. Also suggested were *Bierabende* as a means of maintaining interest in the association's goals and recruiting new members. Following these directives, the Soest branch in Westphalia, for example, held a "patriotic evening" honoring the "heroes" who served in the U-Boats. National headquarters in Berlin constantly reminded branches of the gravity of the situation and the consequent importance of combining instruction and entertainment. It extolled the example of one enthusiastic member who alone had encouraged twenty-four individuals to join the league.[44] But such examples of devotion were rare indeed.

More common as a survival technique was the collaboration of local Army league branches with other patriotic societies. This had already been practiced before 1914, but the war necessitated more intensive and frequent cooperation. Thus associations with similar goals (a Hindenburg Peace) and facing similar problems (dwindling members, funds, public interest) could pool their resources to avoid individual dissolution. The Army League's branches frequently held meetings or planned festivals with local chapters of the Pan-German and Navy leagues, the Eastern Marches Society, the Independent Committee for a German Peace, and, after September 1917, the Fatherland Party (*Vaterlandspartei*).[45] Cooperation also extended to "clearinghouses" for the major patriotic societies, the Information Bureau of the United Associations (*Auskunftsstelle Vereinigter Verbände*), and the Central Coordinating Committee (*Hauptvermittlungsstelle Vaterländische Verbände*).[46]

Sharing goals and members could not by themselves alone alleviate the league's tenuous financial position. Throughout the war it teetered on the brink of bankruptcy. The league's officials agreed to maintain dues at a one mark minimum as long as was financially feasible. They placed frequent notices in *Die Wehr,* urging members to pay their outstanding dues, but with no success.[47] By 1917 the league's treasury had become so depleted that the executive committee voted to abandon paying the postage for subscriptions to *Die Wehr*. Thereafter, regional federations were entrusted with the task of distributing copies of the journal to members, and in most cases, individual subscribers were forced to retrieve the journal's copies at their own expense from the federation offices. Of course, this cost-saving move served to disrupt the valuable lines of communication between rank and file and the executives, and impeded the league's ability to attain its prescribed goals. Efforts to compensate for declining subscriptions by attracting sizable individual donations occasionally bore fruit. For example, Otto Graf v. Baudissin, brother of the league's president, convinced officials of the Gutehoffnungshütte and the Northwest Group of the League of German Iron Industrialists to donate at least ten thousand marks.[48] But the money was too little too late and only served to underscore the inconsistent and insufficient financial support the Army League had received from Germany's wealthy industrialists.

With its membership and finances continuing to dwindle throughout 1917, the

Army League's tirades became more strident, its Anglophobic and racist rhetoric more virulent. Britain and France were not just Germany's military nemeses; their particular cultures posed a threat to Germany's own unique heritage. Even before 1914 the Army League had warned against Germans' allowing foreign words to creep into the vernacular and foreign haberdashery and mores into their homes. The war required even greater vigilance by Germans against any further intrusions of foreign ideology and traditions, for the Allies were bent on subverting Germany from within as well as destroying it from without. "We cannot afford to allow our children to be better educated with the actions and sayings of the ancient Jews, Greeks, and Romans than with our own history, [and to] master foreign languages rather than our own mother tongue," the league insisted. "The German language, German history, German customs and knowledge of our national heritage must be our fulcrum and backbone."[49]

Should Germans not heed the Army League's dire strictures, England would surely impose upon Germany the same treatment it meted out to its vast colonial possessions. England's strength, as the league viewed it, lay in its ability to disseminate English culture throughout an indigenous population, thereby disrupting native traditions and rendering the local community defenseless against their colonial oppressors.[50] The French imitated English methods, whether it was by infiltrating the cultural network of the Walloons in Belgium or subduing African natives.[51] The Allies (but especially the British) were likened by the league to vultures who sought to pick clean the bones of a decaying German nation. Everything was at stake, as the league explained, "For us it does not matter whether we win or lose a few colonies, or if our trade balance will be 20 Milliards . . . or 25 Milliards. . . . What really is at issue is something spiritual, and the enemy . . . is England."[52]

Clearly, the Army League asserted, far-reaching changes were necessary to secure military victory and preserve German culture. In 1917 the league renewed its demand for a comprehensive program to prepare Germany's youth. If not implemented, the nation's prospects were bleak, as they would also be if political changes were not undertaken. "Unfortunately, one looks to the future with great anxiety," wrote Salm-Horstmar to Keim that August. "On the horizon there is no political clairvoyant or resolute individual either in the military high command or in the Wilhelmstrasse."[53] The call for strong, resolute leadership resounded in the platform of the German Fatherland Party, in whose foundation in September 1917 some prominent members of the Army League were instrumental.

Conceived in 1916 by Dr. Wolfgang Kapp, the Fatherland Party elicited the support of Keim, Schäfer, and Salm-Horstmar. After undergoing several name changes—Hindenburg Party, Bismarck Party, German Unity Party—the Fatherland Party emerged to proclaim itself the one party that represented the interests of the German people.[54] Rather than slate candidates for the Reichstag, it preferred to appropriate the nonpartisan image of the patriotic societies. The Party's goals mirrored those of the Army League and the other patriotic associations: only a Hindenburg Peace would be acceptable. Under its auspices, Belgium would be annexed, its Flemish population and resources preserved from Allied pollution and exploitation, and the stranglehold by England would be broken. With these goals achieved, the

Party would become irrelevant. Its constitution, therefore, provided for the Party's existence only until the end of the war, whereupon it would be dissolved.

The founding of the new party, presided over by Admiral v. Tirpitz, met with a varied response. To popular nationalists like Salm-Horstmar, the Party finally offered the prospect of energetic direction of the war effort. He optimistically wrote to Keim, "The public's enthusiasm for the first meeting was very heartening. Moreover, I am firmly convinced that we must immediately launch an assault against the government, if it fails to renounce the parliamentary majority."[55] Indeed, the Party's membership tripled between March and July 1918 from 450,000 to 1,250,000 (roughly the size of the Navy League's prewar combined corporate and individual membership), but then declined to less than 800,000 by September 1918.[56] It seemed briefly in 1917 that the Fatherland Party would be able to achieve what the Army League and the patriotic societies had thus far failed to do—replace war weariness with resolve and unite Germans to insist upon complete victory at the expense of the Allies. As the war wore on and strikes multiplied, however, refusing to accept anything less than a victory with annexations began to seem less plausible. According to the report of the police president of Frankfurt am Main, for example, 90 percent of the 4,000 to 5,000 individuals participating in a Fatherland Party rally in that city on 14 January 1918 were opposition demonstrators, not party enthusiasts. "It was clear that the vast majority of the participants wanted to disrupt the meeting," the police president informed the *Oberpräsident* of the province of Hesse-Nassau. "The urgent appeals for quiet went unheeded, and without the main speaker having uttered a word, the meeting was adjourned."[57] Similar incidents had occurred at rallies in Mannheim and Berlin, the police official added. Already reeling, the Fatherland Party dissolved upon the conclusion of the armistice, in accordance with the provision of its constitution, a mere fourteen months after its foundation.

In anticipation of the impending armistice and upon the occasion of the annual meeting in October 1918 (only the second convened since the war's outbreak), Army League officials revised the league's constitution. The more substantial changes concerned financial matters: annual dues increased from an annual minimum of 1 mark to 3 marks, a donation of 300 marks automatically entitled one to lifetime membership, while 3,000 marks bestowed the title of "honorary league sponsor" upon the generous donor.[58] All were efforts to increase the attractiveness of sponsorship of the league and thus resolve its financial problems. Administratively, the *Ausschuss* (executive council) was enlarged from the original twenty-one to a maximum of thirty individuals. The council, however, continued to be elected for a three-year term by all members present at the annual meeting. The composition of the *Gesamtvorstand* (general council) and the responsibilities of the two governing councils were unaffected.

This reorganization, however, failed to stimulate any new enthusiasm or substantive donations. Of the 350,000 individual members recorded in 1914, 31,000 at best remained in 1919, and only 251 diehards were left by 1922.[59] Gone, too, were many of the league's guiding spirits. In 1919 General Keim returned from Belgium to resume his leadership, but at age seventy-five, persistent pain from old war wounds and cancer forced him to relinquish his position shortly thereafter to retired

Lieutenant General Max Schwarte.[60] Keim, nonetheless, remained on as honorary president until his death in 1926.[61] Eduard v. Liebert found solace in the Pan-German League and the racist *Gobineau Vereinigung*. Karl Litzmann offered his services as an independent lecturer to paramilitary and youth associations and in 1929 joined the Nazis (National Socialist German Workers Party [NSDAP]).[62] Hermann Müller-Brandenburg had served in the war since 1914 and, like many young men of the "Iron Generation," was unable to readjust to civilian society after the war. In the early 1920s he became a police chief in Thuringia, then led a paramilitary association (*Wehrwolf*) between 1926 and 1928, and later accepted the post as press chief of the Brandenburg *Stahlhelm* from 1928 until 1932.[63] Only Kurd v. Strantz remained loyal to the Army League until the bitter end in 1935.

The stipulations of the Treaty of Versailles—a 100,000 man army, reparations payments, and war guilt clause—confirmed the league's dire predictions about Germany's fate in the wake of defeat. General Keim, along with a host of other popular nationalist leaders, led the charge against Germany's internal as well as external enemies.[64] On both accounts, Keim blamed the Allies, but particularly the English, for the outbreak of World War I and the subsequent domestic upheavals. The general explained that, despite the military and economic rivalry that existed between England and Germany before 1914, Germany had not contemplated launching a preemptive strike against the Allies that would lead to war in 1914. To have done so, Keim argued, would have been to commit "economic suicide." The English, on the other hand, had a powerful motive for going to war. The publication of E. E. Williams's *Made in Germany* figured as an example of the prewar paranoia with which the English viewed German economic competition.[65] Furthermore, Keim charged that the German army's drive into Belgium had not violated Belgian neutrality in 1914. Rather, he claimed, Belgium had forfeited its neutral status when in 1906 it had signed a formal agreement with France and Britain against Germany.[66] Thus in 1919 Keim continued to portray Germany as a nation surrounded by enemies eager to destroy the Fatherland. The Army League, therefore, maintained its raison d'être.

The league entered the Weimar Republic with a renewed determination to see its goals to fruition. These now included the revocation of the Treaty of Versailles, the defeat of Bolshevism, and the protection of the rights of veterans.[67] Equally urgent was its demand for the creation of an "Iron Youth" upon which Germany could build its future. As its new motto, the Army League chose "Standing still amounts to retreat [*Stillstand ist Rückschritt*]" to emphasize its resolve to crush the spirit of *Vogel-Strauss Politik* that persisted in the Weimar Republic. All its goals were still cloaked in the image of nonpartisanship, as echoed in the following poem:[68]

Jetzt ist nicht Zeit zum Wühlen,
Nicht Zeit für die Partei.
Jetzt ist es Zeit, zu fühlen,
Dass eins das Grösste sei.

Das Land, aus dessem Schosse,
Uns Leib und Geist erstand,

Das heilige, das grosse,
Das deutsche Vaterland.

As insistent as the Army League was in accomplishing its specific goals, it was especially intent on curing Germany's national malaise. Germany's defeat was in part a failure of will, a distressing lack of national consciousness. "It would appear that [since] . . . the murder of Hermann the Conqueror by his own compatriots . . . this ancient curse has plagued the German people [and] has once again been fulfilled," wrote Keim, adding, "The Germans [are] their own traitors."[69] Likewise, Karl Litzmann bemoaned his countrymen's appalling lack of unity in times of crisis, remarking, "I would characterize the spirit of Bismarck as the fear of God and self-reliance, manliness, military preparedness and loyalty, [and] radiant patriotism . . . [but] Bismarck's heritage was destroyed through the fault of our people; it can only be revived, if the Germans find the Bismarckian spirit once again."[70] For Eduard v. Liebert, "an old man in the twilight of his life, who had followed the spectacular emergence of the Bismarckian Reich [and] who had fought and bled for it," it was "terribly depressing and shameful to have to witness the [German] people in its current deplorable condition."[71] "In no other nation is nationalism so poorly developed as in ours," Dietrich Schäfer explained. "We must fortify [our] national pride and [ensure ourselves] of the basic familiarity with national questions."[72] The most derogatory assessment of all was Kurd v. Strantz's contention that the Germans were a "politically immature people."[73]

But what variables determined political maturity and national consciousness? The Army League and its leaders reserved the right to interpret the ideals of the Iron Chancellor in a way calculated to meet the demands of German public life. For, as it had proclaimed before the war, education of the masses was the proper course by which Germans could be inculcated with the leaders' conception of a true Bismarckian legacy—physical strength, self-discipline, obedience, and nationalism. By 1919 these ideals—army, defense, and honor (*Volksheer, Volkswehr, Volksehr*)— became more explicitly racist.[74] It is perhaps not coincidental that this additional stress on racial purity generally found greatest acceptance among the league's younger leaders. The way to political maturity and national consciousness after 1919, then, could be found in the recognition that Germans belonged to a special race that would emerge someday to inherit its rightful and dominant place in the world community. "What unifies the nation?," one *Die Wehr* article posed: "The knowledge of being a racial community [*Blutgemeinschaft*]. What was it that hindered the Austro-Hungarian Empire in its life and death struggle? The treachery of foreign blood. The war teaches us [the importance] of pursuing '*völkische Politik.*' *Völkisch* is more than just social. National + social = *völkisch.*"[75]

To prevent Germany's further moral, physical, and economic decay, Germans were to be taught that the Allies, Bolsheviks, and especially the Jews were their eternal enemies. Salm-Horstmar wrote Keim in 1920 that the nation's recovery depended on its ability to recognize its enemies and to defeat them:

Even if we must encounter more arduous times, I cannot abandon my hopes for Germany's future and its new ascent. I am entirely convinced that our *Volk* from the worker to the peasantry perceives more and more that its real enemy is Judaism. Not only among our people but also among most other peoples there is the realization that the world's peaceful evolution can be brought about only through their liberation from Judaism. . . . The fight to the finish between the gentiles and the bloodsuckers of mankind is yet to be waged.[76]

The league's anti-Semitic rhetoric was linked to its belief that the Jews, Allies, and Bolsheviks had all along conspired to destroy Germany's imperial government, capitalist economy, and Prussian army. Excerpts from the *Protocols of the Elders of Zion* appeared in a 1920 issue of *Die Wehr* with a brief yet poignant commentary at the end that warned against allowing the Jews to realize their plan of *Weltherrschaft,* world domination.[77] "We view the solution to the Jewish question as one which concerns the very fate of our people," one Army League member charged. "The domination of vital aspects of our economic and public life by Judaism, that racially foreign [self-contained] state within a state, must be prevented under all circumstances because this would endanger German culture and undermine the stability and destroy our people. Our people must be shielded from the putrid elements of materialism and internationalism which are sustained by Judaism."[78]

In 1920 *Die Wehr* served as a platform through which a member of the league, *Volkswirt* Rüse, unveiled his new *Deutsche Gemeinschaft,* a nonpolitical association devoted, as he contended, not to pursuing *Parteipolitik* but rather *Volkspolitik.* Once again the nonpartisan refrain resounded, calling all Army League adherents and other nationally minded Germans to support its effort to forge the long sought-after and seemingly elusive national community. Emphasizing the need to achieve a complete economic recovery and to implement universal military service, Rüse's new *Gemeinschaft* also recognized explicitly the urgency with which to resolve the "Jewish Question," although he offered no details as to how this "fateful question" could be dealt with.[79]

Exactly to what extremes the Army League pursued the racial ideology postulated by Rüse and other members, including Otto Schmidt-Gibichenfels, Friedrich v. Mühlmann, and Georg Wilhelm Schiele, to name just a few, is rather difficult to assess, owing to the destruction of archival material during the Second World War.[80] Above all, one must remember that the Army League throughout the 1920s and until 1935 was incapable of holding its own ground as a popular nationalist association. Its membership and funds drained by the war, the league was forced to rely even more heavily upon corporate memberships with a variety of other right-wing associations. The league continued to maintain its association with the Central Coordinating Committee established in 1917 and branched out from there to corporate membership in the *Stahlhelm,* a paramilitary group, the *Deutscher Offiziersbund* and the *Nationalverband Deutscher Offiziere,* and the *Vaterländische Verbände.*[81] In 1922 the Army League barely clung to life; its 251 members were dispersed throughout sixty branches. Nevertheless, it limped along until the *Gleichschaltung,* and in 1935 was forced into dissolution, disappearing into the murky waters of National Socialism.

# Conclusion

The popular nationalist movement as embodied in the German Army League was devised and orchestrated by an activist minority for whom popular nationalism was a means by which to expand the restrictive ideological and political framework within which they perceived Germans to have been debilitatingly constrained. By mobilizing the opinions of German citizens, in particular those of the middle classes, in order to redirect the course of nationalist politics, the Army League activists intended to prove themselves more effective leaders than Germany's ruling bureaucrats. While the Army League included members of the petite bourgeoisie, it certainly did not represent a petite bourgeois impulse either before or after World War I. The majority of its leading officials at the national and even local level stemmed from middle-class and, upon occasion, aristocratic backgrounds; they were generally well-connected and influential officers, bureaucrats, and businessmen who showed disdain for aristocratic intransigence that obstructed the conduct of foreign and domestic politics. Aristocrats' abhorrence of direct taxation, an increase in middle-class officer recruits, and modern military technology, they insisted, threatened the nation's security. Yet as much as conservative aristocrats posed an obstacle to the Army League's goal of achieving national consensus, the league's leaders readily accepted many of the same values that aristocrats had claimed to embody for centuries—martial virtues, honor, and obedience. Thus by dint of their respectable social origins and their belief that only they comprehended the true meaning of nationalist commitment, Army League activists composed a new kind of notable, the *Verbände Honoratioren*.

Popular nationalism, thus, was a movement based upon the distorted vision of these *Verbände Honoratioren*. By apotheosizing the deeds and intentions of the Iron Chancellor, these men lost their perspective upon the post-1890 decades and, consequently, advocated more radical solutions to older problems. No one could measure up to the "father of the nation"; thus, in comparison, the decades after his departure from politics appeared decadent and chaotic. A frequent complaint was that although Bismarck had consolidated the German Empire, his successors had nearly squandered that precious inheritance by failing to provide comparably firm but decisive leadership. "The basic mistake in our politics," Keim observed, "has been that we have lost sight of an age old proverb that politics is the will to power."[1] "We wanted to avoid a second Jena; after 1890, however, we suffered more than one Olmütz," was v. Strantz's assessment of government policy in the post-Bismarckian era, which, he added, suffered from a "lack of direction [*Ziellosigkeit*]" and conviction.[2]

Yet Bismarck was an appropriate symbol for these men perhaps even aside from his unification of the Empire and the repression of *Reichsfeinde*. Like the Chancellor himself, the *Verbände Honoratioren* struggled to reconcile bourgeois roots with aristocratic traditions.[3] Industry and urban growth produced the sinews of German power. But it was the countryside they associated with communal values. The urban working class continued to be addressed in a paternalistic fashion, its patriotism to be ensured by military indoctrination rather than taken for granted as a consequence of German birth or residence. Parliamentary government was at best a necessary evil whose baneful influence could be moderated by substituting national interests for sectional or partisan ones. As much as the Army League's leaders were interested in courting the masses, though, they neither trusted them nor were willing to delegate power to them. This ambivalence, as well as their devotion to the cult of Bismarck, reflected the Protestant, liberal environment from which so many stemmed.

The ability of the *Verbände Honoratioren* to promote the Army League's goals owed largely to two factors: Germany's misadventures in Morocco in 1911 and a general perception by Germans that the spiraling arms race conducted by France, England, and Russia necessitated immediate qualitative and quantitative improvements in the German army. Many of those individuals who joined the league before 1914 did so because they were apprehensive at the possibility of "encirclement"; by advocating the passage of two consecutive and more extensive army bills in 1912 and 1913, they were hoping to solve a problem that seemed both very real and pressing, and they were demonstrating their patriotism by responding to a tangible objective. Nonetheless, the Army League perceived its goals more broadly. Yet stagnating membership in 1913, followed by precipitously declining figures throughout the war and thereafter, suggested that the league's members remained unconvinced by the league's less tangible aims—the creation of a spiritual *völkisch* community guided by martial and nationalistic precepts. Their nationalistic fervor, as Keim and other popular nationalists complained in 1919, resembled a light switch that was easily turned on and off. Despite the league's impressive propaganda and persistent efforts to secure a German victory in the First World War, members failed to respond to its wider message.

In its strident criticism of the government's conduct of foreign and domestic policies, in its appeal to the *Volk* for justification of its nationalistic demands, and in its excessive use of propaganda, the Army League represented a radical style of politics that was becoming evident by 1890. Circumstances were too grave to allow for compromise in the forging of a new nationalism. "We must prevail and win or . . . lose and suffer." These, as the Army League never tired of repeating, were the alternatives. "We must be either the anvil or the hammer. . . . With sword in hand we *shall* be the hammer and our enemies the anvil."[4] But the league's inability to impose its nationalistic vision upon its members or the German nation as a whole,

and the continued domination of both its leadership and rank and file by the educated middle class, cast doubt on the depth of any petite bourgeois impulse or
breadth of the complete transformation of the Right by 1918.

The Army League and the popular nationalist movement that it represented was a
product of the Wilhelmine age; its survival into the Third Reich, however, raises the
ever-elusive question of whether National Socialism suggested a degree of continuity with the recent past or a departure from that tradition. While this question
cannot be answered satisfactorily in this brief discussion, these reflections are meant
as a point of departure. The circumstances contributing to the NSDAP's ascendancy
differed from those that had predicated the rise of the Wilhelmine patriotic societies.
In 1918, in contrast to the aftermath of the Franco-Prussian War, Germans lan-
guished under a dictated peace and a shattered economy. There was, nonetheless, a
degree of continuity discernible in the responses of both the Army League and the
NSDAP to the particular circumstances each encountered. One thread weaving
together these nationalistic tapestries was the search for a balance between the
forces of modernity and tradition.[5]

Both popular nationalism and National Socialism were products of deeply rooted
structural changes in German life often loosely subsumed under the term "modernization." The shift within a few decades from an agrarian society to an urbanized,
industrialized one, the erection of a national parliamentary system, and the emergence of an avowedly socialist labor movement all transformed much of the nation's
accustomed physical and intellectual landscape. Both movements were ambivalent
toward these changes. For example, industrialization sustained Germany's efforts to
achieve international recognition as a major economic and military power, to engage
in *Weltpolitik*. On the other hand, it aggravated domestic instability, appearing to
accelerate the spread of crime, immorality, squalor, and disease and thereby to
produce fertile soil for socialism. Traditional virtues of order, obedience, and patriotism were assumed to be waning, replaced by materialism, individualism, and
internationalism. The excessive nationalism of the popular nationalist and National
Socialist movements was the response to this perceived decline in the national
character.

Since the nation's malaise could be attributed to capitalism's growth, how did
these movements propose to restore Germany to good health? The remedy certainly
did not involve simply the return to some preindustrial, rural Arcadia. Popular
nationalist and National Socialist propaganda extolled the virtues of the soil and the
values of artisan culture, to be sure, but it also sought to alleviate certain deplorable
aspects of industrial society (materialistic greed and individualistic expression). Of
course, these currents (reverence for the land and the community) predated the
Wilhelmine period and survived the Nazi era. Even today this emphasis on nature is
apparent in many Germans' obsession with tending small plots of land, joining
horticultural or garden associations, and voicing their concerns about the destruction
of Germany's forests by industrial pollutants (as demonstrated by support for the
"Greens.")

Germany's "nationalist revival" ultimately depended upon the condition of its
economy. Given their ambitious foreign policies, the leaders of the popular na-

tionalist and National Socialist movements alike insisted that the German economy function as effectively and efficiently in wartime as in peacetime. Creating a buoyant and invulnerable economy capable of meeting these criteria entailed harmonizing the interests of industry with those of agriculture. It therefore necessitated, in their view, subsuming individual and materialistic desires for the good of the nation. It also meant avoiding possible obstacles to economic autonomy and efficiency. Not only were raw materials and an adequate labor supply essential, but labor's productive capacity and political acquiescence depended upon sufficient and inexpensive food and adequate wages. Achieving this, of course, would necessitate the expansion of German borders; at the very least, it would require soliciting patriotic workers and enlisting civilian experts. The popular nationalist scheme for a Wartime Economic General Staff was evidence of this desire. So, too, despite the absence of a concrete economic program of their own, was the Nazis' commitment to maintain "technological momentum."[6]

The army reflected as well the relentless (if futile) search for a middle ground. The traditions it embodied—authoritarianism, obedience, nationalism—were extolled, as was Frederick the Great, under whose leadership Prussia developed into a first-rate military power. General Keim quoted his maxims frequently in speeches, while Hitler eagerly and frequently compared his hands and skull shape to his illustrious Prussian predecessor. But if these two extreme nationalist movements admired the army as the apotheosis of Prussian traditions, they also promoted notions of military modernization. In particular, the Army League's insistence on infusing the aristocratic officer corps with middle-class candidates and bringing the army in line with the latest military technology can be seen as an attempt to relegate possibly stultifying aspects of Prussia's military traditions in favor of ones more appropriate to contemporary conditions. The NSDAP established its own paramilitary auxiliary which, until the so-called Night of the Long Knives, might have appeared to threaten the army's own monopoly of legitimate force. Clearly, too, the Nazi leadership lacked the patrician bearing characteristic of many of the Wilhelmine era's notables, and Hitler did not hesitate to discredit old-line aristocratic officers when it served his purposes to do so.

Aside from a common interest in synthesizing the forces of modernity and tradition, the leaders of the popular nationalist and National Socialist movements shared a revulsion for parliamentary politics. They both rebuked the Reichstag for failing to provide constructive criticism and effective leadership, condemning it as a banal institution whose politicians greedily pursued sectional and personal interests and ignored the communal interests of their constituents. But popular nationalists and National Socialists approached the issue of parliamentary democracy from different perspectives.

Members of the popular nationalist movement included politicians who served in national or regional parliaments and citizens who considered themselves avid affirmers at and of the ballot box. How can one explain their sustained critique of parliamentary politics in view of this predilection for the political process? Condemnation of the vagaries of parliamentary politics, of the practice of *Kuhhandel*, of the increasing influence of economic interests in the decisions of domestic and foreign policy, was intended by some league members to prod Germans to improve what was in their view a potentially useful forum whose current practice was misguided and materialistic. By subsuming sectional or special interests to the common de-nominator of nationalism, they hoped perhaps to instill a sense of dignity and unity into the political process, without necessarily promoting its demise. The Army League did not advocate, at least not publicly, the elimination of monarchical or parliamentary institutions, nor did it find it necessary to offer any kind of alter-native. Yet undeniably there were others within the league who from the outset vehemently rejected parliamentary politics and advocated its eradication in favor of an authoritarian system.

If popular nationalists could not agree on the fate of parliamentary government, National Socialists, on the other hand, completely repudiated the idea from the start. Throughout its period of gestation (1919–23), the NSDAP adopted the *Putsch* as the primary means by which the Weimar Republic was to be exorcised. But when the *Putsch* failed to accomplish its objective, Hitler abandoned this tactic in favor of ostensibly legitimate means. From 1924 onwards the Nazis used the constitutional framework provided by Weimar to transform themselves into a political party with representation in the Reichstag in order eventually to destroy the system from within. "We shall have to hold our nose and enter the Reichstag against the Catholic and Marxist deputies," Hitler explained from Landsberg prison in 1924, and con-tinued, "If outvoting them takes longer than outshooting them, at least the results will be guaranteed by their own constitution!"[7] By presenting itself as a legitimate and enthusiastic political party and as the only true *Volkspartei,* the NSDAP was able to attract Germans who in the past had just as routinely voted for the parties of the middle. If, however, the Nazis had made their intentions clear from the outset about demolishing the parliamentary system, would these same Germans, some of whom ritualistically came out to vote in Wilhelmine elections, have supported the NSDAP? Hitler observed upon his decision to ban all political parties in 1933: "The political parties have now been finally abolished. This is an historic event, the meaning and significance of which many people have not yet understood."[8]

In 1933 parliamentary government disappeared as quickly as it had been imple-mented in 1871. The end of the political system signaled the Nazification or coordi-nation of so much of that to which Germans had previously been accustomed. Popular nationalists certainly had never been in a position to impose a policy of this magnitude; in retrospect, it appears unlikely they would have done so if they had found themselves in a position of power. The message that its leaders sought to deliver was to be accomplished without eradicating traditional networks of par-ticipation and authority; educating the masses meant instruction by example, not subordination through terror.

# Notes

## Introduction

1. Until the appearance of this book, the Army League largely escaped critical assessment. Erich Schwinn's "Die Arbeit des Deutschen Wehrvereins und die Wehrlage Deutschlands vor dem Weltkriege," (Ph.D. diss., Heidelberg, 1940) is little more than a hagiographic account. Kurt Stenkewitz gives an overview of the league in "Deutscher Wehr-verein, 1912–1935," in Dieter Fricke, ed., *Die bürgerlichen Parteien in Deutschland 1830–1945* (Leipzig, 1968–70), 1: 574–81, as well as in Stenkewitz, *Gegen Bajonett und Dividende: Die politische Krise in Deutschland am Vorabend des ersten Weltkrieges* (Berlin, 1960), 74ff. Roger Chickering offers a more sensitive and accurate account in "Der Deutsche Wehrverein und die Reform der deutschen Armee, 1912–1914," *Militärgeschichtliche Mitteilungen* 25 (1979): 7–33, and idem., *We Men Who Feel Most German: A Cultural Study of the Pan-German League, 1886–1914* (London, 1984), 267–77. For the most detailed examination of the Army League, see my articles, "The Mobilization of the Right? The Deutscher Wehrverein and Political Activism in Württemberg, 1912–14," *European History Quarterly* 15 (1985): 431–52, and with Frans Coetzee, "Rethinking the Radical Right in Germany and Britain before 1914," *Journal of Contemporary History* 21 (1986): 515–37. The remaining works discuss the Army League in passing: Jürgen Kuczynski, *Studien zur Geschichte des deutschen Imperialismus* (Berlin, 1950), 2: 74–81; G. W. F. Hallgarten, *Imperialismus vor 1914* (Munich, 1963), 2: 267–87; Fritz Fischer, *War of Illusions: German Policies from 1911 to 1914* (New York, 1975), 105–9; Gerhard Ritter, *The Sword and the Scepter: The Problem of Militarism in Germany* (Coral Gables, Fla., 1969), 2: 223; Gordon Craig, *Germany, 1866–1945* (Oxford, 1978), 295; Dieter Groh, *Negative Integration und revolutionärer Attentismus: Die deutsche Sozialdemokratie am Vorabend des Ersten Weltkrieg* (Frankfurt a.M., 1973), 341–42; Klaus Wernecke, *Der Wille zur Weltgeltung* (Düsseldorf, 1970), 174–78; Martin Kitchen, *The German Officer Corps, 1890–1914* (Oxford, 1968), 135–39; and Geoff Eley, *Reshaping the German Right: Radical Nationalism and Political Change after Bismarck* (New Haven, 1980), 328–30.

2. Thomas Nipperdey, "Verein als soziale Struktur in Deutschland im späten 18. und frühen 19. Jahrhundert," in Hartmut Boockmann, ed., *Geschichtswissenschaft und Vereinswesen im 19. Jahrhundert* (Göttingen, 1972), 4. See also Otto Dann, "Die Anfänge politischer Vereinsbildung in Deutschland," in Ulrich Engelhardt, Volker Sellen, and Horst Stuke, eds., *Soziale Bewegung und politische Verfassung* (Stuttgart, 1976), 197–232.

3. Nikolai Gogol, *Dead Souls* (Harmondsworth, 1961), 99; "Since a spectacle like that is a real godsend to a peasant, just as a newspaper or club is to a German."

4. Nipperdey, "Verein als soziale Struktur," 10–11.

5. James J. Sheehan, *German Liberalism in the Nineteenth Century* (Chicago, 1978), 14; Nipperdey, "Verein als soziale Struktur," 22.

6. Nipperdey, "Verein als soziale Struktur," 34.

7. On this associational revival, see Ingo Tornow, *Das Münchner Vereinswesen in der ersten Hälfte des 19. Jahrhunderts* (Munich, 1977); Herbert Freudenthal, *Vereine in Hamburg* (Hamburg, 1968); Wolfgang Meyer, *Vereinswesen der Stadt Nürnberg im 19. Jahrhundert* (Nürnberg, 1970); Heinz Schmitt, *Das Vereinsleben der Stadt Weinheim an der Bergstrasse* (Weinheim, 1963); Klaus Tenfelde, "Die Entfaltung des Vereinswesens während der industriellen Revolution in Deutschland (1850–1873)," in Otto Dann, ed., *Vereinswesen und bürgerliche Gesellschaft in Deutschland* (Munich, 1984), 55–114. Figures are from Tornow, *Das Münchner Vereinswesen*, 8. The Hessian university town of Marburg recorded one association for nearly every one hundred inhabitants by 1913, according to Rudy Koshar, *Social Life, Local Politics, and Nazism: Marburg, 1880–1935* (Chapel Hill, 1986), 130.

8. Tornow, *Das Münchner Vereinswesen*, 8.

9. Jonathan Sperber, *Popular Catholicism in Nineteenth-Century Germany* (Princeton, 1984), 81. See also Sperber, "Der Kampf um die Feiertage in Rheinland-Westfalen, 1770–1870," in Wolfgang Schieder, ed., *Volksreligiosität in der modernen Sozialgeschichte* (Göttingen, 1986), 123–36, and "The Transformation of Catholic and Artisan Associations in the Northern Rhineland and Westphalia, 1830–1870," *Journal of Social History* 15 (1981): 253–63.

10. Schmitt, *Das Vereinsleben der Stadt Weinheim*, 97.

11. There is a sizeable literature on the patriotic societies. The best general accounts include the two-volume compilation edited by Dieter Fricke, *Die bürgerlichen Parteien*, which has recently appeared in a new four-volume edition, *Lexikon zur Parteiengeschichte: Die bürgerlichen und kleinbürgerlichen Parteien und Verbände in Deutschland, 1789–1945* (Leipzig, 1983–1986); Dirk Stegmann, *Die Erben Bismarcks: Parteien und Verbände in der Spätphase des wilhelminischen Deutschlands* (Cologne, 1970); idem., "Vom Neokonservatismus zum Proto-Faschismus: Konservative Partei, Vereine und Verbände, 1893–1920," in Dirk Stegmann, ed. *Deutscher Konservatismus im 19. und 20. Jahrhundert* (Bonn, 1983), 199–230; Hartmut Pogge von Strandmann, "Nationale Verbände zwischen Weltpolitik und Kontinentalpolitik," in H. Schottelius and W. Deist, eds., *Marine und Marinepolitik im kaiserlichen Deutschland, 1871–1914* (Düsseldorf, 1972), 296–317; Hans-Ulrich Wehler, "Zur Funktion und Struktur der Nationalen Kampfverbände im Kaiserreich," in Werner Conze, Gottfried Schramm, and Klaus Zernack, eds., *Modernisierung und nationale Gesellschaft im ausgehenden 18. und 19. Jahrhundert* (Berlin, 1979), 113–24; Roger Chickering, "Patriotic Societies and German Foreign Policy, 1890–1914," *International History Review* 1 (1979): 470–89. More recent contributions include Jost Dülffer and Karl Holl, eds., *Bereit zum Krieg. Kriegsmentalität im wilhelminischen Deutschland, 1890–1914* (Göttingen, 1986); David Blackbourn, "The Politics of Demagogy in Imperial Germany," *Past and Present* 113 (1986): 152–84; Coetzee and Coetzee, "Rethinking the Radical Right"; Geoff Eley, "The Wilhelmine Right: How It Changed," in Richard J. Evans, ed., *Society and Politics in Wilhelmine Germany* (London, 1978), 112–35. Recent historiographical surveys include Wolfgang Mock, "'Manipulation von oben' oder Selbstorganisation an der Basis? Einige neuere Ansätze in der englischen Historiographie zur Geschichte des deutschen Kaiserreichs," *Historische Zeitschrift* 232 (1981): 358–75; Robert Moeller, "The Kaiserreich Recast?: Continuity and Change in Modern German History," *Journal of Social History* 17 (1984): 655–83. For specific works on the Society for the Eastern Marches, the Colonial

Society, and the Imperial League against Social Democracy, see Adam Galos, Felix-Heinrich Gentzen, and Witold Jakóbczyk, *Die Hakatisten: Der Deutsche Ostmarkenverein 1894–1934* (Berlin, 1966); Richard W. Tims, *Germanizing Prussian Poland: The H-K-T Society and the Struggle for the Eastern Marches in the German Empire* (New York, 1941); William W. Hagen, *Germans, Poles, and Jews: The Nationality Conflict in the Prussian East, 1772– 1914* (Chicago, 1980). On the Colonial Society, see Woodruff D. Smith, *The German Colonial Empire* (Chapel Hill, 1978); Mary Evelyn Townsend, *The Rise and Fall of Germany's Colonial Empire, 1884–1918* (New York, 1930); Richard V. Pierard, "The German Colonial Society, 1882–1914" (Ph.D. diss., University of Iowa, 1964). Dieter Fricke's studies on the Imperial League against Social Democracy remain the best published sources for this organization: Fricke, "Der Reichsverband gegen die Sozialdemokratie von seiner Gründung bis zu den Reichstagswahlen von 1907," *Zeitschrift für Geschichtswissenschaft* 7 (1959): 237–80, and idem., "Der Reichsverband gegen die Sozialdemokratie, 1904–1918," in Fricke, *Die bürgerlichen Parteien,* 2: 620–30.

12. Membership figures, which have been rounded off to the nearest thousand, are drawn from Eley, *Reshaping the German Right,* 366; Chickering, *We Men Who Feel Most German,* 323; Fricke, "Der Reichsverband gegen die Sozialdemokratie, 1904–1918," 2: 625; and *Die Wehr,* Heft 6 (1914).

13. As cited in Freudenthal, *Vereine in Hamburg,* 445–46. I should like to thank my colleague Jeffrey Sammons for his advice in rendering a felicitous translation of Wriede's poem.

14. Fritz Fischer, *Germany's Aims in the First World War* (New York, 1967), xxii.

15. See, in particular, the discussion of Rosenberg's and Wehler's works in Geoff Eley, *From Unification to Nazism: Reinterpreting the German Past* (London, 1986), and, more generally, David Blackbourn and Geoff Eley, *The Peculiarities of German History: Bourgeois Society and Politics in Nineteenth-Century Germany* (Oxford, 1984).

16. The term "new orthodoxy" was applied by James Sheehan in the *Journal of Modern History* 48 (1976): 566–67.

17. Eley, "The German Navy League in German Politics, 1898–1914" (D. Phil. thesis, University of Sussex, 1974).

18. Geoff Eley, "Sammlungspolitik, Social Imperialism and the Navy Law of 1898," reprinted in idem., *From Unification to Nazism,* 110–53.

19. Ibid., 10. See, in addition, Eckart Kehr, *Economic Interest, Militarism, and Foreign Policy* (Berkeley, 1977), passim.

20. Eley, "Sammlungspolitik," 143.

21. Eley, *Reshaping the German Right,* 41 ff. For insightful reviews that place Eley's work in context, see Richard J. Evans, "From Hitler to Bismarck: Third Reich and Kaiserreich in Recent Historiography: Pt. II," *Historical Journal* 26 (1983), especially 1003–7, and Moeller, "The Kaiserreich Recast?," especially 660–64.

22. Eley's most lucid and concise account of the patriotic societies can be found in his "Some Thoughts on the Nationalist Pressure Groups in Imperial Germany," in Paul Kennedy and Anthony Nicholls, eds., *Nationalist and Racialist Movements in Britain and Germany before 1914* (London, 1981), 40–67.

23. Eley, *Reshaping the German Right,* 15.

24. Ibid., 326–27.

25. Ibid., 24–40.

26. James J. Sheehan, "Political Leadership in the German Reichstag, 1871–1918," *American Historical Review* 74 (1968): 512.

27. Eley, "The German Right: How It Changed," in idem., *From Unification to Nazism,* 243.

28. Ibid., 245–48.

29. Ibid., 246.

30. Ibid., 246–47.

31. Eley, *Reshaping the German Right*, 355.

32. Ibid., 119.

33. Ibid., 48.

34. Roger Chickering also corroborates my conclusion regarding the social origins of these radical nationalists in his *We Men Who Feel Most German*, 110–18.

35. Eley, *Reshaping the German Right*, 201. See also Coetzee and Coetzee, "Rethinking the Radical Right," 526.

36. Eley, "Some Thoughts on the Nationalist Pressure Groups," 53.

37. Eley, *Reshaping the German Right*, 47; idem., "Some Thoughts on the Nationalist Pressure Groups," 51.

38. Sheehan, *German Liberalism in the Nineteenth Century*, 278.

39. I came across this phrase in the *Kölnische Volkszeitung*, no. 1132, 28 December 1907.

40. Coetzee and Coetzee, "Rethinking the Radical Right," 523.

41. Eley, "The German Right," 247.

42. Fischer, *War of Illusions*, 106; Stenkewitz, "Deutscher Wehr-verein," 2: 576.

## Chapter 1

1. Volker Berghahn, *Germany and the Approach of War in 1914* (London, 1973), 76; Peter-Christian Witt, *Die Finanzpolitik des Deutschen Reiches von 1903 bis 1913* (Lübeck, 1970), 380 (Table 14).

2. Adolf Wermuth, *Ein Beamtenleben* (Berlin, 1922), 304.

3. Wermuth as quoted in Berghahn, *Germany and the Approach of War*, 84.

4. Witt, *Die Finanzpolitik*, 17–23.

5. Ibid., 153.

6. Ibid., 199ff.; see also Beverly Heckart, *From Bassermann to Bebel. The Grand Bloc's Quest for Reform in the Kaiserreich, 1900–1914* (New Haven, 1974), 77–82.

7. Heckart, *From Bassermann to Bebel*, 80; Berghahn, *Germany and the Approach of War*, 83.

8. As quoted in Berghahn, *Germany and the Approach of War*, 114.

9. B. S. Townroe, *A Nation in Arms* (London, 1910), 37. Bernard S. Townroe of Warrington, England, was an organizer for the National Service League and a Unionist candidate in Lancashire.

10. Fischer, *War of Illusions*, 117–18.

11. Eley, *Reshaping the German Right*, 48.

12. Chickering, *We Men Who Feel Most German*, 49, 51–52.

13. Ibid., 52.

14. On the league's formative development, see ibid., 53–69.

15. Ibid., 323 (Chart 10.1).

16. Ibid., 62.

17. Eley, *Reshaping the German Right*, 81. The Navy League has been largely the domain of Geoff Eley: "The German Navy League in German Politics"; *Reshaping the German Right;* "Sammlungspolitik"; "Defining Social Imperialism: Use and Abuse of an Idea," *Social History* 3 (1976): 265–90; "Social Imperialism in Germany: Reformist Synthesis or Reactionary Sleight of Hand?" in Joachim Radkau and Imanuel Geiss, eds., *Imperialismus im 20. Jahrhundert: Gedenkschrift für Georg W. F. Hallgarten* (Munich, 1976), 71–86;

"Reshaping the Right: Radical Nationalism and the German Navy League, 1898–1908," *Historical Journal* 21 (1978): 327–54. Wilhelm Deist's *Flottenpolitik und Flottenpropaganda* (Stuttgart, 1976) remains an excellent source on the Navy League as well.

18. Eley, *Reshaping the German Right*, 83.

19. For details on its founding, see Eley, *Reshaping the German Right*, 72–85, and Deist, *Flottenpolitik*, 147–94.

20. Eley, *Reshaping the German Right*, 87.

21. Ibid., 92.

22. The details of the campaign are recounted in Eley, *Reshaping the German Right*, 90–98.

23. Ibid., 336 (Appendix 3).

24. Ibid., 192; Chickering likewise suggests that the Pan-German League lost members to the Navy League; see *We Men Who Feel Most German*, 257.

25. On Würtzburg's role, see Eley, *Reshaping the German Right*, 180–83, 267–79.

26. Ibid., 181. On the Center's arrogance, see Blackbourn, *Class, Religion, and Local Politics in Wilhelmine Germany* (London, 1980), 37–38.

27. Eley, *Reshaping the German Right*, 265.

28. I am grateful to Herr Gerd Keim of Seeheim-Jungenheim for allowing me access to his grandfather's papers, which he has recently deposited in the Bundesarchiv/Militärarchiv, Freiburg. On Keim's life, see also his autobiography, *Erlebtes und Erstrebtes: Lebenserinnerungen* (Hanover, 1925).

29. Keim's efforts with regard to the Army Bill of 1893 are described in J. Alden Nichols, *Germany after Bismarck: The Caprivi Era, 1890–1894* (Cambridge, Mass., 1958), 192–264.

30. Eley, *Reshaping the German Right*, 224.

31. Eley, "The German Navy League in German Politics," 215.

32. On the election of 1907, see George Crothers, *The German Elections of 1907* (New York, 1941). Keim's electoral activities are chronicled in Konrad Schilling, "Beiträge zu einer Geschichte des radikalen Nationalismus in der Wilhelminischen Ära, 1890–1909," (Inaugural diss., Universität Köln, 1968), ch. 3, especially 287–306; Eley, "The German Navy League in German Politics," 218ff., and idem., *Reshaping the German Right*, 271–74; Deist, *Flottenpolitik*, 194–210. In addition, see Bundesarchiv Koblenz (hereafter cited as BAK), Reichskanzlei Akten no. 1807, Keim to v. Loebell, 4 January 1907; Stresemann to Keim, 8 January 1907; and Keim to Günther, 15 January 1907. The Navy League Crisis received considerable press from the Center Party's organ, *Kölnische Volkszeitung*. See especially issue nos. 1072–1130, 9–28 December 1907.

33. Landeshauptarchiv Koblenz, Oberpräsidium der Rheinprovinz, 403/9529, Keim to Cardinal Fischer, 24 May 1907.

34. Ibid.; see as well Fischer to Keim, 4 May 1907. The quotation above reproduces Keim's spelling of the bishop's name, but it is possible that he was in fact referring to Bishop Ketteler. Keim was a member of the *Anti-ultramontaner Reichsverband* (Imperial Anti-Ultramontane Society), which sought to eradicate the political influence in Germany of the Catholic Church. The society claimed a membership of approximately three hundred as of 1912 and was led by retired admiral v. Knorr, this according to the *Kölnische Zeitung*, no. 576, 19 May 1913.

35. Hauptstaatsarchiv Stuttgart (hereafter referred to as HSAS), E 14 Bü 1345, Deutscher Flottenverein, v. Urach to v. Pflaum, 8 January 1908.

36. HSAS, E 14 Bü 1345, Deutscher Flottenverein, v. Urach to v. Pflaum, 8 January 1908.

37. Eley, *Reshaping the German Right*, 278; Deist, *Flottenpolitik*, 247. Deist estimated

that approximately 15,000 or roughly 5 percent of the Navy League's 300,000 members seceded in 1907–8.

38. Heinrich Class, *Wider den Strom* (Leipzig, 1932), 157. For a further assessment of Keim, see Class, 157–60.

39. On the rise of demagogy in German politics, see David Blackbourn, "The Politics of Demagogy in Imperial Germany."

40. Zentrales Archiv Potsdam (hereafter cited as ZAP), ADV no. 192, Geiser to Class, 21 July 1908. A letter dated 4 June 1908 also suggested that by constantly seeking funds for his venture, Keim was provoking dissension (*Zwietracht*) within the Pan-German League.

41. On the league's commitment to maintain its image as a pioneer, see Chickering, *We Men Who Feel Most German,* 192.

42. ZAP, ADV no. 192, Class to Reventlow, 15 July 1908.

43. ZAP, ADV no. 406, Pohl to Class, 3 April 1909.

44. ZAP, ADV no. 406, Putz to Class, 19 November 1910.

45. Ibid.

46. ZAP, ADV no. 194, President of Pan-German League Berlin branch to Class, 18 February 1912. Keim had been suggested as a replacement for Herr Solger. The author of the above remark thought General Hans v. Wrochem would be a more suitable choice. See in addition *Alldeutsche Blätter,* no. 14, 9 April 1910.

47. Keim, *Erlebtes und Erstrebtes,* 159. Keim sat on the executive committee through 1919.

48. Class realized that the "Old Man" was not a Pan-German at heart, yet their friendship persisted. According to Keim's grandson, Class continued to show generosity toward Keim's family after the general's death.

49. Keim, *Erlebtes und Erstrebtes,* 153–58.

50. Ibid., 157–58.

51. Ibid., 153–56.

52. Ibid., 157.

53. Stig Förster, *Der doppelte Militarismus. Die deutsche Heeresrüstungspolitik zwischen Status-quo-Sicherung und Aggression, 1890–1913* (Stuttgart, 1985), 185–86.

54. *Alldeutsche Blätter,* no. 38, 17 September 1910.

55. The crisis is described in full in Klaus Wernecke, *Der Wille zur Weltgeltung* (Düsseldorf, 1970), 26ff., and Emily Oncken, *Panthersprung nach Agadir: Die deutsche Politik während der zweiten Morokkokrise, 1911* (Düsseldorf, 1981); Förster, *Der doppelte Militarismus,* 208–16.

56. *Alldeutsche Blätter,* no. 32, 12 August 1911.

57. *Alldeutsche Blätter,* no. 52, 30 December 1911.

58. Chickering, *We Men Who Feel Most German,* 265.

59. Keim, *Erlebtes und Erstrebtes,* 164–94.

60. In his memoirs Class reveals that he remained behind the scenes and chose not to accept a visible position on the Army League's executive council. Class, *Wider den Strom,* 221. Historians have generally viewed the Army League as a Pan-German puppet. See, for example, most recently, Stig Förster, *Der doppelte Militarismus,* 226–27.

61. *Alldeutsche Blätter,* passim.

62. ZAP, ADV no. 406, Class to Keim, 2 April 1912.

63. ZAP, ADV no. 406, C. C. Eiffe to Class, 4 January 1912.

64. According to Roger Chickering, the Pan-German League "spent the last four years prior to the war . . . swimming in money." Chickering, *We Men Who Feel Most German,* 228.

65. ZAP, ADV no. 406, Class to Keim, 2 April 1912.

66. Chickering, *We Men Who Feel Most German,* 225. In 1909 the Pan-German League had quietly removed funds from the *Wehrschatz* to prevent bankruptcy, but thereafter the fund was replenished with the aid of Alfred Hugenberg and a contingent of other wealthy industrialists.

67. On Possehl's activities in the Pan-German League, see Class, *Wider den Strom,* 229–32. Upon the death of his father in 1875, the twenty-five-year-old Possehl inherited the family iron, tin, and coal company. Helmut Niendorf chronicles Possehl's life in *Geschichte des Handelshauses Possehl, 1847–1919* (Lübeck, 1957). Unfortunately, the Possehl Stiftung of Lübeck has no records pertaining to the Senator's nationalistic activities. There is no comparable biography of Neumann. That Neumann and Class were indeed good friends is suggested by Class's choice of Neumann in June 1913 to represent the Pan-German League in delicate negotiations with the Agrarian League. Class, *Wider den Strom,* 100–01, 271. Neumann (1865–1928) served as a member of the Lübeck Senate and as Mayor of Lübeck and joined the Pan-German League Presidium in 1904.

68. ZAP, ADV no. 406, Class to Keim, 2 April 1912.

69. ZAP, ADV no. 406, Keim to Class, 23 September 1912.

70. Ibid.

71. Ibid.

72. Politisches Archiv/Auswärtiges Amt, Bonn (hereafter cited as PA/AA Bonn), Deutschland 121, no. 33, Deutscher Wehrverein, Poelchau to v. Bülow, 22 February 1912.

73. PA/AA Bonn, Deutschland 121 no. 33, C. Adolph Jacobi to Freiherr Ernst Langwert v. Simmern, 5 March 1913. Ironically, Schäfer was a member of the Pan-German League.

74. On the 1912 elections, see Jürgen Bertram, *Die Wahlen zum deutschen Reichstag vom Jahre 1912* (Düsseldorf, 1964); *Der Tag,* "Wahl und Wehrkraft," 24 December 1911.

75. Keim, *Erlebtes und Erstrebtes,* 165.

76. *Alldeutsche Blätter,* no. 52, 30 December 1911.

77. The best sources on French military expansion remain Gerd Krumeich, *Aufrüstung und Innenpolitik in Frankreich vor dem Ersten Weltkrieg* (Wiesbaden, 1980). Subsequent references are to the recent English translation by Berg Publishers: *Armaments and Politics in France on the Eve of the First World War.* (Leamington Spa, 1984). Douglas Porch, *The March to the Marne: The French Army, 1871–1914* (Cambridge, 1981); and David B. Ralston, *The Army of the Republic: The Place of the French Military in the Political Evolution of France, 1871–1914* (Cambridge, Mass., 1967).

78. The One Percent Law was part of Bismarck's Iron Budget of 1867, which remained in effect from 1867 until 1894, and was the Iron Chancellor's attempt to wrest from the Reichstag control of military matters dealing with peacetime troop strength and military funding. On this point, see Gordon Craig, *Germany, 1866–1945* (Oxford, 1978), 51–53, and idem., *Politics of the Prussian Army* (Oxford, 1955), 220.

79. Keim, *Erlebtes und Erstrebtes,* 170.

80. *Die Wehr,* Heft 3 (1912).

81. Keim, *Erlebtes und Erstrebtes,* 171.

82. *Leipziger Volkszeitung,* "Der Wehrverein," 29 January 1912.

83. *Der Tag,* "Der neue Wehrverein und die Marine," 13 January 1912.

84. Ibid.

85. *Der Tag,* "Ist eine Volksaufklärung über die Armee nötig?" 21 January 1912.

86. Lord Roberts, as cited in *Hansard,* 10 July 1906, col. 658. Keim might also have used Balfour's statement as further ammunition: "Never forget that a fleet without an army is a fleet robbed of half its virtues." Balfour, as cited in the *Annual Report of the National Union of Conservative and Unionist Associations,* 19 November 1908, 42. I should like to thank my husband, Frans, for calling this to my attention.

87. *Der Tag,* "Ist eine Volksaufklärung über die Armee nötig?," 21 January 1912.
88. Deutscher Wehrverein Schrift 2, "Die Notwendigkeit eines Deutschen Wehrvereins," (1912), 9. Keim also claimed that the Navy League's constitution prohibited any such amalgamation.

## Chapter 2

1. Repington is quoted in English in Bernd-Felix Schulte, *Die deutsche Armee, 1900–1914: Zwischen Beharren und Verändern* (Düsseldorf, 1977), 43. For a shrewd characterization of Repington, see A. J. A. Morris, *The Scaremongers* (London, 1984), 111–22, and Repington's own *Vestigia* (London, 1919).
2. Fischer, *War of Illusions,* 119.
3. Details on the rivalry between Tirpitz and Bethmann are found in Deist, *Flottenpolitik,* 292–314; Fischer, *War of Illusions,* 120–21; and Berghahn, *Germany and the Approach of War,* 116–21.
4. As quoted in Fischer, *War of Illusions,* 120.
5. As quoted in Berghahn, *Germany and the Approach of War,* 120.
6. On the Haldane Mission, see Fischer, *War of Illusions,* 123–28.
7. "Warum muss Deutschland sein Heer verstärken?," *Schriften des Deutschen Wehrvereins,* (1912), 2, 3.
8. Ibid., 10.
9. Douglas Porch, *March to the Marne,* 177–78.
10. Ibid., 177.
11. Ibid., 196. See also Allan Mitchell, "'A Situation of Inferiority': French Military Reorganization after the Defeat of 1870," *American Historical Review* 86 (1981): 49–62. *Die Wehr* is filled with articles concerning the plight of the German NCO. See, for example, "Zur Hebung des Unteroffizierstandes in der Armee," Heft 4 (1912); "Der Unteroffizier und Militäranwärterfrage," Heft 1 (1913). Keim was particularly concerned about safeguarding the NCO against socialism and proposed that anyone under the age of twenty-one be legally barred from joining a trade union or political party to ensure that potential recruits were not influenced by socialist ideas. *Jahrbuch für die deutsche Armee,* 1905. For Keim the NCO was "the cement which fortifies the internal structure of the armed forces." *Die Wehr,* Heft 3 (1912).
12. Krumeich, *Armaments and Politics in France,* 22.
13. Porch, *March to the Marne,* 192.
14. Hauptstaatsarchiv Düsseldorf, Schloss Kalkum (hereafter referred to as HSAD), Regierung Düsseldorf, Antilegionsverein, 1907–23, no. 16017.
15. HSAD, Antilegionsverein, *Oberbürgermeister* of Crefeld to *Regierungspräsident,* 4 January 1908. The mayor reported: "Since 1900 we have had only eight young fellows serve in the French Foreign Legion and these were drawn to it by youthful frivolity and a lust for adventure."
16. *Stenographische Berichte über die Verhandlungen des Reichstags,* vol. 264, 24 February 1911.
17. PA/AA Bonn, Deutschland 122, no. 3, Bd. 25, Journalisten, v. Strantz to v. Jagow, 21 January 1913.
18. *Alldeutsche Blätter,* 29 April 1911.
19. According to *Wer ist's* (1912), Ferdinand Graudenz v. Papen was a publicist and held a doctorate.
20. PA/AA Bonn, Frankreich 95, no. 6, Die Französische Fremdenlegion.

21. Ibid.

22. PA/AA Bonn, Frankreich 95, no. 6, Die Französische Fremdenlegion, Schoen to Hollweg, 28 October 1913. Figures for the Legion's second division were not provided.

23. Historisches Archiv der Gutehoffnungshütte Oberhausen (hereafter cited as HA/GHH), no. 300 1071/4, Nordwestliche Gruppe des Vereins deutscher Eisen und Stahlindustrieller, 1913–14.

24. *Kölnische Zeitung*, "Gegen die Fremdenlegion," no. 184, 16 February 1914. Although Army League members agreed upon the dangers of the Foreign Legion, there was no consensus on the best way of combating the problem. For example, some executive members of the Württemberg provincial federation feared that a massive anti-Legion campaign might lead to the opposite of the desired effect. The Württemberg executives failed to agree upon how best to use the issue, concluding only that "the Army League should proceed very cautiously with its anti-Foreign Legion strategy." HSAS, E 14 Bü 1389, Protokoll über die dritte Gesamtvorstandssitzung am 22. Nov. 1913.

25. *Stenographische Berichte*, vol. 284, 22 April 1912. Further details on the Army Bill of 1912 are found in Förster, *Der doppelte Militarismus*, 233–47.

26. *Stenographische Berichte*, vol. 284, 22 April 1912.

27. *Die Wehr*, Heft 3 (1912).

28. *Stenographische Berichte*, vol. 285, 10 May 1912.

29. Ibid., vol. 284, 24 April 1912.

30. Berghahn, *Germany and the Approach of War*, 134–35; Fischer, *War of Illusion*, 205ff., 237, 259ff.

31. Karl Litzmann, *Lebenserinnerungen* (Berlin, 1927–28), 1: 144.

32. A member of the house of Hohenzollern-Sigmaringen, Carol of Romania became king in April 1866. Lothar Gall, *Bismarck: The White Revolutionary* (London, 1986), 1: 345.

33. As quoted in Fischer, *War of Illusions*, 177.

34. Ibid., 179.

35. Ibid., 161–64.

36. As quoted in ibid., 160.

37. Förster, *Der doppelte Militarismus*, 266.

38. Ibid., 267.

39. *Die Wehr*, "Der Unteroffizier und Militäranwärter Frage," Heft 1 (1913), 3–6. Also, see above n. 11. Keim met with Heeringen on two occasions, the 8th and 26th of December, according to Hermann Müller-Brandenburg, *Von Schlieffen bis Ludendorff* (Leipzig, 1925), 27.

40. Förster, *Der doppelte Militarismus*, 271.

41. Ibid., 250.

42. Ibid., passim.

43. Graefe's condemnation was published in *Der Tag*, 8 February 1913. See Förster, *Der doppelte Militarismus*, 276–77.

44. Keim to Eugen Schiffer, 10 February 1913, as quoted in Förster, *Der doppelte Militarismus*, 277.

45. PA/AA Bonn, Deutschland 122, no. 3, Bd. 25, Journalisten, v. Strantz to v. Jagow, 21 January 1913.

46. Förster, *Der doppelte Militarismus*, 271.

47. Ibid., 272.

48. HSAS, E 14 Bü 1389, Protokoll über die zweite Gesamtvorstandssitzung am 5. April 1913; *Die Wehr*, Heft 3 (1913).

49. HSAS, E 14 Bü 1389, Protokoll über die zweite Gesamtvorstandssitzung am 5. April 1913.

50. Berghahn, *Germany and the Approach of War*, 154; Fischer, *War of Illusions*, 182; Förster, *Der doppelte Militarismus*, 256, 273; Witt, *Die Finanzpolitik*, 357.

51. The new bill entailed a nonrecurring expenditure of 884,000 marks and a yearly expenditure of 183,000,000 marks. Förster, *Der doppelte Militarismus*, 272; Witt, *Die Finanzpolitik*, 364; Matthias Erzberger, "Der Wehrbeitrag," in George v. Schanz and Julius Wolf, eds., *Finanzwirtschaftliche Zeitfragen* (Stuttgart, 1913), 2: 1–33. Already at the league's first annual meeting, Adolph Wagner, a member of the *Verein für Sozialpolitik* as well as the Army League, called upon the wealthier classes to pay their fair share of the military burden by means of a direct tax. *Die Wehr*, Heft 3 (1912).

52. "Wer die Wehrvorlage verwirft ist ein Volksfeind!" Schrift 6 (1913): 14–15.

53. *Der Tag*, 3 May 1910.

54. HSAS, E 14 Bü 1389, Protokoll über die zweite Gesamtvorstandssitzung am 5. April 1913.

55. *Die Wehr*, "Gedanken zur Wehrsteuer," Heft 4 (1913).

56. "Wer die Wehrvorlage verwirft ist ein Volksfeind!" 12.

57. Förster, *Der doppelte Militarismus*, 282.

58. Details on the funding for the 1913 Army Bill are found in Witt, *Die Finanzpolitik*, 367–76, and Förster, *Der doppelte Militarismus*, 287–91.

59. Müller-Brandenburg, *Von Schlieffen bis Ludendorff*, 12.

60. Ibid., 13.

61. The French Three-Year Law sought to lengthen the term of service from two to three years, increase the number of men on active duty, and improve the quality of the reserves. See Porch, *The March to the Marne*, 191–212.

62. Militärarchiv Stuttgart, (hereafter referred to as MAS), M 730, Bd. 527, 25 September 1913.

63. Ibid.

64. Ibid.

65. MAS, M 730, Bd. 527, 26 September 1913.

66. Keim, *Erlebtes und Erstrebtes*, 193.

67. MAS, M 730, Bd. 527, 26 September 1913.

68. On the Zabern Affair, see David Schoenbaum, *Zabern 1913: Consensus Politics in Imperial Germany* (London, 1982); Hans-Ulrich Wehler, "Symbol des halbabsolutistischen Herrschaftssytems: Der Fall Zabern von 1913/14 als Verfassungskrise des Wilhelminischen Kaiserreichs," in *Krisenherde des Kaiserreichs, 1871–1918* (Göttingen, 1970), 65–84; Fischer, *War of Illusions*, 287–90; Berghahn, *Germany and the Approach of War*, 174–79.

69. *Stenographische Berichte*, vol. 294, 5 May 1914.

70. Ibid., 6 May 1914; see also "Deutscher Reichstag," *Vossische Zeitung*, no. 229, 7 May 1914.

71. *Stenographische Berichte*, vol. 294, 5 May 1914.

72. Ibid.

73. Ibid., 6 May 1914.

74. Ibid.

75. Ibid.

76. Ibid.

## Chapter 3

1. There is no comprehensive analytical study of propaganda in the prewar period comparable to those by Z. A. B. Zeman, David Welch, Jay Baird, and Ian Kershaw for the Nazi era. Two studies of the topic that are useful for purposes of background or comparison

are Peter Kenez, *The Birth of the Propaganda State: Soviet Methods of Mass Mobilization, 1917–1929* (Cambridge, 1986), and J. A. C. Brown, *Techniques of Persuasion, From Propaganda to Brain-washing* (London, 1972).

2. *10 Jahre Reichsverband gegen die Sozialdemokratie* (Berlin, 1914).

3. Stanley Suval's *Electoral Politics in Wilhelmine Germany* (Chapel Hill, 1985) examines the changes in voter attitudes toward the electoral process.

4. Thomas Kohut, "Mirror Image of the Nation: An Investigation of Kaiser Wilhelm II's Leadership of the Germans," in Charles B. Strozier and Daniel Offer, eds., *The Leader. Psychohistorical Essays* (New York, 1985), 86–107.

5. Gary D. Stark, "Cinema, Society, and the State: Policing the Film Industry in Imperial Germany," in Gary D. Stark and Bede Karl Lackner, eds., *Essays on Culture and Society in Modern Germany* (College Station, Tex., 1982), 126.

6. HSAS, E 14 Bü 1345, Deutscher Flottenverein, "Jahresbericht des Deutschen Flottenverein für das Jahr 1912," 11.

7. *Die Wehr,* Heft 6 (1913).

8. On the notion of the state above politics, see the stimulating discussion in Blackbourn and Eley, *The Peculiarities of German History,* 238–60.

9. Paasche and Dewitz are discussed in Chapter 5. Karl Heckmann (1874–1947), a miner in Bochum, was invalided as a result of a mining accident in 1911 yet managed to get himself elected on a National Liberal platform to the Reichstag (1912–18). According to Socialist Reichstag deputy Hermann Gottfried Sachse, who was also a miner, the National Liberals used Heckmann's injuries to make political capital during the 1912 elections. Sachse recounted how during the campaign Heckmann was carried from one speaking engagement to the next in late 1911, in an attempt to play upon the sympathy of the voters for the National Liberals. Heckmann won the seat for Bochum over his Socialist opponent Hue. *Stenographische Berichte,* vol. 285, 10 May 1912. Von Böhlendorff-Kölpin (1855–1925) was a *Rittergutsbesitzer,* retired major, member of the Prussian House for 1898, and twice a Reichstag deputy for the Conservative Party from 1903 to 1907 and again from 1912 to 1918. Other politicians in the league included Georg Schulenburg (born in 1872), businessman and owner of the wholesale colonial warehouse Gebrüder Schwollmann in Soest, Westphalia, as well as president of the *Krieger-und-Landwehrvereins* Soest and the *Kriegerverein* Soest, who represented the National Liberals in the Reichstag between 1912 and 1918; v. Arnim-Muskau (1839–1919), retired *Legationsrat* and Conservative Reichstag deputy, 1887–1907; Jonathan Roth (1873–1924), lawyer and Reichstag deputy for the Agrarian League and Economic Union (*Wirtschaftliche Vereinigung*) from 1907 to 1911; W. Lattmann (1864–1935), *Amtsrichter* and Reichstag deputy for the Economic Union from 1903 to 1912; and F. Warmuth (born 1870), independent Reichstag deputy, 1912–1918.

10. Members of local councils such as the Senate and City Council generally avoided using partisan labels and used instead the designations left, middle, or right caucuses (*Fraktionen*) to lend the impression of nonpartisanship. Paul de Chapeaurouge, Franz Ferdinand Eiffe, and Freiherr v. Berenberg-Gossler were members of Hamburg's National Liberal association. Haupstaatsarchiv Hamburg (hereafter referred to as SAH), Politische Partei, S 18591, Deutscher Wehrverein; Jürgen Bolland, *Die Hamburgische Bürgerschaft in Alter und Neuer Zeit* (Hamburg, 1959); Ekkehard Böhm, *Überseehandel und Flottenbau: Hanseatische Kaufmannschaft und deutsche Seerüstung, 1879–1902* (Düsseldorf, 1972); Dietrich Kersten, "Die Kriegsziele der Hamburger Kaufmannschaft im Ersten Weltkrieg: Ein Beitrag zur Frage der Kriegszielpolitik im Kaiserlichen Deutschland, 1914–1918" (Diss., University of Hamburg, 1962); Richard J. Evans, *Death in Hamburg. Society and Politics in the Cholera Years, 1830–1910* (Oxford, 1987), 12–27.

11. The best example could be found in the activities of the Tariff Reform League, which

conducted extensive electoral work in the decade after 1903, some of which was designed to drive those Unionists who remained wedded to free trade out of the Conservative Party. Other associations that assisted Conservative candidates included the Primrose League, the Navy League, the National Service League, and the Anti-Socialist Union. On this point, see Coetzee and Coetzee, "Rethinking the Radical Right," 515–37; and Frans Coetzee, *For Party or Country: Nationalism and the Dilemmas of Popular Conservatism in Edwardian England* (New York, 1990).

12. "Die Notwendigkeit eines Deutschen Wehrvereins," 8.

13. Ibid., 9.

14. *Kreuzzeitung*, "Ein Wehrverein," 22 February 1911.

15. *Der Tag*, "Nochmals: Wehrverein und Marine," 3 February 1912.

16. *Das Reichsvereinsgesetz vom 19. April 1908* (Leipzig, 1908). On the changing impact of the associations' laws, see Alfons Hueber, "Das Vereinsrecht im Deutschland des 19. Jahrhunderts," in Otto Dann, ed., *Das Vereinswesen und bürgerliche Gesellschaft in Deutschland* (Munich, 1984), 115–32; and Gerd Fesser, "Von der 'Zuchthausvorlage' zum Reichsvereinsgesetz. Staatsorgane, bürgerliche Parteien, und Vereinsgesetzgebung im Deutschen Reich, 1899–1906," *Jahrbuch für Geschichte* 28 (1983): 107–32.

17. *Das Reichsvereinsgesetz vom 19. April 1908,* passim.

18. BAK, Reichskanzlei Akten no. 1910, Beteiligung von Beamten an Vereinen 1906–18; and Reichskanzlei Akten no. 2242 and no. 2243, Vereins- und Versammlungsrecht; HSAD (Schloss Kalkum), Regierung Düsseldorf no. 15959, Politische Vereine.

19. BAK, Reichskanzlei Akten no. 1910, Beteiligung von Beamten an Vereinen 1906–18, v. Moltke to v. Bülow, 4 May 1910.

20. *Tägliche Rundschau*, "Sankt Bureaukratus und die Nationale Verbände," 25 February 1912; *Berliner Neueste Nachrichten*, "Der Wehrverein ein politischer Verein?" 25 February 1912.

21. BAK, Reichskanzlei Akten, no. 2273.

22. Ibid., 26 February 1912.

23. Ibid.

24. BAK, HO 2–1/22, 386, as cited in Kitchen, *The German Officer Corps,* 138.

25. BAK, Reichskanzlei Akten, no. 2273, v. Jagow to Bethmann Hollweg, 28 February 1912.

26. Ibid., v. Dallwitz to Bethmann Hollweg, 19 March 1912.

27. Ibid.

28. ZAP, ADV no. 406, Keim to Class, 31 March 1912.

29. Ibid.

30. See, for example, the *Deutsche Tageszeitung*, "Niedergang des Liberalismus?" 17 January 1912, in which the Agrarian League commented wryly: "The one thing which Liberalism can still learn is to die in splendor."

31. See Chapter 5 on Paasche.

32. The Agrarian League claimed that the National Liberal Party was run by the Jews.

33. ZAP, ADV no. 406, Class to Keim, 2 April 1912.

34. *Berliner Neueste Nachrichten,* 7 May 1912. Endell was referring to the 5 February vote taken in the Reichstag for the next president and vice president of that elected body. Peter Spahn of the Center Party was elected first vice president, while SPD deputy Bebel received the second vice presidency. According to Gottlob Egelhaaf, 196 votes were cast for Spahn and 175 for Bebel. Fifteen National Liberals reportedly cast their ballots for Bebel, unleashing a crisis within the National Liberal delegation, which was already badly divided. Gottlob Egelhaaf, *Lebens-Erinnerungen,* ed. Adolf Rapp (Stuttgart, 1960), 126. Paasche had been a former vice president of the Reichstag. On Major Endell's role as Agrarian League function-

ary, see Hans-Jürgen Puhle, *Agrarische Interessenpolitik und preussischer Konservatismus im wilhelminischen Reich, 1893–1914,* 2d ed. (Bonn-Bad Godesberg, 1975), 257, 275. Endell's activities in the Eastern Marches Society are chronicled in Hagen, *German, Poles, and Jews,* Chapter 8. On the objectives of the Bund, see James Retallack, *Notables of the Right. The Conservative Party and Political Mobilization in Germany, 1876–1918* (Boston, 1988), especially 92–110.

35. *Berliner Neueste Nachrichten,* 14 May 1912.

36. *Die Wehr,* Heft 3 (1912), Heft 3, 4, 8 (1913).

37. Interestingly, Paasche's name reappeared among the members of the league's *Gesamtvorstand* in 1914. *Die Wehr,* Heft 6 (1914). *Rittmeister a.D.* v. Böhlendorff-Kölpin, a Conservative member of the Reichstag, and Karl Heckmann, a National Liberal deputy, served in the *Ausschuss.*

38. The Pan-German League used the Teutonic knight to convey the image of a pioneer. Chickering, *We Men Who Feel Most German,* 93.

39. *Die Wehr,* "Deutschlands Wehrmacht, ihre Notwendigkeit und Bedeutung für unsere Sozialpolitik," Heft 3 (1912).

40. Use of the term *Deutscher Michel* was not confined to the Right, as evidenced, for example, by Friedrich Engels' reference to it in his study of the English working class. Charles E. McClelland, *The German Historians and England. A Study in Nineteenth-Century Views* (Cambridge, 1971), 122.

41. Ernst v. Heydebrand und der Lasa as quoted in Berghahn, *Germany and the Approach of War,* 114.

42. *Die Wehr,* "Zum volkswirtschaftlichen Wert des Militärdienstes," Heft 7 (1913).

43. On invasion scares, see I. F. Clarke, *Voices Prophesying War* (London, 1966); Samuel Hynes, *The Edwardian Turn of Mind* (Princeton, 1968), 34–53; David French, "Spy Fever in Britain," *Historical Journal* 21 (1978): 355–70.

44. Le Quex's novel was published in 1906. A. J. A. Morris, *The Scaremongers* (London, 1984), 108; Christopher Andrew, *Her Majesty's Secret Service* (New York, 1986), 39–40.

45. The two leagues are discussed at length in Coetzee, *For Party or Country,* passim; Arthur J. Marder's *The Anatomy of British Sea Power* (New York, 1940), 48–55, offers a more conventional approach to the Navy League. See also Anne Summers, "Militarism in Britain before the Great War," *History Workshop* 2 (1976): 104–23, and idem., "The Character of Edwardian Nationalism: Three Popular Leagues," in Paul Kennedy and Anthony Nicholls, eds., *Nationalist and Racialist Movements in Britain and Germany before 1914* (London, 1981), 68–87.

46. The Army League supported a sentence of life imprisonment for most spy offenses and death in the most serious cases. *Die Wehr,* Heft 7 (1913).

47. Keim, *Erlebtes und Erstrebtes,* 166; see also his speech to the Hamburg branch as reported in the *Hamburger Nachrichten,* "Der Deutsche Wehrverein in Hamburg," 13 April 1912.

48. On the impact of Social Darwinism in Germany, see Alfred Kelly, *The Descent of Darwin: The Popularization of Darwinism in Germany, 1860–1914* (Chapel Hill, 1981); H. W. Koch, "Social Darwinism as a Factor in the New Imperialism," in Koch, ed., *Origins of the First World War* (London, 1972), 329–54.

49. *Die Wehr,* "Krieg und Völkerfrieden," Heft 5/6 (1912); "Eine deutsche Schmach," Heft 8 (1913).

50. Friedrich v. Bernhardi, *Germany and the Next War* (London, 1914), 18.

51. "Krieg und Völkerfrieden."

52. "Der Krieg als Kulturfaktor, als Schöpfer und Erhalter der Staaten," first appeared in

the *Politisch-Anthropologische Revue,* nos. 8 and 9 (November and December 1912): 393–407 and 449–61. Gibichenfels's Army League article was entitled "Wehrmacht und Volkskraft," *Die Wehr,* Heft 2 (1912).

53. *Die Wehr,* "Das Volk und sein Treiber," Heft 9 (1913); "Wehrmacht und Volkskraft," Heft 2 (1912).

54. "Wehrmacht und Volkskraft."

55. *Schriften des Deutschen Wehrvereins 10,* "Die Friedensbewegung und ihre Gefahren für das deutsche Volk," (1913): 5–6. The pamphlet comprised four individual essays by Keim, General Litzmann, D. Rogge, and Hermann Müller-Brandenburg. The Peace Movement responded to the pamphlet's accusations with its own propaganda, "Der Wehrverein, eine Gefahr für das deutsche Volk" (Esslingen, 1914). See, in addition, Otfried Nippold, *Der deutsche Chauvinismus* (Berlin, 1913), especially 79ff.; and *Die Friedenswarte,* "Von Wehrverein," (April 1914), 147–48.

56. "Die Friedensbewegung und ihre Gefahren."

57. Keim's address to the annual meeting is in *Die Wehr,* Heft 6 (1913).

58. Ibid. See also v. Strantz, *Ein starkes Volk—ein starkes Heer* (Berlin, 1914), 10.

59. Abbé Wetterlé, *Behind the Scenes in the Reichstag: Sixteen Years of Parliamentary Life in Germany* (London, 1918), and Heinrich Class, *Wider den Strom,* 188–96, offer different perspectives of the incident.

60. *Der Tag,* "Schwoben und Alsässer," 9 January 1914.

61. The Abbé had served a sentence for slandering a Herr Gneisse, director of a Gymnasium, as a "passionate Pan-German pedagogue."

62. *Schwäbische Merkur,* "Wetterlé gegen Gen. Keim," 14 May 1914.

63. *Die Wehr,* "Waffenfähige Jugend," Heft 5 (1913).

fEN64. Ibid.

65. Richard Nordhausen, *Zwischen 14 und 18* (Leipzig, 1910).

66. Ibid., 52. Nordhausen's complaints against what he considered scurrilous literature were echoed by the general public as well. For example, in the city of Göppingen in Württemberg, a committee calling itself the "Komitee zur Bekämpfung von Schund-Literatur und Errichtung einer Freien öffentlichen Bibliothek," which was headed by the city's Rabbi and consisted of local citizens from diverse religious and social backgrounds, voiced concerns about precisely the same literature and its deleterious effect on the youth. *Göppinger Zeitung,* 7 April 1911.

67. Ibid., 10–11.

68. Ibid., 58.

69. Ibid., 13.

70. The idea of using the army to neutralize socialist influence on workers was already practiced in the army. See Kitchen, *The German Officer Corps,* 143–86.

71. *Die Wehr,* "Arbeiterschaft und Wehrfrage," Heft 4 (1912).

72. Nordhausen, *Zwischen 14 und 18,* 88, 97. See also *Die Wehr,* "Der Geburtenrückgang," Heft 9 (1912), and *Hamburger Echo,* "Die Geburtshelfer des Rüstungsfanatismus," 9 April 1913. Nordhausen's attitude toward urbanization resembled those theories propounded by Georg Hansen, who warned against the evils of city life. On this point, see Andrew Lees, *Cities Perceived* (New York, 1985), 142–48, 158–64.

73. *Die Wehr,* "Wehrfähigkeit-Wehrmacht," Heft 1 (1913); *Die Wehr* also called attention to the Austrian army's attempt to prevent drunkeness among its troops and noted that at lunch its troops were served water as a beverage. *Die Wehr,* Heft 2 (1913).

74. Details on this association, founded in Cassel in March 1883, are found in James S. Roberts, *Drink, Temperance, and the Working Class in Nineteenth-Century Germany* (London, 1984), 55–82.

75. Roberts, *Drink, Temperance, and the Working Class,* 58–66. Both organizations

recruited heavily from the *Bildungsbürgertum,* the academically trained civil servants, professors, and professionals.

76. Roberts, *Drink, Temperance, and the Working Class,* 64.

77. Eley, *Reshaping the German Right,* 224.

78. James S. Roberts, "Drink and the Labour Movement: The Schnaps Boycott of 1909," in Richard J. Evans, ed., *The German Working Class, 1888–1933* (London, 1982), 80–107.

79. Ibid., 99.

80. *Die Wehr,* "Deutschlands Wehrmacht, ihre Notwendigkeit und Bedeutung für unsere Sozialpolitik," Heft 3 (1912).

81. Lutz Niethammer, "Wie wohnten Arbeiter im Kaiserreich?" *Archiv für Sozialgeschichte* 16 (1976): 61–134; Franz J. Brüggemeier and Lutz Niethammer, "Lodgers, Schnapps-Casinos, and Working-Class Colonies in a Heavy-Industrial Region: Aspects of Working-Class Housing in the Ruhr prior to the First World War," in Georg Iggers, ed., *The Social History of Politics* (Leamington Spa, 1985), 217–58.

82. "Brief eines Rekruten an seine Mutter" (1913) was perhaps the most successful piece of anti-Socialist propaganda published by the league. Eley discusses the Navy League's anti-Socialist rhetoric in *Reshaping the German Right,* 218–26.

83. *Die Wehr,* "Ferdinand Lassalle der Kriegsherold," Heft 1 (1913).

84. Richard J. Evans, "Liberalism and Society: The Feminist Movement and Social Change," in Evans, ed., *Society and Politics in Wilhelmine Germany,* 190. See also idem., *The Feminist Movement in Germany, 1894–1933* (London, 1976), for an in-depth study of the German feminist movement.

85. Unfortunately, little is known about the Women's League. Evans, *The Feminist Movement in Germany,* 199. Marie v. Alten penned several articles in *Die Wehr* on women's patriotic duties (Heft 10, 1913). She was the wife of Lieutenant General v. Alten. The German-Evangelical Women's League (*Deutsch-evangelischer Frauenbund*) was probably a corporate member of the Army League since it had ties to the German League for the Prevention of the Emancipation of Women. See Richard Evans, "The Concept of Feminism: Notes for Practicing Historians," in Ruth-Ellen B. Joeres and Mary Jo Maynes, eds., *German Women in the Eighteenth and Nineteenth Centuries* (Bloomington, Ind., 1986), 251.

86. *Die Wehr,* Heft 2 (1913); Heft 5 (1913); Heft 9 (1913).

87. *Die Wehr,* Heft 6 (1914).

88. Nordhausen, *Zwischen 14 und 18,* 89. For his rebuttal of the suffrage movement, see 92–100.

89. Ibid., 101–13.

90. *Die Wehr,* "Ein Aufruf an die deutsche Frau," Heft 1 (1913); see also "Zur Wehrhaftmachung der Frau," Heft 1 (1916).

91. *Die Wehr,* "Eine deutsche Frau an die deutschen Frauen," Heft 9 (1912); "Unbekannte vaterländische Männer und Frauen," Heft 3 (1914).

92. There are stimulating discussions of this and other images in Klaus Theweleit's *Male Fantasies,* vol. 1 (Minneapolis, 1987), especially 90–100, 125–38. Theweleit emphasizes the sexual roots of this imagery, but I hesitate to draw any further parallels.

93. On the German Language Association, see Hermann Dunger, *Die deutsche Sprachbewegung und der Allgemeiner Deutsche Sprachverein, 1885–1910: Festschrift zur 25. Jahrfeier des Allgemeinen Deutschen Sprachvereins* (10 September 1910) (Berlin, 1910); *Zeitschrift des Allgemeinen Deutschen Sprachvereins, 1911–1914.*

94. *Die Wehr,* "Eine oft aber nie genug gerügte, deutsche Ansitte," Heft 9 (1913).

95. Stark, *Entrepreneurs of Ideology: Neoconservative Publishers in Germany, 1890–1933* (Chapel Hill, 1981), 120–22, 186.

96. See Chapter 5 for brief biographical sketches.

97. *Wer ist's*, 1912.
98. See Chapter 5 for details on his background.
99. *Die Wehr*, passim.
100. HSAS, E 14 Bü 1345, Deutscher Flottenverein, Jahresbericht des Deutschen Flotten-verein für das Jahr 1912, 7.
101. Ibid., 7–8.
102. Ibid., 18–21.
103. All figures are from *Die Wehr*, Heft 6 (1913).
104. Eley, *Reshaping the German Right*, 119.

## Chapter 4

1. Otto Umfrid, a Stuttgart pastor and leading figure in the German Peace Society, sadly noted that the founding of the Army League in Württemberg was proof that many Swabians "believed themselves to be more Prussian than the Prussians." Umfrid, "Der deutsche Wehrverein," in *Die Friedenswarte*, Heft 2 (1912), 47.

2. On the development of the early liberal movement in Württemberg, see in particular Dieter Langewiesche, *Liberalismus und Demokratie in Württemberg zwischen Revolution und Reichsgründung* (Düsseldorf, 1974); Gerlinde Runge, *Die Volkspartei in Württemberg von 1864 bis 1871* (Stuttgart, 1970); Hans Fenske, *Der liberale Südwesten. Freiheitliche und demokratische Traditionen in Baden und Württemberg, 1790–1933* (Stuttgart, 1981), especially 110–45; Friedrich Henning, "Liberalismus und Demokratie im Königreich Württemberg," in Paul Rothmund and Erhard R. Wiehn, eds., *Die F.D.P./D.V.P. in Baden-Württemberg und ihre Geschichte* (Stuttgart, 1979), 59–78.

3. Runge, *Die Volkspartei in Württemberg*, 32–52; Henning, "Liberalismus und Demokratie," 62–65; Langewiesche, *Liberalismus und Demokratie in Württemberg*, 285ff.

4. Unfortunately, we still lack a comprehensive study of the National Liberals in Württemberg. Wilhelm Lang (himself a National Liberal) offers a brief history of the party in *Die Deutsche Partei in Württemberg, 1866–1891* (Stuttgart, 1891), which commemorates the twenty-fifth anniversary of its founding. Klaus Simon compares the two liberal movements in "Württembergischer Liberalismus in der Zeit der Demokratisierung und Parlamentarisierung," in Rothmund and Wiehn, eds., *Die F.D.P./D.V.P. in Baden-Württemberg*, 97–115.

5. James C. Hunt, *The People's Party in Württemberg and Southern Germany, 1890–1914* (Stuttgart, 1975), and Klaus Simon, *Die württembergischen Demokraten: Ihre Stellung und Arbeit im Parteien und Verfassungsystem in Württemberg und im Deutschen Reich, 1890–1920* (Stuttgart, 1969) remain the best sources on the state's left-liberal movement.

6. Karl Bachem referred to Württemberg at the height of the *Kulturkampf* as an "oasis of peace." As cited in Blackbourn, *Class, Religion, and Local Politics*, 62.

7. On the SPD in Württemberg, see Jörg Schadt and Wolfgang Schmierer, eds., *Die SPD in Baden-Württemberg und ihre Geschichte* (Stuttgart, 1979), especially the contributions by Schmierer, "Die Anfänge der Arbeiterbewegung und der Sozialdemokratie in Baden-Württemberg vom Vormärz zum Sozialistengesetz von 1878," 35–63, and Maja Christ-Gmelin, "Die Württembergische Sozialdemokratie, 1890–1914," 107–27; see also Maja Christ-Gmelin, "Die Württembergische Sozialdemokratie, 1890–1914. Ein Beitrag zur Geschichte des Reformismus und Revisionismus in der deutschen Sozialdemokratie" (Ph.D. Diss., University of Stuttgart, 1975); Christof Rieber, *Das Sozialistengesetz und die Sozialdemokratie in Württemberg, 1878–1890*, 2 vols. (Stuttgart, 1984). The Center's fortunes are revealed most judiciously in Blackbourn, *Class, Religion, and Local Politics*, as well as in his article "The Political Alignment of the Center Party in Wilhelmine Germany: A Study of the Party's Emergence in Nineteenth-Century Württemberg," *Historical Journal* 18

(1975): 821–50, and "Class and Politics in Wilhelmine Germany: The Center Party and the Social Democrats in Württemberg," *Central European History* 9 (1976): 220–49. The Agrarian League is discussed in James Hunt, "The 'Egalitarianism' of the Right: The Agrarian League in Southwest Germany, 1893–1914," *Journal of Contemporary History* 10 (1975): 513–30.

8. The Pan-German League, Colonial Society, Navy League, the Imperial League against Social Democracy, and the Society for Germandom Abroad were well represented throughout the state. On occasion, Army League branches shared offices and more often members with these associations. HSAS, E 14 Bü 1344 and 1345, Deutscher Flottenverein; E 14 Bü 1361, Deutscher Kolonialgesellschaft.

9. On the Peace Movement, see Roger Chickering, *Imperial Germany and a World without War: The Peace Movement and Germany, 1892–1914*, (Princeton, 1975), and Friedrich-Karl Scheer, *Die deutsche Friedensgesellschaft (1892–1933): Organisation, Ideologie, politische Ziele* (Frankfurt, 1981).

10. Umfrid as quoted in Chickering, *Imperial Germany*, 72. Figures for the Peace Society are from Chickering, *Imperial Germany*, 62, 59.

11. HSAS, E 14 Bü 1389, Jahresbericht für 1912: Deutscher Wehrverein Ortsgruppe Stuttgart.

12. The number of participants for the February meeting rose to 112.

13. HSAS, J 150 no. 191/2, Satzung der Ortsgruppe Stuttgart.

14. Compiled from HSAS, E 14 Bü 1389, Wehrverein protocols.

15. *Schwäbische Tagwacht*, "Dem Wehrverein an der Arbeit," 8 February 1912.

16. *Hof und Staatshandbuch des Königreichs Württemberg, 1911*; HSAS, E 14 Bü 1067, Politische Vereine. *Privatier* Gustav Kienzle, *Gutsbesitzer* Gustav Graf v. Adelmannsfelden and *Gutsbesitzer* Adorno, members of the executive committee, also belonged to the Racing Club.

17. HSAS, E 14 Bü 1389, Jahresbericht für 1912: Deutscher Wehrverein Ortsgruppe Stuttgart.

18. HSAS, E 14 Bü 1389, Protokoll über die zweite Gesamtvorstandssitzung am 5. April 1913.

19. Hübner was one of the league's most widely used and valuable circuit lecturers.

20. HSAS, E 14 Bü 1389, Protokoll über die zweite Gesamtvorstandssitzung am 5. April 1913.

21. *Schwäbische Merkur* (*Schwäbische Kronik*), "General Keim im Deutschen Wehrverein," 30 November 1912.

22. *Schwäbische Merkur* (*Schwäbische Kronik*), "Weltlage und Weltpolitik," 27 November 1912.

23. HSAS, E 14 Bü 1389, Jahresbericht für 1912: Deutscher Wehrverein Ortsgruppe Stuttgart. Von Soden and Dörtenbach were simultaneously executives of the Württemberg provincial federation of the Navy League (v. Soden as a member of the *Gesamtausschuss* and Dörtenbach as a member of the *Präsidium*). HSAS, E 14 Bü 1345, Deutscher Flottenverein, Rechenschaftbericht für das Jahr 1912. Von Soden (born 1856), served also as president and honorary president of the *Württembergischer Kriegerbund*. HSAS, J 150 no. 191/1–6, Flugschriften Krieger und Wehrverbände; MAS, Nachlass-Mappe Soden.

24. *Schwäbische Merkur* (*Schwäbische Kronik/Mittagsblatt*), "Deutscher Wehrverein," 30 March 1912; *Schwäbische Tagwacht*, "Der Deutsche Wehrverein," 1 April 1912.

25. Ibid.

26. *Schwäbische Merkur* (*Schwäbische Kronik*), "Deutscher Wehrverein," 9 May 1912.

27. Born in 1848, Egelhaaf was rector of Karlsgymnasium in Stuttgart, a member of the prestigious *Württembergische Kommission für Landesgeschichte*, and a National Liberal. He

served the league as a primary lecturer. Details of his life are found in Egelhaaf, *Lebens-Erinnerungen.*

28. *Schwäbische Merkur* (*Schwäbische Kronik*), "Deutscher Wehrverein," 9 May 1912.

29. Ibid.

30. HSAS, E 14 Bü 1389, Protokoll über die zweite Gestamvorstandssitzung am 5. April 1913.

31. Ibid.

32. I have used the map of Württemberg's religious distribution in Blackbourn, *Class, Religion, and Local Politics,* 242, as a reference.

33. *Schwäbische Merkur* (*Schwäbische Kronik*), "Politische Nachrichten," 25 July 1914. Of the 2,550 residents of Tettnang, only 185 were Protestant.

34. Adorno evidently had hoped to become the Center candidate for a substitute Reichstag election to be held on 21 August 1914. The Württemberg Centrists chose instead *Katholischer Volksverein* secretary Stiegele to run as their candidate.

35. Heinrich Graf v. Adelmannsfelden, "Ursprung und älteste Geschichte der Grafen A. von Adelmannsfelden und deren Beziehungen zu Hohenstadt," *Württembergische Vierteljahrsheft für Landesgeschichte* 16 (1908): 301ff.

36. Gustav was born in 1850. *Wer ist's,* 1912, summarizes his accomplishments.

37. Statistics I consulted did not give a breakdown for Hohenstadt's population under eighteen. Nevertheless, since we know that on the national level 34.2 percent of the German population was fifteen and under and 9.7 percent was between the ages of fifteen and twenty, a figure of between 30 percent and 40 percent seems reasonable for those under eighteen in the town. Thus somewhere between 60 percent and 70 percent of Hohenstadt's inhabitants were eligible to join the Army League and about 18 percent actually did. G. Hohorst, J. Kocka, and G. A. Ritter, eds., *Sozialgeschichtliches Arbeitsbuch* (Munich, 1975), 24.

38. Perhaps it is no coincidence that Adorno and v. Adelmannsfelden seemed to move in the same circles, both participating in the Association for the Breeding of Pure Racing Hounds in 1910.

39. *Hof und Staatshandbuch des Königreichs Württemberg, 1912.* Von Schleich was born in 1851 near Waldenbuch and died in 1928 in Tübingen.

40. Roth ran unsuccessfully in the 1907 Reichstag election for Württemberg electoral district IV (Vaihingen, Böblingen, Leonberg, Maulbronn), losing to *Volkspartei* challenger Leo.

41. HSAS, E 14 Bü 1389, Protokoll über die dritte Gesamtvorstandssitzung am 22. Nov. 1913.

42. Ibid., letter of Franz v. Soden to Julius v. Soden, 8 January 1913.

43. HSAS, E 14 Bü 1389, Protokoll über die dritte Gesamtvorstandssitzung am 22. Nov. 1913.

44. Ibid. The nine new branches were Neuenbürg, Korntal, Sulz, Oberndorf, Freudenstadt, Isny, Waldsee, Tettnang, and Reutlingen.

45. Even provincial federations had a difficult time remembering the precise names of all the Army League's pamphlets. *Schriften des Deutschen Wehrvereins* 6, "Wer die Wehrvorlage verwirft ist ein Volksfeind," was incorrectly referred to in the protocol as "Wer die Wehrvorlage annimt, ist ein Volksfeind."

46. HSAS, E 14 Bü 1389, Jahresbericht für 1913: Deutscher Wehrverein Ortsgruppe Stuttgart.

47. HSAS, E 14 Bü 1389, Protokoll über die dritte Gesamtvorstandssitzung am 22. Nov. 1913.

48. Ibid.

49. Ibid.

50. HSAS, E 14 Bü 1389, Protokoll über die zweite Gesamtvorstandssitzung am 5 April 1913.

51. HSAS, E 14 Bü 1389, Jahresbericht für 1912/1913: Deutscher Wehrverein Ortsgruppe Stuttgart.

52. *Die Wehr,* Heft 9 (1912).

53. Chapter 5 will examine the Army League's finances in detail.

## Chapter 5

1. HSAS, J 150 no. 191/2, Satzung des Deutschen Wehrvereins.

2. For example, Warner Poelchau (Hamburg), Graf Adelmann v. Adelmannsfelden (Hohenstadt), Major General Heckert (Aachen), and *Landgerichtsdirektor* Hahn (Kiel) were responsible for establishing some of the first Army League branches and regional federations.

3. HSAS, J 150 no. 191/2, Satzung des Deutschen Wehrvereins.

4. Stadtarchiv Essen (hereafter referred to as SAE), Rep. 102, Abt. 1, no. 850.

5. Wertheimer, *The Pan-German League, 1890* (New York, 1924), 54.

6. *Die Wehr,* Heft 3 (1912).

7. See Table 9.

8. Chickering, *We Men Who Feel Most German,* 142; Eley, *Reshaping the German Right,* 125.

9. *Die Wehr,* Heft 2 (1913).

10. As in the case of the Württemberg branches, those in the two Saxonies were founded primarily between spring 1912 and May 1913.

11. *Die Wehr,* Heft 3 (1913), Heft 3 (1914), Heft 5/6 (1912). Population statistics are for 1910 as indicated in *Statistisches Jahrbuch für das deutsche Reich,* 1912.

12. *Die Wehr,* Heft 2 (1913) and Heft 3 (1914).

13. ZAP, ADV no. 197, Hofmeister to Class, 9 February 1913.

14. According to Mildred Wertheimer, the Pan-German League had twenty-eight foreign branches at its peak in 1897 and 1900, but thereafter their number steadily declined to only eleven by 1913. Wertheimer, *Pan-German League,* 55.

15. Of the Army League officials discussed in this section, only Hans v. Wrochem was not a member of the *Ausschuss,* which consisted of a maximum of twenty-one individuals.

16. David Blackbourn explores this motif in his "Politics as Theatre: Metaphors of the Stage in German History, 1848–1933," *Transactions of the Royal Historical Society* 37 (1987): 149–67.

17. Schäfer was the only academic to have served in the elite inner circle, although two other university professors were members of the extended *Ausschuss.*

18. Dietrich Schäfer, *Mein Leben* (Berlin, 1926), 29.

19. Ibid., 67.

20. Ibid., 72.

21. Ibid., 100.

22. Ibid., 110.

23. Ibid., 129.

24. Ibid., 120.

25. Ibid., 150–54. Schäfer also discusses his role in the Navy League on pp. 130–32.

26. Ibid., 32; 80.

27. Ibid., 81.

28. Accounts of both men are found in *Wer ist's,* 1912.

29. Details on Rippler's background are culled from *Wer ist's,* 1912.

30. Eley, *Reshaping the German Right,* 92–93.

31. These details are reconstructed from *Wer ist's*, 1912. Although Müller-Brandenburg left no actual memoir, his *Von Schlieffen bis Ludendorff* (Leipzig, 1925) and *Irrungen und Wirrungen: Schlaglichter auf den Zusammenbruch unserer Aussenpolitik* (Berlin 1919) offer some insight into his character.

32. *Wer ist's*, 1912; Dankwart Guratzsch, *Macht durch Organization* (Düsseldorf, 1974), 297–99; Wernecke, *Der Wille zur Weltgeltung*, 13–15.

33. Baltazzi was a *Legations-Rat, Kaiserlicher Gesandter*, and *Bevollmächtiger Minister*. *Wer ist's*, 1912.

34. Ibid.

35. Eduard v. Liebert, *Aus einem bewegten Leben: Erinnerungen* (Munich, 1925), 9; see also v. Liebert's contribution in Hans v. Arnim and Georg v. Below, *Deutscher Aufstieg. Bilder aus der Vergangenheit und Gegenwart der rechtstehenden Parteien* (Berlin, 1925), 404–13.

36. Von Liebert, *Aus einem bewegten Leben*, 10.

37. Ibid., 11.

38. Ibid.

39. Ibid., 22.

40. Ibid., 94; while serving with the General Staff in Berlin, v. Liebert became acquainted with Friedrich Lange, one of the newspaper's editors.

41. Ibid.

42. Ibid., 158–68.

43. Ibid., 169.

44. Ibid., 173.

45. Ibid., 174. The successful Socialist challenger was Heinrich Pëus.

46. Ibid., 175.

47. Ibid., 183. Von Liebert brought a libel suit against his Socialist opponent, Herr Schöpflin, for calling him a liar. The court in Leipzig ruled in the general's favor, requiring Schöpflin to pay 400 marks in "damages."

48. Ibid., 190.

49. Ibid., 87.

50. Karl Litzmann, *Lebenserinnerungen* (Berlin, 1927), 1: 12–13; 135.

51. Ibid., 62.

52. Ibid., 125–28.

53. Ibid., 135.

54. Hans v. Wrochem, *Erinnerungen eines "Chinesen"* (Berlin, 1910).

55. *Alldeutsche Blätter*, passim.

56. *Wer ist's*, 1911.

57. Ibid.

58. The exception here was Schäfer, whose roots were in the working class.

59. Litzmann, *Lebenserinnerungen*, 64. Litzmann bemoaned the fact that the German public had lost the Bismarckian spirit of patriotism and military preparedness, remarking: "Bismarck's successors destroyed our *Volk* through their own devices; [the *Volk*] can be rewon only when the Germans return to the Bismarckian spirit" (314). Von Liebert praised the Age of Bismarck as a time when Germany was at the center of international attention. Von Liebert, *Aus einem bewegten Leben*, 76.

60. Von Liebert, *Aus einem bewegten Leben*, 128.

61. Roger Chickering independently compiled figures on the Army League's social composition that generally agree with my own. Chickering, *We Men Who Feel Most German*, 325–28.

62. Hans-Joachim Henning, *Das Westdeutsche Bürgertum in der Epoche der Hochindustrialisierung, 1860–1914* (Wiesbaden, 1972), 1: 172.

63. According to the 1910 census, Posen's Polish population constituted 64.7 percent or 1,352,650 inhabitants, whereas the German population comprised only 34 percent or 720,650. These figures are from Hagen, *Germans, Poles, and Jews,* 217. See also, Hagen, Chapters 5–8; Tims, *Germanizing Prussian Poland;* Galos, Gentzen, and Jakóbczyk, *Die Hakatisten;* and Richard Blanke, *Prussian Poland in the German Empire, 1871–1900* (Boulder, Colo., 1981).

64. *Die Wehr,* Heft 8 (1912). The city of Posen was the seat of the higher provincial authority and the Royal Colonization Commission as well as the headquarters of the 5th Army Corps.

65. The Eastern Marches Society also recruited heavily from among Posen's bureaucracy, according to Hagen, *Germans, Poles, and Jews,* 281; Tims, *Germanizing Prussian Poland,* 66, 221–23; Galos, Gentzen and Jakóbczyk, *Die Hakatisten,* 56ff., 148ff. According to Galos, there were approximately a thousand *Gutsbesitzer* in Posen in 1906–7, most of whom were aligned with the *Bund der Landwirte* (148).

66. See for example, *Die Wehr,* "Der Unteroffizier und Militäranwärter Frage," Heft 1 (1913).

67. *Die Wehr,* Heft 3 (1912). In the 1905 edition of the *Jahrbuch für die deutsche Armee,* Keim proposed his plan for safeguarding the young noncommissioned officer against socialism, advocating that anyone under twenty-one be legally barred from joining a trade union or political party. On this point, see Kitchen, *The German Officer Corps,* 143–86.

68. Veterans, too, were highly visible in the league's branches. As the Württemberg Federation reminded its chapters: "It is of the utmost importance that the Army League interests the *Kriegervereine* in its work. In those places where it is impossible to solicit corporate membership, individual members must be persuaded [to join]." HSAS, E 14 Bü 1389, Jahresbericht für 1913: Deutscher Wehrverein Ortsgruppe Stuttgart.

69. *Die Wehr,* passim.

70. *Die Wehr,* Heft 2 (1913).

71. See, for example, Rüdiger vom Bruch, *Wissenschaft, Politik, und öffentliche Meinung: Gelehrtenpolitik im wilhelminischen Deutschland* (Husum, 1980), and idem., " 'Deutschland und England: Heeres oder Flottenverstärkung?' Politische Publizistik deutscher Hochschullehrer, 1911/12," *Militärgeschichtliche Mitteilungen* 29 (1981): 7–35.

72. Schäfer, *Mein Leben,* 67.

73. Egelhaaf, *Lebens-Erinnerungen,* 14–15.

74. *Die Wehr,* passim.

75. *Die Wehr,* Heft 4 (1913).

76. *Die Wehr,* "Zur Veteranenfrage," Heft 9 (1912).

77. HA/GHH, 300 127/4, Deutscher Wehrverein; *General-Anzeiger für Oberhausen, Sterkrade, Osterfeld, Bottrop, und Umgegend,* 28 November 1913; *Neue Oberhausener Zeitung,* 28 November 1913.

78. *General-Anzeiger,* 2 January 1914.

79. Stadtarchiv Oberhausen, Nachlass Gehne, no. 54. Becker died in 1936.

80. SAH, S 18591, Deutscher Wehrverein.

81. SAH, S 18591, Deutscher Wehrverein.

82. PA/AA Bonn, Hamburg, no. 1, Bd. 4, Innere Verhältnisse Hamburgs, v. Bülow to Bethmann Hollweg, 23 October 1912. The forty-six-year-old v. Berenberg-Gossler requested a full pardon from Kaiser Wilhelm, noting in his request that his opponent had not been injured.

83. *Die Wehr*, Heft 2 (1913).

84. SAE, Rep. 102, Abt. 1, no. 850.

85. *Die Wehr*, Heft 7 (1913). This branch was founded in April 1913 with twenty-two members.

86. *Die Wehr*, Heft 3 (1913). At the time of its founding in February 1913, the branch recorded over one hundred members.

87. *Die Wehr*, Heft 5 (1913).

88. The Hamburg branch advertised a 10 percent reduction at the Karstadt department store for members.

89. *Die Wehr*, Heft 9 (1912).

90. On the relationship between workers and employers in Oberhausen, see Heinz Reif, "Arbeiter und Unternehmer in Städten des westlichen Ruhrgebiets, 1850–1930," in Jürgen Kocka, ed., *Arbeiter und Bürger im 19. Jahrhundert* (Munich, 1986), 151–81.

91. *Schwäbische Tagwacht,* "Dem Wehrverein an der Arbeit," 8 February 1912. On socialist culture in Imperial Germany, see Günther Roth's now classic study, *The Social Democrats in Imperial Germany* (Totowa, N.J., 1963); the critical comments in Richard J. Evans's introduction to *The German Working Class* (London, 1982); and Vernon Lidtke, *The Alternative Culture: Socialist Labor in Imperial Germany* (Oxford, 1985).

92. Dates of birth were available for eleven of the sixteen members.

93. Chickering, *We Men Who Feel Most German,* 312 (Table 5.4).

94. Ibid., 315, 316; Tables 5.7, 5.8.

95. *Politisches Handbuch der Nationalliberalen Partei* (1907), 1219–22; W. Kulemann, *Zusammenschluss der Liberalen* (Dresden, 1905), 27–30.

96. HSAS, E 14 Bü 1344, Deutscher Flottenverein, Württembergischer Landesverband des Deutschen Flottenvereins—Ausflug nach Bremen, Helgoland, Kiel, und Hamburg, 1905.

97. HSAS, E 14 Bü 1361, Deutsche Kolonialgesellschaft, Abteilung Stuttgart, 1902–13.

98. *Alldeutsche Blätter,* 4 December 1909 and 30 March 1912.

99. PA/AA Bonn, Deutschland 138, no. 5, Deutscher Flottenverein. See Chickering, *We Men Who Feel Most German,* 322 (Table 9) for the correlation of overlapping memberships among Hamburg members of the patriotic societies.

100. *Alldeutsche Blätter,* 4 September 1909.

101. James Q. Wilson, *Political Organizations* (New York, 1973); Mancur Olson, *The Logic of Collective Action* (Cambridge, 1965); and Terry Moe, *The Organization of Interests* (Chicago, 1980), provide a point of departure for assessing the complex issues of incentives to participation.

102. *Die Wehr*, Heft 6 (1913).

103. Ibid., Heft 10 (1915).

104. Ibid., Heft 3 (1912).

105. Chickering, *We Men Who Feel Most German,* 186.

106. HSAS, E 14 Bü 1345, Deutscher Flottenverein, Jahresbericht des Deutschen Flottenverein für das Jahr 1912, 11–12. In 1901 the Colonial Society held 279 lectures and 247 slide shows. HSAS, E 14 Bü 1361, Deutsche Kolonialgesellschaft, Abteilung Stuttgart, Jahresbericht der Deutschen Kolonialgesellschaft 1901.

107. *Die Wehr*, Heft 1 (1913).

108. Ibid.

109. The Navy League had a similar arrangement so as to facilitate the use of slide programs.

110. *Die Wehr*, Heft 7 (1912).

111. *Hamburgischer Korrespondent,* 9 April 1912; *Hamburger Fremdenblatt,* 9 April

1912; *General Anzeiger,* 10 April 1912; *Hamburger Echo,* "Die Kriegsmente bellt," 14 April 1912.

112. *Die Wehr,* Heft 5 (1913).

113. Ibid., Heft 4 (1913).

114. Ibid., Heft 2 (1913).

115. Wolfgang Kaschuba and Carola Lipp make precisely this point regarding the Württemberg village of Kiebingen, where memberships in local associations, they argue, were a useful means by which a nontown citizen could become integrated socially into the community. Moreover, one of the best ways to assure acceptance was by marrying into the *Vereinsfamilie.* Wolfgang Kaschuba and Carola Lipp, *Dörfliches Überleben, Zur Geschichte materieller und sozialer Reproduktion ländlicher Gesellschaft im 19. und frühen 20. Jahrhundert* (Tübingen, 1982), 595. The issue of sociability remains a part of German culture today; newspaper advertisements for spouses abound and beerhalls, discos, cafes, and associational meetings offer Germans an opportunity to meet potential mates.

116. Germans' fascination with monuments is explored in Thomas Nipperdey, "Nationalidee und Nationaldenkmal in Deutschland im 19. Jahrhundert," *Historische Zeitschrift* 206 (1968): 559–85, and Eric Hobsbawm, "Mass-Producing Traditions: Europe, 1870–1914," in Eric Hobsbawm and Terence Ranger, eds., *The Invention of Tradition* (Cambridge, 1983), 263–307.

117. HSAS, E 14 Bü 1344, Deutscher Flottenverein, Württembergischer Landesverband des Deutschen Flottenvereins–Ausflug nach Bremen, Helgoland, Kiel, und Hamburg 1905 (Teilnehmer Liste).

118. *Die Wehr,* Heft 3 (1913).

119. Ibid., Heft 6 (1913).

120. HSAS, E 14 Bü 1389, Franz Freiherr v. Soden to Julius v. Soden, 8 January 1913.

121. Galos, Gentzen, and Jakóbczyk, *Die Hakatisten,* 140.

122. Chickering, *We Men Who Feel Most German,* 226.

123. Eley, *Reshaping the German Right,* 145.

124. Chickering, *We Men Who Feel Most German,* 227. See also Wertheimer, *Pan-German League,* 75–89.

125. ZAP, ADV no. 406, Class to Keim, 2 April 1912.

126. Ibid., Keim to Class, 23 September 1912. Of course, occasionally wealthy businessmen contributed considerable funds to the local Army League chapter, as was the case in Stuttgart, where an unidentified "industrialist" donated 1,000 marks to the branch. *Die Wehr,* Heft 9 (1912). According to *Die Wehr,* Heft 6 (1914), Frau v. Swiderska donated 5,000 marks. By and large, however, such donations proved to be the exception to the rule before the First World War.

### Chapter 6

1. Von Strantz, *Ein starkes Volk,* 39.

2. Possehl served on the presidium of the Hansabund from 1909 to 1914.

3. Class, *Wider den Strom,* 229; Alfred Kruck, *Geschichte des Alldeutschen Verbandes, 1890–1939* (Wiesbaden, 1954), 68. Class described Possehl as an "economic philosopher" and "entrepreneur of the grand style."

4. The complete text of his speech was reprinted in *Die Wehr,* Heft 8 (1917) and in *The Times,* "Through German Eyes: Results of Trade War. A Forecast of Ruin," 29 December 1914.

5. In 1913 Germany imported nearly three times the value of raw materials as it exported. Hohorst, Kocka, and Ritter, *Sozialgeschichtliches Arbeitsbuch,* 85–86.

6. *Die Wehr,* Heft 2 (1913).

7. Class, *Wider den Strom,* 229; Lothar Burchardt, *Friedenswirtschaft und Kriegsvorsorge: Deutschlands wirtschaftliche Rüstungsbestrebungen vor 1914* (Boppard, 1968), 138ff.

8. Clemens v. Delbrück, *Die wirtschaftliche Mobilmachung in Deutschland 1914* (Munich, 1924), 64.

9. Ibid., 69, 78.

10. Keim, *Erlebtes und Erstrebtes,* 179.

11. Gerald Feldman, *Army, Industry, and Labor in Germany, 1914–1918* (Princeton, 1966), 51.

12. Class, *Wider den Strom,* 231; Niendorf, *Geschichte des Handelshauses Possehl.*

13. HSAS, E 130a no. 1241, "Denkschrift des Deutschen Wehrvereins: Die Notwendigkeit eines Kriegswirtschaftsstabes." The importance of a strong army, economy, and nationalist sentiment are outlined in v. Strantz, *Ein starkes Volk, passim.*

14. *Die Wehr,* Heft 1 (1917).

15. Ibid.

16. On Keim's activities in Belgium see his *Erlebtes und Erstrebtes,* 195–234, and Gatzke, *Germany's Drive to the West* (Baltimore, 1950), 86.

17. See, for example, v. Strantz, *Belgien als Sklave Englands im Lichte der Geschichte* (Leipzig, 1918), *passim;* idem., *Unser völkisches Kriegsziel* (Leipzig, 1918), 113–47; Hans Gatzke, *Germany's Drive,* 92–99, 158–61; Fischer, *Germany's Aims,* 495–550.

18. As quoted in *Alldeutsche Blätter,* "Ein neutrales Lob für General Keim," 25 November 1916.

19. Fischer, *Germany's Aims,* 445.

20. Keim, *Erlebtes und Erstrebtes,* 211–14.

21. *Die Wehr,* "Englands irischer Gefahr," Heft 11/12 (1914); v. Strantz, *Belgien als Sklave,* 33.

22. Fischer, *Germany's Aims,* 120–31.

23. v. Strantz, *Unser völkisches Kriegsziel,* 62. He estimated that there were at least 14 million Irish immigrants living in the U.S. who shared the German-American community's hatred of England.

24. On Germany and the Irish question before 1914, see Wolfgang Hünseler, *Das deutsche Kaiserreich und die irische Frage, 1900–1914* (Frankfurt a.M., 1978); James Joll, *The Origins of the First World War* (London, 1984), 97.

25. PA/AA Bonn, Deutschland 121, no. 33, Consul General to Bethmann Hollweg, 23 March 1914.

26. Ibid., telegram of Count Bernstorff, 18 November 1916.

27. Ibid., n.d.

28. I should like to thank Ed Milne for providing me with a copy of his University of Virginia master's thesis, "The Irish-German Alliance, 1907–1917."

29. Milne, "The Irish-German Alliance," 46.

30. PA/AA Bonn, Deutschland 121, no. 33, v. Strantz to v. Jagow, 21 May 1915. Von Strantz estimated that the United States had an army of 80,000 men, of which 40,000 were stationed in the Philippines and in the reserves. *Ein starkes Volk,* 15.

31. See, for example, *New York Times,* 22 October 1916.

32. Fischer, *War of Illusions,* 280–309.

33. PA/AA Bonn, Deutschland 121, no. 33, v. Strantz to ?, 7 April 1917 and 18 April 1917; see also v. Strantz, *Belgien als Sklave,* 33.

34. As quoted in Fischer, *Germany's Aims,* 396.

35. PA/AA Bonn, Deutschland 121, no. 33, v. Strantz to v. Jagow, 12 June 1915 and letter of 21 July 1917; v. Strantz, *Unser völkisches Kriegsziel,* 43.

36. v. Strantz, *Unser völkisches Kriegsziel*, 33.

37. Ibid., 29; v. Strantz, *Ein starkes Volk*, 18.

38. *Die Wehr*, Heft 6 (1914).

39. Fischer, *Germany's Aims*, 460, 456–72.

40. G. Horst Sieber was born in Dresden in 1864 but subsequently moved to the United States where he received his medical degree from the University of Chicago and interned at hospitals in Arkansas, California, and Pennsylvania. He was also an avid traveler and explorer who participated in expeditions in Africa. *Wer ist's*, 1912.

41. Born in 1852 at Gut Schierensee, Kreis Rendsburg, Schleswig-Holstein, v. Baudissin pursued a naval career, entering the Prussian navy in 1867 and naval academy in the 1870s. *Wer ist's*, 1912.

42. As president of the Röchling iron and steel works, Röchling's income was estimated at 5–6 million marks, according to Hans Jaeger, *Unternehmer in der deutschen Politik, 1890–1918* (Bonn, 1967), 65. On the Röchling family's close ties with the National Liberal Party, see Hartwig Thieme, *Nationaler Liberalismus in der Krise: Die nationalliberale Fraktion des preussischen Abgeordnetenhauses, 1914–1918* (Boppard, 1963), 33, 25. Poensgen, born in Cologne in 1873, was the son of a manufacturer and received a university education. He was also a member with Keim of the *Anti-Ultramontane Reichsverband* and later joined the Young Liberal Movement, becoming its leader in 1912, the same year in which he ran unsuccessfully as a National Liberal candidate for Wahlkreis Arnswalde-Friedeberg in Brandenburg.

43. *Die Wehr*, Heft 2 (1916).

44. Ibid., Heft 7 (1917).

45. So similar were the composition and aims of these associations that a Socialist Reichstag deputy charged in 1917 that "Pan-German League, Army League, Navy League, Colonial Society, League of the Eastern Marches, Independent Committee for a German Peace— they are always the same men, only the name of the firm changes." As quoted in Gatzke, *Germany's Drive*, 207.

46. The Information Bureau was founded on 22 February 1915, the Independent Committee on 13 July 1916, and the Central Coordinating Committee on 10 January 1917. British Library of Political and Economic Science (hereafter cited as BLEPES), Misc. Collection no. 84; Karl Heinz Schädlich, "Der 'Unabhängige Ausschuss für einen deutschen Frieden' als ein Zentrum der Annexionspropaganda des deutschen Imperialismus im ersten Weltkrieg," in Fritz Klein, ed., *Politik im Krieg, 1914–1918* (Berlin, 1964), 50–65; Dietrich Woygod, "Unabhängiger Ausschuss für einen deutschen Frieden, 1916–1918," in Fricke, *Die bürgerlichen Parteien*, 2:681–83. Dietrich Schäfer claimed to be one of the founders of the Central Coordinating Committee. Schäfer, *Mein Leben*, 221. Based upon a 1916 balance sheet (for a two-month period) of the Central Coordinating Committee, the league probably had an income of anywhere between 40,000 marks and 70,000 marks. BAK, Nachlass Alfred Hugenberg, Auskunftsstelle Vereinigter Verbände balance sheet for 31 August 1916. In October 1917, Hugenberg donated 50,000 marks to Poensgen's association. Letter of 23 October 1917, Poensgen to Hugenberg.

47. See, for example, *Die Wehr*, Heft 11 (1917). The league was so desperate for funds that members were urged to make provision in their wills to assist it. *Die Wehr*, Heft 9 (1918).

48. On two occasions, the Graf secured sums of 10,000 marks each from the Gelsenkirchen and Erhardt branches of the Gutehoffnungshütte, but in general, donations were considerably smaller, usually less than 1,000 marks. HA/GHH, no. 300 127/4, letter of Lohmann, 8 April 1918; letters of Mehner and Kalthoff, 9 April 1918; letter of Reusch and Kalthoff to v. Baudissin, 28 December 1917 and letters of 8 January 1918 and 1 February 1918.

49. *Die Wehr*, Heft 1 (1916).

50. See, for example, v. Strantz, *Belgien als Sklave*, 11–12.

51. Ibid., 14.

52. *Die Wehr*, Heft 1/2 (1915).

53. Keim papers, Otto zu Salm-Horstmar to Keim, 30 September 1917.

54. On the *Vaterlandspartei*, see Karl Wortmann, *Geschichte der deutschen Vaterlands-Partei, 1917–1918* (Halle, 1926); Stegmann, *Die Erben Bismarcks*, 497–519; Robert Ullrich, "Deutsche Vaterlandspartei, 1917-1918," in Fricke, *Die bürgerlichen Parteien*, 1: 620–28; and "Warum muss ich der Vaterslandpartei beitreten?" (Landesverband der Provinz Ostpreussen, 1918).

55. Keim papers, Salm-Horstmar to Keim, 30 September 1917. He was instrumental in organizing the *Vaterslandpartei* in Westphalia.

56. These figures are from Ullrich, "Deutsche Vaterlandspartei," 1: 620.

57. Hessisches Staatsarchiv Marburg, Vaterlandsverein 150/662, Police President of Frankfurt to *Oberpräsident* der Provinz Hessen-Nassau, 15 January 1918. The Police Chief also reported that the demonstrators were members of the Social Democratic Party and of the *Mittelstand*, who sang the "Marseilles" to disrupt the meeting.

58. *Die Wehr*, Heft 11 (1918).

59. Ibid., Heft 6 (1919); Kurt Stenkewitz, "Der Deutsche Wehrverein," in Fricke, *Die bürgerlichen Parteien*, 1: 574.

60. Schwarte (born in Solingen in 1860) was a military journalist and former instructor at the Military Academy who served as president of the Army League from 1920 until 1926. He was, coincidentally, a former student of Karl Litzmann at the Military Academy. Litzmann, *Lebenserinnerungen*, 2: 305; *Wer ist's*, 1922.

61. In line with his earlier experiences as a military journalist, Keim accepted the editorship of the *Monatsheft für Politik und Wehrmacht*, formerly the *Jahrbücher für deutsche Armee und Marine*, from 1919 until 1926.

62. In 1932 Litzmann was elected to the Prussian Landtag and in 1933 campaigned as a member of the NSDAP for a Reichstag seat in Wahlkreis 5 Frankfurt (Oder) and won. In November 1933 he represented Wahlkreis 4 Potsdam I until his death in June 1936. Hoover Institution, NSDAP Hauptarchiv; *Wer ist's* 1935.

63. *Wer ist's* 1935.

64. Keim, "Die Schuld am Weltkriege," (Berlin, 1919), and *Reichsverderber: Prinz Max von Baden und das Kriegskabinett*, 2 vols. (Berlin, 1922); Dietrich Schäfer, *Die Schuld am Krieg* (Berlin, 1919) and "Wie wurden wir ein Volk? Wie können wir es bleiben?" (Munich, 1919); Müller-Brandenburg, *Irrungen und Wirrungen;* Eduard v. Liebert, *Nationale Forderungen und Pflichten* (Munich, 1920).

65. Keim, "Die Schuld am Weltkriege," 9–12.

66. Ibid., 24–31; v. Strantz made the same contention in his *Belgien als Sklave*, 20–21, and in *Unser völkisches Kriegsziel*, 122.

67. *Die Wehr*, Heft 6 (1919).

68. Ibid., Heft 1 (1919).

69. Keim, *Erlebtes und Erstrebtes*, 256.

70. Litzmann, *Lebenserinnerungen*, 314.

71. v. Liebert, *Aus einem bewegten Leben*, 222–23.

72. Schäfer, *Mein Leben*, 151–52.

73. v. Strantz, *Unser völkisches Kriegsziel*, 229.

74. *Die Wehr*, Heft 3 (1919).

75. Ibid., "Der Krieg als Lehrer und Erzieher in Wirtschaftsleben," Heft 8 (1918).

76. Keim papers, Salm-Horstmar to Keim, 26 April 1920.

77. *Die Wehr,* "Die Geheimnisse der Weisen von Zion," Heft 2 (1920).

78. Ibid., "Der Weg zur Gesundung," Heft 6 (1920).

79. Ibid.

80. In 1928 the Army League continued to operate a *Landesverband* Hessen-Nassau und Waldeck through its Cassel branch and president Dr. Overbeck, the branch's original founder. This according to *Adresse-und-Einwohnerbuch der Stadt Cassel, 1928.* Dr. Overbeck also served as president of the local Pan-German League: *Alldeutsche Blätter,* no. 19, 19 June 1920. The Hamburg chapter, one of its largest before 1914, was no longer listed in the *Hamburger Adresse-Buch* after 1922.

81. The Army League also collaborated with the Young Germany Movement, whose *Geschäftsführer,* retired Major General Ludwig Vogt, served as Army League president from 1927 until 1935.

## Conclusion

1. *Schwäbische Merkur,* no. 182, 22 April 1913.

2. v. Strantz, *Unser völkisches Kriegsziel,* 226, 208.

3. On Bismarck's inner struggle, see Lothar Gall, *Bismarck. The White Revolutionary* (London, 1986), vol. 1 especially Chapters 1 and 2.

4. *Die Wehr,* Heft 2 (1917).

5. This theme is also developed in Detlev J. K. Peukert, *Inside Nazi Germany. Conformity, Opposition, and Racism in Everyday Life* (New Haven, 1987).

6. R. J. Overy, *The Nazi Economic Recovery, 1932–1938* (London, 1982), 54.

7. As quoted in J. Noakes and G. Pridham, eds., *Nazism, 1919–1945* (Exeter, 1983), 1: 37.

8. Ibid., 170.

# Bibliography

## Archival Sources

Hauptstaatsarchiv Stuttgart, (HSAS)

| | |
|---|---|
| J 150 no. 191/1/-6 | Deutscher Wehrverein |
| E 14 Bü 1389 | Deutscher Wehrverein, Landesverband Württemberg |
| E 130a no. 1241 | Deutscher Wehrverein |
| E 74 no. 314 | Wehrvorlage, 1913 |
| E 14 Bü 1344, 1345 | Deutscher Flottenverein, Landesverband Württemberg |
| E 14 Bü 1361 | Deutsche Kolonialgesellschaft, Landesverband Württemberg |
| E 14 Bü 1067 | Politische Vereine |
| Nachlass Konrad Haussmann | |

Militärarchiv Stuttgart (MAS)

| | |
|---|---|
| M 730 Bd. 527 | Deutscher Wehrverein, 1912–14 |
| M 1/2 Bd. 129 | Unabhängiger Ausschuss für einen deutschen Frieden |
| M 1/3 Bd. 54 | Deutscher Wehrverein, Landesverband Württemberg |
| M 1/3 Bd. 55 | Deutscher Wehrverein, Landesverband Württemberg |
| M 1/4 Bd. 4 | Deutscher Wehrverein, Landesverband Württemberg |
| M 1/4 Bd. 550 | Deutscher Wehrverein, Landesverband Württemberg |
| M 1/4 Bd. 558 | Deutscher Wehrverein, Landesverband Württemberg |
| M 1/11 Bd. 461 | Deutscher Wehrverein, Landesverband Württemberg |
| Mappe Soden | |

Staatsarchiv Hamburg (SAH)

| | |
|---|---|
| S 18591 | Deutscher Wehrverein |
| S 11792 | Reichsverband gegen die Sozialdemokratie |
| S 20648 | Unabhängiger Ausschuss für einen deutschen Frieden |
| S 20640 | Vaterlandspartei |
| S 6545 | Alldeutscher Verband |
| Vers. 452 | Alldeutscher Verband, Hamburg |

Hauptstaatsarchiv Düsseldorf, Schloss Kalkum (HSAD)

Regierung Aachen, Präsidialbüro 1092 III/7a    Kriegervereine Bd. 2, 1910–14
                                924 II/318      Deutscher Flottenverein, Bd. 1,
                                                  1898–1916
Regierung Düsseldorf            16017           Antilegionsverein, 1907–23
Regierung Düsseldorf            15959           Politische Vereine, 1910–16
Regierung Köln                  7755            Deutscher Flottenverein, 1905–10


Hessisches Staatsarchiv Marburg

150/665      Deutscher Wehrverein, 1912–14
150/651      Deutscher Flottenverein
150/662      Vaterlandsverein
180/4001     Konservativer Verein, Gelnhausen


Historisches Archiv der Gutehoffnungshütte, Oberhausen (HA/GHH)
(as of 1986 Haniel-Archiv, Duisburg-Ruhrort)

300 127/4        Deutscher Wehrverein, 1913–18
300 127/1        Nationale Vereine, 1910–13
300 127/0        Reichsverband gegen die Sozialdemokratie, 1907–16
300 106/34       Krieger und Militärvereine, 1908–29
300 106/65       Unterstützungen an Vereine, Verbände, 1909–22
300 106/82       Jungdeutschlandbund Sterkrade, 1913
300 106/114      Nationalliberale Partei, 1908–14
300 1012/28      Nationalliberale Partei, Oberhausen, 1913–14
300 19326/1      Deutscher Ostmarken-Verein, Berlin, 1910–12
300 19326/16–17  Verschiedene Vereine, 1912–13; 1920–22
300 19390/23     Fürst zu Salm Horstmar, 1915–17
300 1071/4       Nordwestliche Gruppe des Vereins deutscher Eisen und
                   Stahlindustrieller, 1913–14


Bundesarchiv Koblenz (BAK)

Nachlass Alfred Hugenberg
Nachlass Friedrich Wilhelm von Loebell
Nachlass Max Bauer
K1. Erw. 353, Paul Rohrbach
K1. Erw. 383, Akten der Fortschrittlichen Volkspartei (Pfarrer Traub)
Sgl-130, Reichsverband gegen die Sozialdemokratie, 1907–13


Reichskanzlei Akten

No. 2273      Wehrvereine, 1912–18
No. 2259a     Kriegervereine, 1909–12, Bd. 5
No. 2259b     Kriegervereine, 1912–18, Bd. 6
No. 2242      Vereins- und Versammlungsrecht, 1908–13, Bd. 5
No. 2243      Vereins- und Versammlungsrecht, 1913–16, Bd. 6
No. 1910      Beteiligung von Beamten an Vereinen, 1906–18
No. 1807      General Keim, 1906–7
No. 1415F     Die Alldeutschen, 1908–15, Bd. 1
No. 43 1/770  Vaterländische Vereine, 1923–33, Bd. 1

Generallandesarchiv Karlsruhe

    60/1616     Deutscher Wehrverein

Stadtarchiv Konstanz

    S II, No. 5812     Deutscher Wehrverein, Konstanz

Politisches Archiv/Auswärtiges Amt, Bonn (PA/AA Bonn)

    Deutschland 121, no. 33, Bd. 1 and 2     Deutscher Wehrverein
    Deutschland 122, no. 3, Bd. 25 and 33     Journalisten
    Deutschland 122, geheim Bd. 1     Journalisten
    Deutschland 121, no. 7, Bd. 5     Personalien von Offizieren und Leute der Armee, 1912–16
    Deutschland 138, no. 5     Deutscher Flottenverein
    Deutschland 169, no. 7, Bd. 4     Alldeutscher Verband
    Lübeck, no. 1, Bd. 1     Innere Verhältnisse Lübecks, 1895–1919
    Bremen, no. 1, Bd. 1     Innere Verhältnisse Bremen, 1890–1918
    Hamburg, no. 1, Bd. 4     Innere Verhältnisse Hamburgs, 1907–18
    Frankreich 95, no. 6     Die Französische Fremdenlegion
    Akten betr. den Deutschen Schulverein, Bd. 3, no. 101

    Nachlass Eisendecher

Bayerisches Staatsarchiv Coburg

    LA AI 28b 22/149     Deutscher Wehrverein, 1914–17

Stadtarchiv Coburg

    Vereinsregister Deutscher Wehrverein Coburg, 1914

Landeshauptarchiv Koblenz

    Oberpräsidium der Rheinprovinz, 403/9529     Deutscher Flottenverein

Stadtarchiv Oberhausen

    Nachlass Gehne, no. 54

Stadtarchiv Essen (SAE)

    Rep. 102, Abt. 1, no. 850     Deutscher Wehrverein

Zentrales Archiv Potsdam (ZAP) (Microfilm copies courtesy of Roger Chickering)

    Akten des Alldeutschen Verbandes: ADV nos. 192, 194, 197, 198, 406
    Nachlass Gebsattel

British Library of Political and Economic Science, London School of Economics (BLEPES)

    Misc. Collections, nos. 84, 111

Hoover Institution, Stanford University

NSDAP Hauptarchiv

Privately Held Collection

August Keim Papers

## Primary Sources

### Books and Articles

v. Arnim, Hans, and v. Below, Georg. *Deutscher Aufstieg: Bilder aus der Vergangenheit und Gegenwart der rechtstehenden Parteien.* Berlin: Franz Scheider, 1925.

Bechtold, Konrad. *Die deutsche Vaterlandspartei: Ihre Entstehung und Aufgaben.* Berlin: Carl Heymann, 1918.

Bernhardi, Friedrich A. J. v. *Germany and the Next War.* London: Longmans, Green & Co., 1914.

———. *Eine Weltreise 1911/12 und der Zusammenbruch Deutschlands.* Leipzig: Hirzel, 1920.

———. *Denkwürdigkeiten aus meinem Leben.* Berlin: E. S. Mittler, 1927.

v. Bissing, General. *Political Testament: A Study of German Ideals.* London: T. F. Unwin, 1917.

Class, Heinrich. *Wider den Strom.* Leipzig: K. F. Koehler, 1932.

Collenberg, Rüdt Freiherr v. *Generalfeldmarschall v. Mackensen.* Berlin: Karl Siegismund, 1935.

Dawson, William Harbutt. *What Is Wrong With Germany?* London: Longmans, Green & Co., 1915.

Delbrück, Clemens v. *Die wirtschaftliche Mobilmachung in Deutschland, 1914.* Munich: Verlag für Kulturpolitik, 1924.

Deutsche Vaterlandspartei. *Das deutsche Volk und der Friede.* Berlin: K. Curtius, 1918.

Deutsche Vaterlandspartei, Landesverein der Provinz Ostpreussen. *Warum muss ich der Vaterlandspartei beitreten?* Königsberg: Vaterlandspartei, 1917(?).

Egelhaaf, Gottlob. *Lebens-Erinnerungen.* Edited by Adolf Rapp. Stuttgart: W. Kohlhammer, 1960.

Einem, Karl v. *Erinnerungen eines Soldaten, 1853–1933.* Leipzig: K. F. Koehler, 1933.

Erzberger, Matthias. "Der Wehrbeitrag." In *Finanzwirtschaftliche Zeitfragen,* ed. Georg v. Schanz and Julius Wolf, 2 (1913): 1–33.

Goltz, Colmar Freiherr v. *The Nation in Arms.* English translation by Philip Ashworth. London: Longmans, Green & Co., 1906.

———. *Denkwürdigkeiten.* Edited by Friedrich Freiherr von der Goltz. Berlin: E. S. Mittler, 1929.

Hobohm, Martin, and Rohrbach, Paul. *Die Alldeutschen.* Vol. 2. Berlin: Hans R. Engelmann, 1919.

Keim, August. *Die Schuld am Weltkriege.* Berlin: Verlag der deutschen Zeitung, 1919.

———. *Reichsverderber: Prinz Max von Baden und das Kriegskabinett.* 2 vols. Berlin: Bath, 1922.

———. *Erlebtes und Erstrebtes: Lebenserinnerungen.* Hannover: Ernst Letsch, 1925.

Klingemann, Karl. *Glaube und Vaterlandsliebe.* Essen: G. D. Baedeker, 1915.

Lehmann, J. F. *Germany's Future with a Good Peace and a Bad Peace.* Translated by Edwyn Bevan. London: Darling & Son, 1918.

————. *Vierzig Jahre Dienst am Deutschtum, 1890–1930.* Munich: J. F. Lehmann, 1930.

Liebert, Eduard v. *Nationale Forderungen und Pflichten.* Munich: J. F. Lehmann, 1920.

————. *Aus einem bewegten Leben: Erinnerungen.* Munich: J. F. Lehmann, 1925.

Litzmann, Karl. *Lebenserinnerungen.* 2 vols. Berlin: R. Eisenschmidt, 1927–28.

Misch, Carl. *Geschichte des vaterländischen Frauen-Verein, 1866–1916.* Berlin: Carl Heymann, 1917.

Most, Otto. "Zur Wirtschafts- und Sozialstatistik der höheren Beamten in Preussen." *Schmollers Jahrbuch* 39 (1915): 181–218.

Müller-Brandenburg, Hermann. *Russland und Wir: Volkswirtschaftliche, politische und militärische Schlaglichter.* Berlin: Politik, 1914.

————. *Irrungen und Wirrungen: Schlaglichter auf den Zusammenbruch unserer Aussenpolitik.* Berlin: Politik, 1919.

————. *Offizier und Republik: Schlaglichter auf die Revolution.* Berlin: Verlag für Sozialwissenschaft, 1919.

————. *Von Schlieffen bis Ludendorff.* Leipzig: Ernst Oldenburg, 1925.

————. *Die Schuld der Anderen und der Betrug von Versailles.* Berlin: Schlieffen, 1931.

Naumann, Friedrich. "Die Partei der Nichtwähler." *Süddeutsche Monatsheft* (March 1907): 257–62.

Nippold, Otfried. *Der deutsche Chauvinisimus.* Berlin: W. Kohlhammer, 1913.

————. *Meine Erlebnisse in Deutschland vor dem Weltkriege, 1909–1914.* Bern: Der Freie Verlag, 1918.

Nordhausen, Richard. *Zwischen 14 und 18.* Leipzig: Fritz Eckardt, 1910.

Oncken, Hermann. *Historisch-politische Aufsätze und Reden.* Vol. 1. Munich: R. Oldenburg, 1914.

*Das Reichsvereinsgesetz vom 19. April 1908.* Leipzig: C. L. Hirschfeld, 1908.

Renner, Wilhelm. *Feldmarschall v. Mackensen: Ein Leben Charaktersbild.* Berlin: August Scherl, 1915.

Schäfer, Dietrich. *Unser Recht auf die Ostmarken: Vortrag gehalten am 4 März 1911 in der Berliner Ortsgruppe des Ostmarkenvereins.* 1911.

————. *Aufsätze, Vorträge und Reden.* 2 vols. Jena: Gustav Fischer, 1913.

————. *Das deutsche Volk und der Osten.* Leipzig: Teubner, 1915.

————. *Das Reichsland.* Berlin: G. Grote, 1917.

————. *Durch deutschen Sieg zum deutschen Frieden.* Berlin: K. Curtius, 1917.

————. *Die Schuld am Kriege.* Berlin: Gerhard Stalling, 1919.

————. *Wie wurden wir ein Volk? Wie können wir es bleiben?* Munich: J. F. Lehmann, 1919.

————. *Mein Leben.* Berlin: K. F. Koehler, 1926.

Schmidt-Gibichenfels, Otto. *Der tiefste Sinn des gegenwärtigen Krieges.* Berlin-Steglitz: Politisch-Anthropologischer Verlag, 1915.

Specht, Fritz. *Die Reichstagswahlen von 1867 bis 1897.* Berlin: Carl Heymann, 1898.

Stalling, Heinrich. *Ein deutscher Verleger.* Oldenburg: Gerhard Stalling, 1935.

Strahl, Fedor. "Der Streit um die Wehrsteuer." In *Finanzwirtschaftliche Zeitfragen*, ed. Georg v. Schanz and Julius Wolf, 7 (1913): 11–175.

Strantz, Kurd v. *Ihr wollt Elsass und Lothringen? Wir nehmen ganz Lothringen und mehr! Antwort auf das französische Rachegeschrei!* Berlin: Politik, 1912.

————. *Ein starkes Volk—ein starkes Heer.* Berlin: Politik, 1914.

————. *Unser völkisches Kriegsziel.* Leipzig: Reichenbach, 1918.

————. *Belgien als Sklave Englands im Lichte der Geschichte.* Leipzig: Reichenbach, 1918.

Unabhängiger Ausschuss für einen deutschen Frieden. *Die Neuordnung unserer östlichen Nachbargebiete—Ansprache und Reden.* Berlin: 1918.

Wermuth, Adolf. *Ein Beamtenleben.* Berlin: August Scherl, 1922.

Wetterlé, Abbé. *Behind the Scenes in the Reichstag: Sixteen Years of Parliamentary Life in Germany.* London: Hodder & Stoughton, 1918.

v. Wrochem, Hans. *Erinnerungen eines 'Chinesen.'* Berlin: Edwin Runge, 1910.

### Journals and Statistical Reference Works

*Alldeutsche Blätter,* 1908–22.

*Alldeutscher Verband: Flugschriften,* 1896–1913.

*Baedecker's Northern Germany,* 1904.

*Baedecker's Southern Germany,* 1910.

*Das Deutschtum im Auslande,* 1909–19.

*Deutsche Kolonial Zeitung,* 1911–14.

*Deutsche Revue über das gesamte nationale Leben der Gegenwart,* 1910–14.

*Deutsches Kolonial-Addressbuch,* 1908–11.

*Deutschlands Erneuerung,* 1917–18.

*Die Friedenswarte,* 1912–14.

*Festschrift zur 25. Feier des Allgemeiner Deutsche Sprachverein,* 1910.

*Gemeinde und Ortsverzeichnis für das Königreich Sachsen,* 1904.

*Gross Berlin Statistische Monatsberichte,* 1912–14.

Grosse, C., and Raith, C. *Beiträge zur Geschichte und Statistik des Reichstags und Landtagswahlen in Württemberg seit 1871* (1912).

*Handbuch der Provinz Sachsen,* 1912–14.

*Handbuch des Deutschtums im Auslande,* 1906.

*Hof und Staats-Handbuch des Königlichen Württemberg,* 1911–14.

*Jahrbuch für die deutsche Armee,* 1905.

Jahresbericht des Deutschen Flottenvereins für 1912.

*Militär-Handbuch des Königreichs Württemberg,* 1913.

National Service League. *The Nation in Arms,* 1907–14.

*Politisch-Anthropologische Revue,* 1912–15.

*Das Reichsland Elsass-Lothringen: Landes und Ortsbeschreibung,* 1898–1903.

*Reichstags Handbuch,* 1912.

*Schriften des Deutschen Wehrvereins,* 1912–14.

*Staatshandbuch für das Königreich Sachsen* 1912–14.

*Statistisches Handbuch,* 1912–14.

*Statistisches Jahrbuch der Stadt Berlin,* 1912–14.

*Statistisches Jahrbuch der Stadt Stuttgart,* 1902–13.

*Statistisches Jahrbuch für das deutsche Reich,* 1912–14.

*Statistisches Jahrbuch für das Königreich Sachsen,* 1912–13.

*Statistisches Jahrbuch für den Preussischen Staat,* 1912–14.

*Stenographische Berichte über die Verhandlungen des Reichstags,* 1911–14.

*Die Wehr,* 1912–20.

*Wehrkalender des Deutschen Wehrvereins,* 1914.

*Wer ist's,* 1912, 1922, 1935.

*Württembergische Vierteljahrshefte für Landesgeschichte,* 1908, 1916.

*Zeitschrift des Allgemeinen Deutschen Sprachvereins,* 1908–20.

### Newspapers

*Berliner Neueste Nachrichten.*

*Deutsche Tageszeitung.*

*Frankfurter Zeitung.*
*General-Anzeiger für Oberhausen, Sterkrade, Osterfeld, Bottrop und Umgegend.*
*Hamburger Echo.*
*Hamburger Fremdenblatt.*
*Hamburger General Anzeiger.*
*Hamburger Nachrichten.*
*Hamburgischer Korrespondent.*
*Kölnische Volkszeitung.*
*Kölnische Zeitung.*
*Konstanzer Zeitung.*
*Kreuzzeitung.*
*Leipziger Neueste Nachrichten.*
*Neue Hamburger Zeitung.*
*Neue Oberhausener Zeitung.*
*Neue Preussische Zeitung.*
*New York Times.*
*Norddeutsche Allgemeine Zeitung.*
*Die Post.*
*Rheinisch-Westfälische Zeitung.*
*Schwäbische Merkur.*
*Schwäbische Tagwacht.*
*Tägliche Rundschau.*
*Der Tag.*
*The Times* (London).
*Vorwärts.*
*Vossische Zeitung.*

## Secondary Sources

Balfour, Michael. *The Kaiser and His Times.* London: Cresset Press, 1964.

Barkin, Kenneth. *The Controversy over German Industrialization, 1890–1902.* Chicago: University of Chicago Press, 1970.

Berghahn, Volker. *Der Stahlhelm: Bund der Frontsoldaten, 1918–1935.* Düsseldorf: Droste, 1966.

———. *Germany and the Approach of War in 1914.* London: Macmillan, 1973.

———. "Militär, industrialisierte Kriegführung und Nationalismus." *Neue Politische Literatur* 26 (1981): 20–41.

Berghahn, V. R., and Kitchen, Martin, eds. *Germany in the Age of Total War.* London: Croom Helm, 1981.

Bertram, Jürgen. *Die Wahlen zum deutschen Reichstag vom Jahre 1912.* Düsseldorf: Droste, 1964.

Bessel, Richard. "Militarismus in innenpolitischen Leben der Weimarer Republik: von den Freikorps zur SA." In *Militär und Militarismus in der Weimarer Republik,* ed. Klaus-Jürgen Müller and Eckart Opitz, 193–222. Düsseldorf: Droste, 1978.

Bessel, Richard, and Feuchtwanger, E. J., eds. *Social Change and Political Development in Weimar Germany.* London: Croom Helm, 1981.

Blackbourn, David. "The Political Alignment of the Center Party in Wilhelmine Germany: A Study of the Party's Emergence in Nineteenth-Century Württemberg." *Historical Journal* 18 (1975): 821–50.

————. "Class and Politics in Wilhelmine Germany: The Center Party and the Social Democrats in Württemberg." *Central European History* 9 (1976): 220–49.

————. "The Mittelstand in German Society and Politics, 1871–1919." *Social History* 4 (1977): 409–33.

————. *Class, Religion, and Local Politics in Wilhelmine Germany*. London: Yale University Press, 1980.

————. "The Discreet Charm of the Bourgeoisie: Some Recent Works on German History." *European Studies Review* 11 (1981): 243–55.

————. "Between Resignation and Volatility: The German Petite Bourgeoisie in the Nineteenth Century." In *Shopkeepers and Master Artisans in Nineteenth-Century Europe*, ed. Geoffrey Crossick and Heinz-Gerhard Haupt, 35–61. London: Methuen, 1984.

————. "The Politics of Demagogy in Imperial Germany." *Past and Present* 113 (1986): 152–84.

————. "Politics as Theatre: Metaphors of the Stage in German History, 1848–1933." *Transactions of the Royal Historical Society* 37 (1987): 149–67.

————. *Populists and Patricians. Essays in Modern German History*. Boston: Allen & Unwin, 1987.

Blackbourn, David, and Geoff Eley. *The Peculiarities of German History: Bourgeois Society and Politics in Nineteenth-Century Germany*. Oxford: Oxford University Press, 1984.

Blanke, Richard. *Prussian Poland in the German Empire, 1871–1900*. Boulder, Colo.: East European Monographs/Columbia University Press, 1981.

Blessing, Werner K. "The Cult of Monarchy, Political Loyalty, and the Workers' Movement in Imperial Germany." *Journal of Contemporary History* 13 (1978): 357–75.

Böhm, Ekkehard. *Überseehandel und Flottenbau: Hanseatische Kaufmannschaft und deutsche Seerüstung, 1879–1902*. Düsseldorf: Bertelsmann, 1972.

Bolland, Jürgen. *Die Hamburgische Bürgerschaft in Alter und Neuer Zeit*. Hamburg: Auerdruck, 1959.

Bruch, Rüdiger vom. *Wissenschaft, Politik, und öffentliche Meinung: Gelehrtenpolitik im wilhelminischen Deutschland*. Husum: Mattiesen Verlag, 1980.

————. "'Deutschland und England: Heeres oder Flottenverstärkung?' Politische Publizistik deutscher Hochschullehrer, 1911/1912." *Militärgeschichtliche Mitteilungen* 29 (1981): 7–35.

Burchhardt, Lothar. *Friedenswirtschaft und Kriegsvorsorge: Deutschlands wirtschaftliche Rüstungsbestrebungen vor 1914*. Boppard: Harald Boldt, 1968.

Büsch, Otto, Wölk, Monika, and Wölk, Wolfgang, eds. *Wählerbewegung in der deutschen Geschichte*. Berlin: Colloquium, 1978.

Caplan, Jane. "The Imaginary Universality of Particular Interests: The 'Tradition' of the Civil Service in German History." *Social History* 4 (1977): 298–317.

Carsten, F. L. *War against War: British and German Radical Movements in the First World War*. Berkeley: University of California Press, 1982.

Cecil, Lamar. *Albert Ballin: Business and Politics in Imperial Germany, 1888–1918*. Princeton: Princeton University Press, 1967.

Chickering, Roger. *Imperial Germany and a World without War: The Peace Movement and Germany, 1892–1914*. Princeton: Princeton University Press, 1975.

————. "Der Deutsche Wehrverein und die Reform der deutschen Armee, 1912–1914." *Militärgeschichtliche Mitteilungen* 25 (1979): 7–33.

————. "Patriotic Societies and German Foreign Policy, 1890–1914." *The International History Review* 1 (1979): 470–89.

————. *We Men Who Feel Most German. A Cultural Study of the Pan-German League, 1886–1914*. London: Allen & Unwin, 1984.

———. "Die Alldeutschen erwarten den Krieg." In *Bereit zum Krieg. Kriegsmentalität im Wilhelminischen Deutschland 1890–1914*, ed. Jost Dülffer and Karl Holl, 20–32. Göttingen: Vandenhoeck and Ruprecht, 1986.

———. "'Casting Their Gaze More Broadly': Women's Patriotic Activism in Imperial Germany." *Past and Present* 118 (1988): 156–85.

Childers, Thomas. "The Social Bases of the National Socialist Vote." *Journal of Contemporary History* 11 (1976): 17–42.

———. "National Socialism and the New Middle-Class." In *Die Nationalsozialisten: Analysen faschistischer Bewegungen*, ed. Reinhard Mann, 14–33. Stuttgart: Klett-Cotta, 1980.

———. *The Nazi Voter. The Social Foundations of Fascism in Germany, 1919–1933*. Chapel Hill: University of North Carolina Press, 1983.

Coetzee, Frans. *For Party or Country: Nationalism and the Dilemmas of Popular Conservatism in Edwardian England*. New York: Oxford University Press, 1990.

Coetzee, Marilyn Shevin. "The Mobilization of the Right? The Deutscher Wehrverein and Political Activism in Württemberg, 1912–14." *European History Quarterly* 15 (1985): 431–52.

Coetzee, Marilyn Shevin, and Coetzee, Frans. "Rethinking the Radical Right in Germany and Britain before 1914." *Journal of Contemporary History* 21 (1986): 515–37.

Craig, Gordon. *The Politics of the Prussian Army*. Oxford: Oxford University Press, 1955.

———. *Germany, 1866–1945*. Oxford: Oxford University Press, 1978.

———. *The Germans*. New York: Putnam, 1982.

Crew, David. *Town in the Ruhr: A Social History of Bochum, 1860–1914*. New York: Columbia University Press, 1979.

Crothers, George D. *The German Elections of 1907*. New York: Columbia University Press, 1941.

Dahrendorf, Ralf. *Society and Democracy in Germany*. Garden City, N.Y.: Doubleday, 1967.

Dann, Otto. "Die Anfänge politischer Vereinsbildung im Deutschland." In *Soziale Bewegung und politische Verfassung*, ed. Ulrich Engelhardt, Volker Sellin, and Horst Stuke, 197–232. Stuttgart: Ernst Klett, 1976.

Deist, Wilhelm. *Flottenpolitik und Flottenpropaganda*. Stuttgart: Deutsche Verlagsanstalt, 1976.

Diehl, James. "Germany: Veterans' Politics under Three Flags." In *The War Generation: Veterans of the First World War*, ed. Steven R. Ward, 135–86. Port Washington, N.Y.: Kennikat Press, 1975.

———. *Paramilitary Politics in Weimar Germany*. Bloomington, Ind.: Indiana University Press, 1977.

———. "Von der 'Vaterlandspartei' zur 'Nationalen Revolution': Die Vereinigten Vaterländischen Verbände Deutschlands (VVVD), 1922–1932." *Vierteljahrhefte für Zeitgeschichte* 33 (1985): 617–39.

Dülffer, Jost, and Karl Holl, eds., *Bereit zum Krieg. Kriegsmentalität im wilhelminischen Deutschland, 1890–1914*. Göttingen: Vandenhoeck & Ruprecht, 1986.

Eley, Geoff. "The German Navy League in German Politics, 1898–1914." D. Phil. thesis, University of Sussex, 1974.

———. "Sammlungspolitik, Social Imperialism, and the Navy Law of 1898." *Militärgeschichtliche Mitteilungen* 15 (1974): 29–63.

———. "Defining Social Imperialism: Use and Abuse of an Idea." *Social History* 3 (1976): 265–90.

———. "Social Imperialism in Germany: Reformist Synthesis or Reactionary Sleight of

Hand?" In *Imperialismus im 20. Jahrhundert: Gedenkschrift für Georg W. F. Hallgarten,* ed. Joachim Radkau and Imanuel Geiss, 71–86. Munich: C. H. Beck, 1976.

―――. "Reshaping the Right: Radical Nationalism and the German Navy League, 1898–1908." *Historical Journal* 21 (1978): 327–54.

―――. "Some Thoughts on German Militarism." In *Militär und Militarismus,* ed. Klaus-Jürgen Müller and Eckart Opitz, 223–35. Düsseldorf: Droste, 1978.

―――. "The Wilhelmine Right: How It Changed." In *Society and Politics in Wilhelmine Germany,* ed. Richard J. Evans, 112–35. London: Croom Helm, 1978.

―――. *Reshaping the German Right: Radical Nationalism and Political Change after Bismarck.* New Haven: Yale University Press, 1980.

―――. *From Unification to Nazism. Reinterpreting the German Past.* London: Allen & Unwin, 1986.

Elliot, C. J. "The Kriegervereine and the Weimar Republic." *Journal of Contemporary History* 10 (1975): 109–29.

Evans, Richard J. *The Feminist Movement in Germany, 1894–1933.* London: Sage, 1976.

―――., ed. *Society and Politics in Wilhelmine Germany.* London: Croom Helm, 1978.

―――. *Rethinking German History.* London: Allen & Unwin, 1987.

―――. *Death in Hamburg. Society and Politics in the Cholera Years, 1830–1910.* Oxford: Oxford University Press, 1987.

Feld, M. D. "Professionalism, Nationalism, and the Alienation of the Military." In *Armed Forces and Society,* ed. Jacques Van Doorn, 55–70. The Hague: Mouton, 1967.

Feldman, Gerald. *Army, Industry, and Labor in Germany, 1914–1918.* Princeton: Princeton University Press, 1966.

―――. "Economic and Social Problems of the German Demobilization, 1918–19." *Journal of Modern History* 47 (1975): 1–47.

Fenske, Hans. *Der liberale Südwesten: Freiheitliche und demokratische Traditionen in Baden und Württemberg, 1790–1933.* Stuttgart: W. Kohlhammer, 1981.

Fesser, Gerd. "Von der 'Zuchthausvorlage' zum Reichsvereinsgesetz. Staatsorgane, bürgerliche Parteien, und Vereinsgesetzgebung im Deutschen Reich, 1899–1906." *Jahrbuch für Geschichte* 28 (1983): 107–32.

Fischer, Fritz. *Germany's Aims in the First World War.* New York: W. W. Norton, 1967.

―――. *War of Illusions: German Policies from 1911 to 1914.* New York: W. W. Norton, 1975.

―――. "Der Stellenwert des Ersten Weltkrieges in der Kontinuitätsproblematik der deutschen Geschichte." *Historische Zeitschrift* 229 (1979): 25–53.

Fischer, Joachim. "Das württembergische Offizierkorps, 1866–1918." In *Das deutsche Offizierkorps, 1860–1960,* ed. Hans Hubert Hofmann, 99–138. Boppard: Harald Boldt, 1980.

Förster, Stig. *Der doppelte Militarismus. Die deutsche Heeresrüstungspolitik zwischen Status-quo-Sicherung und Aggression, 1890–1913.* Wiesbaden: Franz Steiner, 1985.

Freudenthal, Herbert. *Vereine in Hamburg: Ein Beitrag zur Geschichte und Volkskunde der Geselligkeit.* Hamburg: Museum für Hamburgische Geschichte, 1968.

Fricke, Dieter. "Der Reichsverband gegen die Sozialdemokratie von seiner Gründung bis zu den Reichstagswahlen von 1907." *Zeitschrift für Geschichtswissenschaft* 7 (1959): 237–80.

―――. *Die bürgerlichen Parteien in Deutschland, 1830–1945.* 2 vols. Leipzig: Verlag Enzyklopädie, 1968–1970.

Fritsch-Seerhausen, Thomas Freiherr v. "Das sächsische Offizierkorps, 1867–1918." In *Das deutsche Offizierkorps, 1866–1960,* ed. Hans Hubert Hofmann, 59–73. Boppard: Harald Boldt, 1980.

Gall, Lothar. "Liberalismus und 'Bürgerliche Gesellschaft': Zur Charakter und Entwicklung der Liberalen Bewegung in Deutschland." *Historische Zeitschrift* 220 (1975): 324–56.

———. *Bismarck. The White Revolutionary*. 2 vols. London: Allen & Unwin, 1986.

Galos, Adam; Gentzen, Felix-Heinrich; and Jakóbczyk, Witold. *Die Hakatisten: Der deutsche Ostmarkenverein (1894–1934)*. Berlin: VEB Deutscher Verlag der Wissenschaften, 1966.

Gatzke, Hans. *Germany's Drive to the West*. Baltimore: Johns Hopkins University Press, 1950.

Geary, Dick. *European Labor Protest, 1848–1939*. London: Croom Helm, 1981.

Gellately, Richard. *The Politics of Economic Despair: Shopkeepers and German Politics, 1890–1914*. London: Sage, 1974.

Gordon, Michael R. "Domestic Conflict and the Origins of the First World War: The British and German Cases." *Journal of Modern History* 46 (1974): 191–226.

Groh, Dieter. *Negative Integration und revolutionärer Attentismus: Die deutsche Sozialdemokratie am Vorabend des Ersten Weltkriegs*. Frankfurt a.M.: Ullstein, 1973.

Grupp, Peter. "Die deutsche Kolonialgesellschaft in der Agadirkrise." *Francia* 7 (1979): 285–307.

Guratzsch, Dankwart. *Macht durch Organisation*. Düsseldorf: Bertelsmann, 1974.

Gutsche, Willibald. "Zu einigen Fragen der staatsmonopolistischen Verflechtung in den ersten Kriegsjahren am Beispiel der Ausplünderung der belgischen Industrie und der Zwangsdeportation von Belgien." In *Politik im Krieg, 1914–1918: Studien zur Politik der deutschen herrschenden Klassen im ersten Weltkrieg,* ed. Fritz Klein, 66–89. Berlin: Akademie Verlag, 1964.

Guttsman, W. L. *The German Social Democratic Party, 1875–1933: From Ghetto to Government*. London: Allen & Unwin, 1981.

Hagen, William. *Germans, Poles, and Jews: The Nationality Conflict in the Prussian East, 1772–1914*. Chicago: University of Chicago Press, 1980.

Hallgarten, G. W. F. *Imperialismus vor 1914*. Munich: C. H. Beck, 1963.

Hamel, Iris. *Völkischer Verband und nationale Gewerkschaft: Der Deutschnationale Handlungsgehilfen-Verband, 1893–1933*. Frankfurt a.M.: Europäische Verlagsanstalt, 1967.

*Handbuch zur deutschen Militärgeschichte, 1648–1939: Von der Entlassung Bismarcks bis zum Ende des Ersten Weltkrieges (1890–1918)*. Vol. 5. Frankfurt a.M.: Bernard & Graefe, 1968.

Hardach, Gerd. *The First World War, 1914–1918*. Berkeley: University of California Press, 1977.

Hartwig, Edgar. "Zur Politik des Alldeutschen Verbandes von seiner Gründung bis zum Beginn des Ersten Weltkrieges, 1891–1914." Ph.D. diss., University of Jena, 1966.

Heckart, Beverly. *From Basserman to Bebel: The Grand Bloc's Quest for Reform in the Kaiserreich, 1900–1914*. New Haven: Yale University Press, 1974.

Henning, Hans-Joachim. "Kriegervereine in den Preussischen Westprovinzen: Ein Beitrag zur preussischen Innenpolitik zwischen 1860 und 1914." *Rheinische Vierteljahrblätter* 32 (1968): 430–75.

———. *Das Westdeutsche Bürgertum in der Epoche der Hochindustrialisierung, 1860–1914*. Vol. 1. Wiesbaden: Franz Steiner, 1972.

Herwig, Holger. *The German Naval Officers Corps: A Social and Political History, 1890–1918*. Oxford: Oxford University Press, 1973.

Herzfeld, Hans. *Die deutsche Rüstungspolitik vor dem Weltkriege*. Bonn & Leipzig: K. Schroeder, 1923.

Hobsbawn, Eric. "Mass-Producing Traditions: Europe, 1870–1914." In *The Invention of*

*Tradition,* ed. Eric Hobsbawm and Terence Ranger, 263–307. Cambridge: Cambridge University Press, 1983.

Hoehn, Reinhard. *Die Armee als Erziehungsschule der Nation: Das Ende einer Idee.* Bad Harzburg: Verlag für Wissenschaft, Wirtschaft, und Technik, 1963.

Hofmann, Wolfgang. *Zwischen Rathaus und Reichskanzlei: Die Oberbürgermeister in der Kommunal- und Staatspolitik des deutschen Reiches von 1890 bis 1933.* Stuttgart: W. Kohlhammer, 1974.

Hohorst, Gerd; Kocka, Jürgen; and Ritter, Gerhard A. *Sozialgeschichtliches Arbeitsbuch: Materialien zur Statistik des Kaiserreichs, 1870–1914.* Munich: C. H. Beck, 1975.

Holl, Karl, and List, Gunther, eds. *Liberalismus und imperialistischer Staat.* Göttingen: Vandenhoeck & Ruprecht, 1975.

Hopwood, Robert. "Paladins of the Bürgertum: Cultural Clubs and Politics in Small German Towns, 1918–1925." *Canadian Historical Association Historical Papers* (1974): 213–35.

Hueber, Adolf. "Das Vereinsrecht im Deutschland des 19. Jahrhunderts." In *Das Vereinswesen und bürgerliche Gesellschaft in Deutschland,* ed. Otto Dann, 115–32. Munich: R. Oldenbourg, 1984.

Hull, Isabel V. *The Entourage of Kaiser Wilhelm II, 1888–1918.* Cambridge: Cambridge University Press, 1982.

Hunt, James C. "The 'Egalitarianism' of the Right: The Agrarian League in Southwest Germany, 1893–1914." *Journal of Contemporary History* 10 (1975): 513–30.

———. *The People's Party in Württemberg and Southern Germany, 1890–1914.* Stuttgart: Ernst Klett, 1975.

———. "The Bourgeois Middle in German Politics, 1871–1933: Recent Literature." *Central European History* 11 (1978): 83–106.

Jaeger, Hans. *Unternehmer in der deutschen Politik, 1890–1918.* Bonn: Ludwig Röhrscheid, 1967.

Jarausch, Konrad. "The Illusion of Limited War: Chancellor Bethmann Hollweg's Calculated Risk, July 1914." *Central European History* 2 (1969): 48–76.

———. *The Enigmatic Chancellor: Bethmann Hollweg and the Hubris of Imperial Germany.* New Haven: Yale University Press, 1973.

———. "From Second to Third Reich: The Problem of Continuity in German Foreign Policy." *Central European History* 12 (1979): 68–82.

———. *Students, Society, and Politics in Imperial Germany.* Princeton: Princeton University Press, 1982.

Jochmann, Werner. "Struktur und Funktion des deutschen Antisemitismus." In *Juden im wilhelminischen Deutschland, 1890–1914,* ed. Werner E. Mosse, 389–477. Tübingen: J. C. B. Mohr, 1976.

John, Hans-Georg. *Politik und Turnen: Die deutsche Turnerschaft als Nationale Bewegung im Deutschen Kaiserreich, 1871–1914.* Ahrensburg bei Hamburg: Ingrid Czwalina, 1976.

John, Hartmut. *Das Reserveoffizierkorps im Deutschen Kaiserreich, 1890–1914: Ein Sozialgeschichtlicher Beitrag zur Untersuchung der Gesellschaftlichen Militärisierung im wilhelminischen Deutschland.* Frankfurt a.M.: Campus, 1981.

Joll, James. *The Origins of the First World War.* London: Longman, 1984.

Jones, Larry E. "'The Dying Middle': Weimar Germany and the Fragmentation of Bourgeois Politics." *Central European History* 5 (1972): 23–54.

Kaelble, Hartmut. *Industrielle Interessenpolitik in der wilhelminischen Gesellschaft: Zentralverband Deutscher Industriellen, 1895–1914.* Berlin: de Gruyter, 1967.

————. "Industrielle Interessenverbände vor 1914." In *Zur soziologischen Theorie und Analyse des 19. Jahrhunderts,* ed. W. Rüegg and O. Neuloh, 180–92. Göttingen: Vandenhoeck & Ruprecht, 1971.

————. "Sozialer Aufstieg in Deutschland, 1850–1914." *Vierteljahrschrift für Sozial und Wirtschafts Geschichte* 60 (1973): 41–71.

Kaulisch, Baldur. "Die Auseinandersetzungen über den uneingeschränkten U-Boot-Krieg innerhalb der herrschenden Klassen im zweiten Halbjahr 1916 und seine Eröffnung im Februar 1917." In *Politik im Krieg, 1914–1918: Studien zu Politik der deutschen herrschenden Klassen im ersten Weltkrieg,* ed. Fritz Klein, 90–117. Berlin: Akademie Verlag, 1964.

Kehr, Eckart. *Battleship Building and Party Politics in Germany, 1894–1901.* Chicago: Midway Reprints, 1975.

————. *Economic Interest, Militarism, and Foreign Policy.* Berkeley: University of California Press, 1977.

Kelly, Alfred. *The Descent of Darwin: The Popularization of Darwinism in Germany, 1860–1914.* Chapel Hill: University of North Carolina Press, 1981.

Kennedy, Paul M. *The Rise of the Anglo-German Antagonism, 1860–1914.* London: Allen & Unwin, 1980.

Kennedy, Paul M., and Nicholls, Anthony, eds. *Nationalist and Racialist Movements in Britain and Germany before 1914.* London: Macmillan, 1981.

Kersten, Dietrich. "Die Kriegsziele der Hamburger Kaufmannschaft im Ersten Weltkrieg: Ein Beitrag zur Frage der Kriegszielpolitik im Kaiserlichen Deutschland, 1914–1918." Ph.D. diss., University of Hamburg, 1962.

Kitchen, Martin. *The German Officer Corps, 1890–1914.* Oxford: Oxford University Press, 1968.

————. *The Silent Dictatorship: The Politics of the German High Command under Hindenburg and Ludendorff, 1916–1918.* New York: Holmes & Meier, 1976.

Klein, Thomas. "Reichstagswahlen-und-Abgeordnete der Provinz Sachsen und Anhalts, 1867–1918: Ein Überblick." In *Festschrift für Friedrich von Zahn,* ed. Walter Schlesinger, 1: 65–141. Cologne: Böhlau, 1968.

Koch, H. W. ed. *Origins of the First World War.* London: Macmillan, 1972.

Kocka, Jürgen. *Klassengesellschaft im Krieg, 1914–1918.* Göttingen: Vandenhoeck & Ruprecht, 1973.

————. "The First World War and the 'Mittelstand': German Artisans and White-Collar Workers." *Journal of Contemporary History* 8 (1973): 101–23.

————. *Die Angestellten in der deutschen Geschichte, 1850–1980.* Göttingen: Vandenhoeck & Ruprecht, 1981.

————. "Der 'deutsche Sonderweg' in der Diskussion." *German Studies Review* 5 (1982): 365–79.

Kocka, Jürgen, ed. *Arbeiter und Bürger im 19. Jahrhundert.* Munich: R. Oldenbourg, 1986.

Koshar, Rudy. "Two Nazisms: The Social Context of Nazi Mobilization in Marburg and Tübingen." *Social History* 7 (1982): 27–42.

————. *Social Life, Local Politics, and Nazism. Marburg, 1880–1935.* Chapel Hill: University of North Carolina Press, 1986.

Kruck, Alfred. *Geschichte des Alldeutschen Verbandes, 1890–1939.* Wiesbaden: Franz Steiner, 1954.

Krumeich, Gerd. *Armaments and Politics in France on the Eve of the First World War.* Leamington Spa: Berg, 1984.

Kuczynski, Jürgen. *Studien zur Geschichte des deutschen Imperialismus.* Vol. 2. Berlin: Dietz, 1950.

Lebovics, Herman. *Social Conservatism and the Middle Classes in Germany, 1914–1933.* Princeton: Princeton University Press, 1969.

Leed, Eric. *No Man's Land: Combat and Identity in World War I.* Cambridge: Cambridge University Press, 1979.

Levy, Richard S. *The Downfall of the Anti-Semitic Political Parties in Imperial Germany.* New Haven: Yale University Press, 1975.

Lidtke, Vernon. *The Alternative Culture: Socialist Labor in Imperial Germany.* New York: Oxford University Press, 1985.

Lohalm, Uwe. *Völkischer Radikalismus: Die Geschichte des Deutschvölkischen Schutz und Trutz Bundes.* Hamburg: Leibniz-Verlag, 1976.

Maier, Charles S. *Recasting Bourgeois Europe: Stabilization in France, Germany, and Italy in the Decade after World War I.* Princeton: Princeton University Press, 1975.

Marsh, David. "On Joining Interest Groups: An Empirical Consideration of the Work of Mancur Olson Jr." *British Journal of Political Science* 6 (1976): 257–71.

Mayer, Arno. *The Persistence of the Old Regime: Europe to the Great War.* London: Croom Helm, 1981.

Meyer, Wolfgang. *Vereinswesen der Stadt Weinheim an der Bergstrasse.* Weinheim: Stadt Weinheim a.d.B., 1963.

Mielke, Siegfried. *Der Hansabund für Gewerbe, Handel, und Industrie, 1909–1914.* Göttingen: Vandenhoeck & Ruprecht, 1976.

Mitchell, Allan. "A 'Situation of Inferiority': French Military Reorganization after the Defeat of 1870." *American Historical Review* 86 (1981): 49–62.

Mock, Wolfgang. "'Manipulation von oben' oder Selbstorganisation an der Basis? Einige neuere Ansätze in der englischen Historiographie zur Geschichte des deutschen Kaiserreichs." *Historische Zeitschrift* 232 (1981): 358–75.

Moe, Terry. *The Organization of Interests.* Chicago: University of Chicago Press, 1980.

Mommsen, Hans; Petzina, D.; and Weisbrod, Bernd, eds. *Industrielles System und politische Entwicklung in der Weimarer Republik.* Düsseldorf: Droste, 1974.

Mommsen, Wolfgang. "Domestic Factors in German Foreign Policy before 1914." *Central European History* 6 (1973): 3–43.

———. "The Topos of Inevitable War in Germany in the Decade before 1914." In *Germany in the Age of Total War,* ed. Volker Berghahn and Martin Kitchen, 23–45. London: Croom Helm, 1981.

Moses, John. *The Politics of Illusion: The Fischer Controversy in German Historiography.* London: George Prior, 1975.

Müller, Klaus-Jürgen, and Opitz, Eckardt, eds. *Militär und Militarismus in der Weimarer Republik.* Düsseldorf: Droste, 1978.

Muncy, Lysbeth W. "The Prussian Landräte in the Last Years of the Monarchy: A Case Study of Pomerania and the Rhineland in 1890–1918." *Central European History* 6 (1973): 299–338.

Nichols, J. Alden. *Germany after Bismarck: The Caprivi Era, 1890–1894.* Cambridge, Mass.: Harvard University Press, 1958.

Niendorf, Helmut. *Geschichte des Handelshauses Possehl, 1847–1919.* Lübeck: Possehl Stiftung, 1957.

Nipperdey, Thomas. *Die Organisation der deutschen Parteien.* Düsseldorf: Droste, 1961.

———. "Interessenverbände und Parteien in Deutschland vor dem Ersten Weltkrieg." *Politische Vierteljahrschrift* 2 (1961): 262–80.

———. "Nationalidee und Nationaldenkmal in Deutschland im 19. Jahrhundert," *Historische Zeitschrift* 206 (1968): 559–85.

———. "Verein als soziale Struktur in Deutschland im späten 18. und frühen 19. Jahrhundert." In *Geschichtswissenschaft und Vereinswesen im 19. Jahrhundert*, ed. Hartmut Boockmann, 1–44. Göttingen: Vandenhoeck & Ruprecht, 1972.

Nusser, Horst G. W. *Konservative Wehrverbände in Bayern, Preussen, und Österreich, 1918–1933*. Munich: Nusser, 1973.

O'Donnell, Anthony. "National Liberalism and the Mass Politics of the German Right, 1890–1907." Unpubl. Ph.D. diss., Princeton University, 1974.

Olson, Mancur. *The Logic of Collective Action*. Cambridge, Mass.: Harvard University Press, 1965.

Oncken, Emily. *Panthersprung nach Agadir: Die deutsche Politik während der zweiten Morokkokrise, 1911*. Düsseldorf: Droste, 1981.

Peck, Abraham J. *Radicals and Reactionaries: The Crisis of Conservatism in Wilhelmine Germany*. Washington: University Press of America, 1978.

Pierard, Richard V. "The German Colonial Society, 1882–1914." Ph.D. diss., University of Iowa, 1964.

Porch, Douglas. *The March to the Marne: The French Army, 1871–1914*. Cambridge: Cambridge University Press, 1981.

Puhle, Hans-Jürgen. "Parlament, Parteien, und Interessenverbände, 1890–1914." In *Das Kaiserliche Deutschland*, ed. Michael Stürmer, 340–77. Düsseldorf: Droste, 1970.

———. *Agrarische Interessenpolitik und preussischer Konservatismus im wilhelminischen Reich, 1893–1914*. 2d ed. Bonn-Bad Godesberg: Verlag Neue Gesellschaft, 1975.

———. "Conservatism in Modern German History." *Journal of Contemporary History* 13 (1978): 689–720.

Pulzer, Peter G. J. *The Rise of Political Anti-Semitism in Germany and Austria*. New York: Wiley, 1964.

Ralston, David B. *The Army of the Republic: The Place of the French Military in the Political Evolution of France, 1871–1914*. Cambridge, Mass.: M.I.T. Press, 1967.

Retallack, James N. *Notables of the Right. The Conservative Party and Political Mobilization in Germany, 1876–1918*. Boston: Unwin Hyman, 1988.

Ringer, Fritz. *The Decline of the German Mandarins*. Cambridge, Mass.: Harvard University Press, 1969.

Ritter, Gerhard. *The Sword and the Scepter: The Problem of Militarism in Germany*. Vol. 2. Coral Gables, Fla.: University of Florida Press, 1969.

———, ed. *Die deutsche Parteien vor 1918*. Cologne: Kiepenheuer & Witsch, 1973.

Roberts, James S. "Drink and the Labour Movement: The Schnaps Boycott of 1909." In *The German Working Class, 1888–1933*, ed. Richard J. Evans, 80–107. London: Croom Helm, 1982.

———. *Drink, Temperance, and the Working Class in Nineteenth-Century Germany*. London: Allen & Unwin, 1984.

Röhl, J. C. G. *Germany without Bismarck: The Crisis of Government in the Second Reich, 1890–1900*. Berkeley: University of California Press, 1967.

———. "Higher Civil Servants in Germany, 1890–1900." In *Imperial Germany*, ed. James J. Sheehan, 129–51. New York: Franklin Watts, 1976.

Röhl, J. C. G., and Werner Sombart, eds. *Kaiser Wilhelm II: New Interpretations: The Corfu Papers*. Cambridge: Cambridge University Press, 1982.

Rosenberg, Hans. *Grosse Depression und Bismarckzeit*. Berlin: Walter de Gruyter, 1967.

Ross, Ronald. *Beleaguered Tower: The Dilemma of Political Catholicism in Wilhelmine Germany*. Notre Dame: University of Notre Dame Press, 1976.

Saul, Klaus. "Der deutsche Kriegerbund: Zur innenpolitischen Funktion eines nationalen Verbandes im kaiserlichen Deutschland." *Militärgeschichtliche Mitteilungen* 2 (1969): 95–130.

————. *Staat, Industrie, Arbeiterbewegung im Kaiserreich.* Düsseldorf: Bertelsmann, 1974.

Schädlich, Karl Heinz. "Der 'Unabhängige Ausschuss für einen deutschen Frieden' als ein Zentrum der Annexionspropaganda des deutschen Imperialismus im ersten Weltkrieg." In *Politik im Krieg, 1914–1918,* ed. Fritz Klein, 50–65. Berlin: Akademie Verlag, 1964.

Scheer, Friedrich-Karl. *Die deutsche Friedensgesellschaft (1892–1933): Organisation, Ideologie, politische Ziele.* Frankfurt: Haag & Herchen, 1981.

Schellenberg, Johanna. "Die Herausbildung der Militärdiktatur in den ersten Jahren des Krieges." In *Politik im Krieg, 1914–1918,* ed. Fritz Klein, 22–49. Berlin: Akademie Verlag, 1964.

Schilling, Konrad. "Beiträge zu einer Geschichte des radikalen Nationalismus in der Wilhelminischen Ära, 1890–1909." Inaugural diss., Universität Köln, 1968.

Schmidt, Gustav. "Innenpolitische Blockbildungen am Vorabend des Ersten Weltkrieges." *Das Parlament,* Beiheft 20 (1972): 1–32.

————. "Parlamentarisierung oder 'Präventive Konterrevolution'? Die deutsche Innenpolitik im Spannungsfeld konservativer Sammlungsbewegungen und latenter Reformbestrebungen, 1907–1914." In *Gesellschaft, Parlament und Regierung: Zur Geschichte des Parlamentarismus in Deutschland,* ed. Gerhard A. Ritter, 249–70. Düsseldorf: Droste, 1974.

Schoenbaum, David. *Zabern 1913: Consensus Politics in Imperial Germany.* London: Allen & Unwin, 1982.

Schröter, Klaus. "Chauvinism and its Tradition: German Writers and the Outbreak of the First World War," *The Germanic Review* 43 (1968): 120–35.

Schulte, Bernd-Felix. *Die deutsche Armee, 1900–1914, Zwischen Beharren und Verändern.* Düsseldorf: Droste, 1977.

Schwabe, Klaus. *Wissenschaft und Kriegsmoral: Die deutschen Hochschullehrer und die politischen Grundfragen des Ersten Weltkrieges.* Göttingen: Musterschmidt, 1969.

Schwarz, Max. *MdR:Biographisches Handbuch der Reichstage.* Hannover: Verlag für Literatur und Zeitgeschehen, 1965.

Schwinn, Erich. "Die Arbeit des Deutschen Wehrvereins und die Wehrlage Deutschlands vor dem Weltkriege." Ph.D. diss., University of Heidelberg, 1940.

Sheehan, James J. "Political Leadership in the German Reichstag, 1871–1918." *American Historical Review* 74 (1968): 511–28.

————. *German Liberalism in the Nineteenth Century.* Chicago: University of Chicago Press, 1978.

Silverman, Dan P. *Reluctant Union: Alsace-Lorraine and Imperial Germany.* College Park, Penn.: Penn State University Press, 1972.

Simon, Klaus. *Die württembergischen Demokraten: Ihre Stellung und Arbeit im Parteien und Verfassungsystem in Württemberg und im Deutschen Reich, 1890–1920.* Stuttgart: W. Kohlhammer, 1969.

Smith, Woodruff D. *The German Colonial Empire.* Chapel Hill: University of North Carolina Press, 1978.

————. *The Ideological Origins of Nazi Imperialism.* Oxford: Oxford University Press, 1985.

Spencer, Elaine Glovka. "Rulers of the Ruhr: Leadership and Authority in German Big Business before 1914." *Business History Review* 53 (1979): 41–64.

Stark, Gary D. *Entrepreneurs of ideology: Neoconservative Publishers in Germany, 1890–1933.* Chapel Hill: University of North Carolina Press, 1981.

————. "Cinema, Society, and the State: Policing the Film Industry in Imperial Germany." In *Essays on Culture and Society in Modern Germany,* ed. Gary D. Stark and Bede Karl Lackner, 123–66. College Station: Texas A&M Press, 1982.

Stearns, Peter N. "The Middle Class: Toward a Precise Definition." *Comparative Studies in Society and History* 21 (1979): 377–96.

Stegmann, Dirk. *Die Erben Bismarcks: Parteien und Verbände in der Spätphase des wilhelminischen Deutschlands.* Cologne: Kiepenheuer & Witsch, 1970.

———. "Zwischen Repression und Manipulation: Konservative Machteliten und Arbeiter- und Angestelltenbewegung, 1910–1918: Ein Beitrag zur Vorgeschichte der DAP/NSDAP." *Archiv für Sozialgeschichte* 12 (1972): 351–432.

———. "Vom Neokonservatismus zum Proto-Faschismus: Konservative Partei, Vereine und Verbände, 1893–1920." In *Deutscher Konservatismus in 19. und 20. Jahrhundert,* ed. Dirk Stegmann, 199–230. Bonn: Verlag Neue Gesellschaft, 1983.

Stenkewitz, Kurt. *Gegen Bajonett und Dividende: Die politische Krise in Deutschland am Vorabend des ersten Weltkrieges.* Berlin: Rütten & Loenig, 1960.

———. "Deutscher Wehr-Verein, 1912–1935." In *Die bürgerlichen Parteien in Deutschland,* ed. Dieter Fricke, 1: 574–81. Leipzig: Verlag Enzyklopädie, 1969.

Stern, Fritz. *The Politics of Cultural Despair.* Berkeley: University of California Press, 1961.

———. *The Failure of Illiberalism: Essays on the Political Culture of Modern Germany.* New York: Alfred A. Knopf, 1972.

Strandmann, Hartmut Pogge von. "Staatsstreichpläne, Alldeutsche und Bethmann Hollweg." In *Die Erforderlichkeit des Unmöglichen: Deutschland am Vorabend des ersten Weltkrieges,* ed. Hartmut Pogge von Strandmann and Imanuel Geiss, 7–45. Frankfurt a.M.: Europäische Verlagsanstalt, 1965.

———. "Nationale Verbände zwischen Weltpolitik und Kontinentalpolitik." In *Marine und Marinepolitik im kaiserlichen Deutschland, 1871–1914,* ed. H. Schottelius and W. Deist, 296–317. Düsseldorf: Droste, 1972.

Struve, Walter. *Elites against Democracy: Leadership Ideals in Bourgeois Political Thought in Germany, 1890–1933.* Princeton: Princeton University Press, 1973.

Stürmer, Michael. "Machtgefüge und Verbandsentwicklung in Deutschland." *Neue Politische Literatur* 14 (1969): 490–507.

Summler, David F. "Domestic Influences on the Nationalist Revival in France, 1909–1914." *French Historical Studies* 6 (1970): 517–37.

Suval, Stanley. *Electoral Politics in Wilhelmine Germany.* Chapel Hill: University of North Carolina Press, 1985.

Tenfelde, Klaus. "Die Entfaltung des Vereinswesens während der industriellen Revolution in Deutschland (1850–1873)." In *Vereinswesen und bürgerliche Gesellschaft in Deutschland,* ed. Otto Dann, 55–114. Munich: R. Oldenbourg, 1984.

Thieme, Hartwig. *Nationaler Liberalismus in der Krise: Die nationalliberale Fraktion der preussischen Abgeordnetenhauses, 1914–1918.* Boppard: Harald Boldt, 1963.

Tims, Richard W. *Germanizing Prussian Poland: The H-K-T Society and the Struggle for Eastern Marches in the German Empire.* New York: Columbia University Press, 1941.

Tipton, Frank. "The National Consensus in German Economic History." *Central European History* 7 (1974): 195–225.

———. *Regional Variations in the Economic Development of Germany during the Nineteenth Century.* Middletown, Conn.: Wesleyan University Press, 1976.

Tornow, Ingow. *Das Münchner Vereinswesen in der ersten Hälfte des 19. Jahrhunderts.* Munich: Stadtarchiv München, 1977.

Townsend, Mary Evelyn. *The Rise and Fall of Germany's Colonial Empire, 1884–1918.* New York: Macmillan, 1930.

Ullmann, Hans Peter. *Der Bund der Industriellen: Organisation, Einfluss und Politik klein- und mittelbetrieblicher Industrieller in deutschen Kaiserreich, 1895–1914.* Göttingen: Vandenhoeck & Ruprecht, 1976.

Vagts, Alfred. *A History of Militarism.* New York: Meridian, 1937.

Varain, Heinz Josef, ed. *Interessenverbände in Deutschland*. Cologne: Kiepenheuer & Witsch, 1973.

Volkov, Shulamit Angel. *The Rise of Popular Anti-Modernism in Germany*. Princeton: Princeton University Press, 1978.

Waite, R. G. L. *Vanguard of Nazism: The Free Corps Movement in Postwar Germany, 1918–1923*. Cambridge, Mass.: Harvard University Press, 1952.

Warren, Donald. *The Red Kingdom of Saxony*. The Hague: Martinus Nijhoff, 1964.

Wehler, Hans-Ulrich. *Bismarck und der Imperialismus*. Cologne: Kiepenheuer & Witsch, 1969.

———. *Krisenherde des Kaiserreichs, 1871–1918*. Göttingen: Vandenhoeck & Ruprecht, 1970.

———. *Das deutsche Kaiserreich*. Göttingen: Vandenhoeck & Ruprecht, 1973.

———. "Zur Funktion und Struktur der Nationalen Kampfverbände im Kaiserreich." In *Modernisierung und nationale Gesellschaft im ausgehenden 18. und im 19. Jahrhundert*, ed. Werner Conze, Gottfried Schramm, and Klaus Zernack, 113–24. Berlin: Duncker & Humblot, 1979.

———. "Deutscher Sonderweg oder allgemeine Probleme des westlichen Kapitalismus?" *Merkur* 35 (1981): 478–87.

Weidenfeller, Gerd. *VDA: Verein für das Deutschtum im Ausland*. Bern & Frankfurt a.M.: Lang, 1976.

Wernecke, Klaus. *Der Wille zur Weltgeltung*. Düsseldorf: Droste, 1970.

Wertheimer, Mildred. *The Pan-German League, 1890–1914*. New York: Columbia University Press, 1924.

Whalen, Robert. *Bitter Wounds: German Victims of the Great War, 1914–1939*. Ithaca, N.Y.: Cornell University Press, 1984.

White, Dan. *The Splintered Party: National Liberalism in Hessen and the Reich, 1867–1918*. Cambridge, Mass.: Harvard University Press, 1976.

Wiedner, Hartmut. "Soldatenmisshandlungen im wilhelminischen Kaiserreich (1890–1914)." *Archiv für Sozialgeschichte* 22 (1982): 159–99.

Wilson, James Q. *Political Organizations*. New York: Basic Books, 1973.

Witt, Peter-Christian. *Die Finanzpolitik des Deutschen Reiches von 1903 bis 1913*. Lübeck: Matthiesen, 1970.

Wohl, Robert. *The Generation of 1914*. Cambridge, Mass.: Harvard University Press, 1979.

Wortmann, Karl. *Geschichte der deutschen Vaterlands-Partei, 1917–1918*. Halle: Otto Hendel, 1926.

Zeender, John K. *The German Center Party, 1890–1906. Transactions of the American Philosophical Society*, vol. 66, pt. 1. Philadelphia: The Society, 1976.

# Index